ALEXANDRIA

ALEXANDRIA

The Quest for the Lost City

EDMUND RICHARDSON

BLOOMSBURY PUBLISHING
LONDON · OXFORD · NEW YORK · NEW DELHI · SYDNEY

BLOOMSBURY PUBLISHING
Bloomsbury Publishing Plc
50 Bedford Square, London, WC1B 3DP, UK
29 Earlsfort Terrace, Dublin 2, Ireland

BLOOMSBURY, BLOOMSBURY PUBLISHING and the Diana logo are
trademarks of Bloomsbury Publishing Plc

First published in Great Britain 2021

ISBN: HB: 978-1-5266-0378-4; TPB: 978-1-5266-0381-4; EBOOK: 978-1-5266-0379-1

2 4 6 8 10 9 7 5 3 1

Typeset by Newgen KnowledgeWorks Pvt. Ltd., Chennai, India
Printed and bound in Great Britain by CPI Group (UK) Ltd, Croydon CR0 4YY

To find out more about our authors and books visit www.bloomsbury.com
and sign up for our newsletters

Contents

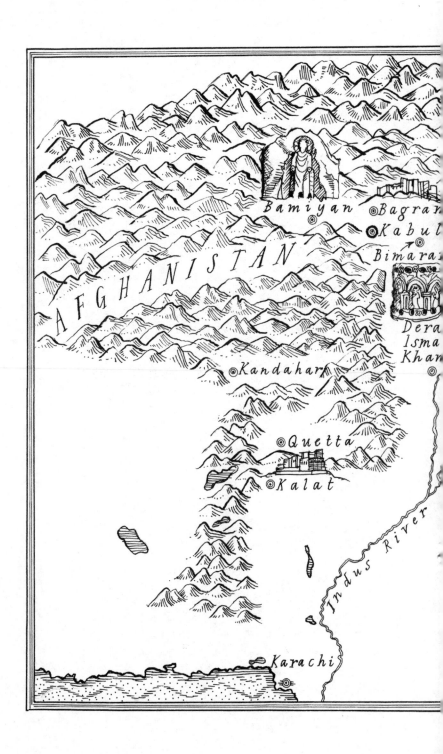

AFGHANISTAN

Bamiyan

Bagram

Kabul

Bimaran

Dera
Isma
Khan

Kandahar

Quetta

Kalat

Indus River

Karachi

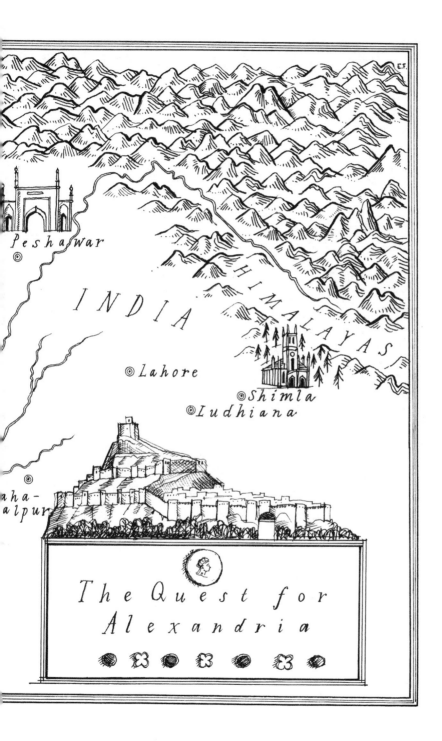

The Quest for Alexandria

I

The Runaway

4 July 1827. Dawn smelled of sweat, incense and horseshit.

Private James Lewis, an unremarkable member of the British East India Company's army, awoke in Agra.[1] In India, but not of it, the army camp was a miniature world of snoring soldiers, cooking fires, cannonballs and gunpowder. In the distance, with flocks of tiny birds whirling around its dome, the Taj Mahal loomed up in silhouette. By 6 a.m., the sun was well over the horizon, breaking through the mist on the Yamuna River, and turning the ancient red walls of Agra Fort to flaming gold. At the top of the fort's towers, the last of the night's bats flapped home.

For Lewis, it was independence day. He pulled on his uniform, walked out of the gate past the sleepy guards and never went back. By evening, he would be a wanted man

Lewis picked his way through Agra, putting as much distance between himself and his regiment as he could. Squat British bungalows clustered around the whitewashed bulk of St George's Cathedral, completed the previous year. Closer to the river, the old city slipped back into view. Bright green parrots peered down from the trees. Half-ruined mansions and tombs lined the riverside. Agra's star had been fading for almost 200 years: its brief reign as the capital of the Mughal Empire was long past.

The British treated the city as a colossal playground. The imperial apartments of Agra Fort – where Shah Jahan spent the final years of his life imprisoned, staring out through the lattice windows at the tomb of his beloved Mumtaz Mahal – had been taken over by Major Taylor, of the Bengal Engineers. People had started to grumble, so the Major was setting up a second home. This one was in the Taj Mahal.[2]

As he left Agra behind, Lewis had no way of knowing that he was walking into one of history's most incredible stories. He would beg by the roadside and take tea with kings. He would travel with holy men and become the master of a hundred disguises. He would see things no westerner had ever seen before, and few have glimpsed since. And, little by little, he would transform himself from an ordinary soldier into one of the greatest archaeologists of the age. He would devote his life to a quest for Alexander the Great.

His quest would take him across snow-covered mountains, into hidden chambers filled with jewels, and to a lost city buried beneath the plains of Afghanistan. He would unearth priceless treasures and witness unspeakable atrocities. He would unravel a language which had been forgotten for over a thousand years. He would be blackmailed and hunted by the most powerful empire on earth. He would be imprisoned for treason and offered his own kingdom. He would change the world – and the world would destroy him.

This is a story about following your dreams to the ends of the earth – and what happens when you get there.

Had he known what was coming, Lewis might have stayed in bed.

James Lewis was born in London, when the nineteenth century was just a few weeks old, on 16 February 1800.[3] London was a fetid, heaving thing: twice the size of Paris, growing in all directions, and the dirtiest city in the world. Lewis was brought up in its rotten heart, in the shadow of the Tower of London: a labyrinth of streets, lightless and reeking, littered with dead animals and menaced by gangs. 'The most bare-faced villains, swindlers, and thieves, walk about the streets in the daytime,' wrote Pierce Egan in 1821. 'The most vicious and abandoned wretches, who are lost to every friendly tie that binds man to man, are to be found in swarms in the metropolis.'[4] The air was full of soot. The Thames was a ribbon of sewage. London stank. Wandering the streets, amidst 'that huge fermenting mass of human-kind', Wordsworth felt horrified and utterly alone. 'How oft, amid those overflowing streets, / Have I gone forward with the crowd, and said / Unto myself, "The face of every one / That passes by me is a mystery!" '[5]

Even as a child, Lewis knew that Britain was not kind to people like him. To survive London you needed money, family connections, or cartoonish reserves of rage and guile. 'It seems,' Egan wrote, 'some poet has humorously described London as "the Devil!" '[6]

When Lewis was a teenager, the British economy was teetering on the brink of collapse. London's streets filled up with the newly homeless. Leigh Hunt, first publisher of Keats and Shelley, wrote of protests at 'bankruptcies, seizures, executions, imprisonments … great arrears of rent'.[7] The government responded with the sympathy which has marked British attitudes to the poor for centuries: they announced a plan to execute the protesters. Lord Byron, speaking in Parliament in 1812, tried in vain to raise some sympathy: 'Nothing but absolute want could have driven a large, and once honest and industrious, body of the people, into the commission of excesses so hazardous to themselves, their families, and the community. They were not ashamed to beg, but there was none to relieve them … Can you commit a whole county to their own prisons? Will you erect a gibbet in every field and hang up men like scarecrows?'[8] Lewis could see no future for himself in this broken land. On 5 October 1821, at the age of twenty-one, he enlisted in the army of the British East India Company, hoping for a better life.

The East India Company began life as a trading company, running ships back and forth between Britain and the East. But, propelled by fear and greed, it gradually expanded from its coastal trading posts. Local rulers were bullied, blackmailed and deposed, one after another. Horace Walpole called the Company 'a crew of monsters'[9] in the 1770s, but it was just getting started then. By the 1820s, the Company was the dominant power in India. No multinational corporation today could match it at its height.[10] The Company had a gigantic private army. It had spies everywhere. It was the largest drug dealer in history, pushing tons of opium every year. It cared only for profit. It was the god of capitalism.

Many of the Company's officials returned to Britain laden with gold: the spoils of trade, and loot from a hundred Indian treasuries. 'They have,' wrote William Cobbett, 'long been cooking and devouring the wretched people of both England and India.'[11] But Lewis quickly realised that fame and fortune were reserved for his betters, not for private soldiers like him. His job in the Bengal Artillery was to fight, sweat, cheer, swear, bleed and, if necessary, die, for the greater good of the Company's accounts. Years of marching up and down India turned him into a slight, shy, anxious young man, scraggly and red-haired, with blue-grey eyes that noticed things. Most private soldiers could barely read or write. Lewis read Latin and Greek, borrowing books from anyone who would lend them. Today, a soldier like that would be noticed, trained and put to work. But Lewis was only there to fill out the ranks: grist for the imperial mill. After sweating through six summers, he was just as poor and just as ignored as he had been when he first joined up. (An officer let him arrange some dead butterflies once, but that was about it.)[12]

It wasn't fair, but the East India Company had never promised fairness. Lewis watched his superiors get rich. In 1825, he spent a hair-raising Christmas at the siege of Bharatpur. The massive fortress, around thirty miles from Agra, had sent a British army packing in 1805, and the East India Company was determined not to risk a second humiliation. When the dust settled over the ruins of Bharatpur, on 16 January 1826, the British divided up the treasure within. The commanding officer, Lord Combermere, walked away with 595,398 rupees. Lewis and the rest of the ordinary soldiers got 40 rupees each.[13] (Today, this would be equivalent to approximately £6 million or $7.5 million for the commanding officer, and £400 or $500 for the ordinary soldiers.)[14] Even the drunks and the idiots among the officers lived far better lives than he ever would. And when they gave him an order, he had to obey. He was not, by nature, a patient man. He had probably heard of the concept of suffering fools gladly, but he never seems to have understood it. He began to mutter under his breath. He dreamed about life on his own terms. In July 1827, after years of thankless service, something snapped.

What happens when you decide to walk away from your entire life? Lewis was about to find out.

The punishing summer heat was beginning to break when he left Agra. The monsoon had swept up from the Bay of Bengal a few days earlier, and the rains, when they came, were cool and blindingly strong. But for the rest of the day, the hills of northern India were brown and bare, and shimmered with heat. Each step raised clouds of dust. Lewis had no money or food. 'I was now destitute, a stranger in the centre of Asia, unacquainted with the language – which would have been most useful to me – and from my colour exposed on all occasions to notice.'[15] Staying alive was going to be a problem.

Lewis had a bigger problem, though: the East India Company. As soon as his absence was discovered, his description was sent out across India far faster than he himself could travel. Towns, garrisons and frontier officials were put on alert. The Company's vast network of spies took pleasure in hunting deserters down and delivering them over to military justice. If Lewis was caught, he might be flogged to the point of death, revived, then flogged again. Or he might be put to death in a particularly unpleasant manner. The Company was known for tying its Indian soldiers to the mouths of cannon, and quite literally blasting them into smithereens. They would just hang Lewis, but that was cold comfort. Either way, the birds that haunted the Company's places of execution would be waiting.

'A number of kites (a bird of prey very common in India) actually accompanied the melancholy party in their progress to the place of execution,' wrote one horrified British soldier, 'as if they knew what was going on, and then kept hovering over the guns from which the culprits were to be blown away, flapping their wings, and shrieking, as if in anticipation of their bloody feast, till the fatal flash, which scattered the fragments of bodies in the air; when, pouncing on their prey, they positively caught in their talons many pieces of the quivering flesh before they could reach the ground.'[16]

Lewis had seen what the East India Company did to deserters. At the siege of Bharatpur, one of his fellow artillerymen, a man named Herbert, had slipped through the British patrols and gone over to the other side. The first the British knew of this was when a cannonball from the fort ripped through the air and flew straight at the commanding officer's observation post, missing Lord Combermere by inches and dismembering one of his servants. It was, all things considered, quite a way for Herbert to resign. Day after day, on the battlements of Bharatpur, he 'was seen, in his English uniform, parading the ramparts, and pointing the enemy's guns upon his countrymen',[17] 'coolly exposing himself to all risks'.[18] The British could not believe it: Herbert had fought at Waterloo, 'his character was fair; he was well spoken of by those with whom he served; and was believed to have supported his mother', but still, here he was, trying to kill them – and doing uncomfortably well.[19] A few days later, another lucky shot from the fort ignited 20,000 pounds of British gunpowder, and blew everyone in the vicinity sky-high.[20] When the East India Company captured Bharatpur, they made it their business to hunt down Herbert. He was captured alive and, after the briefest of trials, was put to death in front of the assembled army.[21]

Lewis kept moving. He headed west, navigating by the sun and the stars. He begged for food in villages, slept in ditches, and stayed out of sight. The countryside around Agra was eerily quiet. Cholera had struck, and every village was filled with the dying. Lewis looped around Delhi, city of poets and magicians, where the Mughal Emperor Akbar II held court in the Red Fort. There, the eyes of the Company were too numerous and too sharp for him to survive. His only hope was to slip through the borders and put himself beyond their reach. So he struck out into the great wastelands of the Thar Desert, with no water, no backup plan and no map.

The desert crept up on Lewis. Fields gave way to scrubland, herds of cows to flocks of goats. The golden city of Bikaner loomed up on the horizon: a shimmering fort, seemingly carved out of the desert sand. Lewis did not dare to approach it. Instead, he pressed on into the heart of the desert. Villages became further and further apart. Hills began to look more like dunes. The landscape changed colour imperceptibly, from green to brown to dirty yellow to gold. Dust began to cling to him, coating his nostrils and settling in the folds of his clothes. Days went by without another sign of human life. The sun hung malevolently in the sky. It was too hot for tigers, so at least he could sleep soundly. That was the only good news.

This was the true desert. Even today, the Thar is one of the most isolated and desolate parts of India. The temperature can reach 50° Centigrade (122° Fahrenheit). The occasional rusty train rattles by, paralleling the border with Pakistan, scattering bottles of water and samosa wrappers across the sands, but people are otherwise few and far between. In the afternoon heat, even the camels struggle, panting in scraps of shade, leathery grey tongues lolling from their mouths. The nights are full of silence and ten thousand stars. The odds of anyone surviving the journey on foot seem impossibly low.

But, somehow, Lewis did. Several weeks after he left Bikaner behind, rumours began to spread at the court of Ahmedpur in present-day Pakistan. A very strange man had been seen emerging from the desert. He called himself Charles Masson.

Lewis – for it was he – limped along on blistered feet, covering less than a mile a day. The journey had almost killed him. His clothes were in rags, he was shivering with fever and barely able to walk. 'I found it impossible to travel after sunrise, when I was compelled, wherever I might be, to seek the nearest shade and throw myself on the ground beneath it.'[22] Eventually, he staggered into a frontier town, hoping to stay out of sight and recover.

This Charles Masson may have looked like a red-haired scarecrow with heatstroke, but appearances could be deceptive. The Khan of Ahmedpur was keeping a close eye on his frontiers. So Lewis was ceremoniously welcomed by a courtier, who 'was very anxious to know my business, and could hardly believe that I had none, or that I had not brought some message to the Khan. It was in vain I appealed to the negative evidences of my poverty, and my trudging alone, and on foot.'[23]

Lewis did not know it yet, but he was not the only western traveller in Ahmedpur. There was one other man, a sallow, forbidding, bearded figure. His name was Josiah Harlan – and the East India Company had asked him to be on the lookout for deserters. When Harlan heard about the new arrival, he smiled to himself, and made it his business to meet Mr Masson.

Lewis appeared at Harlan's tent 'in the dress of a native with his head shorn'. But Harlan was not fooled for a second. 'The light and straggling hair upon the upper lip in conjunction with the blue eyes at once revealed the true nativity of his caste. I addressed him without hesitation as a European deserter from the Horse Artillery … of whom I had already read a description.'[24] Lewis's jaw dropped. Harlan loomed over him, huge and wild-looking. Already, Lewis could feel the rope around his neck, and hear the vultures circling.

Visibly shaking, he stammered out his cover story 'asserting that he belonged to Bombay and was merely travelling for amusement in this direction with the intention … of proceeding home over land'.[25] Harlan almost laughed aloud. He had heard many lies in his time – and had told more than a few himself. But this wretched-looking man had to be the worst liar he had ever met.

Josiah Harlan had set out from America at the age of twenty-one, with the modest ambition of making himself a king. His father secured him a job on a merchant ship bound for the East. Harlan learned how to haggle with traders in China and bluff his way through a card game in the back streets of Calcutta. He came back to America richer and hairier, and promptly fell in love. He and the lady agreed that he would make one more voyage, then return to America and marry her. He embarked again for Calcutta, but when his ship reached India, he found a letter waiting for him. His fiancée had, with remarkable efficiency, broken off the engagement and married someone else.

Heartbroken, Harlan walked away from his ship. Without any training, he bluffed his way into a job as a surgeon with the East India Company, armed with little more than a saw and an unshakeable self-regard.[26] When that posting came to an end, instead of returning to America he struck out into northern India to make his fortune.

In the city of Ludhiana in the Punjab, one of the last British outposts in India, Harlan met the exiled king of Afghanistan, Shah Shujah. The Shah was desperate to reclaim his throne – and Harlan thought he might be able to help. When he met Lewis, Harlan was heading to Afghanistan with a ragged bunch of mercenaries, a giant American flag and his beloved dog, Dash. He would go on to plant his flag atop the Hindu Kush mountains, and proclaim himself a prince. He thought he was the nineteenth century's answer to Alexander the Great.

Now, looking the trembling Lewis up and down, Harlan scented an opportunity. It would be useful to sell this wretch out to the East India Company. But it would be even more beneficial to have a trained soldier at his side in the weeks to come, even a sorry-looking specimen like this one. 'Perceiving his extremely uncomfortable position by the tremor of his voice and personal demonstrations of alarm,' Harlan wrote, 'I quieted his terror with the assurance that I was not an Englishman and had no connection with the British government, and consequently neither interest nor duty could induce me to betray him now or hereafter.'[27] Lewis barely had time to stammer out his thanks before Harlan had signed him up to his Afghan expedition, as the American's 'confidential retainer'. There wasn't much Josiah Harlan didn't know about leverage.

On 10 December 1827, Harlan's little army prepared to leave Ahmedpur.[28] As the American pulled on his giant boots, Lewis felt that he had swapped his former military life for an even crazier one. Harlan had dressed him in his battered old Bengal Artillery uniform, broadsword and all. He let him keep the name Charles Masson – and Lewis decided that he liked it better than his old one. (Harlan himself, with customary chutzpah, had outfitted himself as a British officer.) Still stricken from the fever, red-eyed and unshaven, this Masson was a grotesque parody of the well-groomed soldier he had been a few months ago. But he was happy to be alive, and happier still to be mounted on one of Harlan's horses, even if he did keep falling off.

Soon, the unlikely expedition was making good progress. Harlan's force now amounted to around a hundred men, though he didn't trust a single one of them. He and his second-in-command, Gul Khan, bickered constantly. Gul Khan was a fat fifty-something, missing a hand and an eye, but magnificently moustached and armed to the teeth. He specialised in passive-aggressive speeches about his own unshakeable loyalty, which drove Harlan to distraction. 'Death to the King's enemies and may his salt become dirt in the mouths of traitors! Twenty years have I been a faithful servant to his Majesty – an unrewarded slave – but let that pass. Now is the time for duty – what though the King never distinguished his friend from his foe – thank God the King is a great King!'[29] Gul Khan could never quite remember how he had lost his hand: he told a different story every time. In Ludhiana, the rumour was that Shah Shujah had cut it off.

Harlan fussed and worried every mile of the way. If he spotted a single bundle tied up sloppily, he would start ranting. 'There will be great waste of physical power, destruction of property, suffering to man and beast . . . These minute considerations control the success of the military operations!'[30] His speeches were not short, and brought in everyone from the Romans to Napoleon.[31] All the sound and fury concealed a deep anxiety: Harlan suspected it had been a very bad idea to pay his men in advance. Gul Khan had hardly been able to believe it. The moment Harlan's money was in his hand, his decades-long loyalty to Shah Shujah vanished into thin air. 'This much of his [the Shah's] salt have I eaten,' he told Harlan, with a grin, 'and now I commit him to the mercy of God – let the brave serve the brave – demand mercy of the merciful – 'tis to ask a handful of dust from the mountain. Have I been but two days in the sahib's service and have earned two months' pay in advance – may his house flourish!'[32] At the time, Harlan had not wondered how quickly Gul Khan's loyalties might shift again.

Beyond the frontiers of the East India Company, power was seemingly there for the taking. To the east was Lahore, capital of the one-eyed Sikh Maharaja, Ranjit Singh, one of history's smartest and most ruthless empire builders. The Maharaja drank British envoys under the table, helped himself to the Koh-i-Noor diamond and terrified every power within range of his vast and meticulously drilled armies, from the East India Company on down. (His favourite sunset cocktail: whisky, meat juice, opium, musk and crushed pearls.)[33] To the north, Dost Mohammad Khan ruled Afghanistan uneasily from Kabul. ('He had foiled his competitors, and elevated himself to power, the great object of his ambition,' reflected Masson later. 'To attempt to delineate the character of a man who has none, would be ridiculous. He was good or bad as it suited his interests.')[34] But, in between, in the borderlands and the mountain passes, their influence was little felt. A patchwork of small-time chiefs still held sway, each with his own crumbling fort, band of underpaid retainers and rusting cannon. Against such opposition, even a ten-cent Machiavelli like Harlan stood a decent chance.

Harlan went through life with his hand on his pistol, but his head in the clouds. As his band of mercenaries headed towards Afghanistan, 'my mind was full of contemplations of the past,' he wrote. 'I was about to enter the country and become familiar with the objects which have been made conspicuous to the world as the arena and subject of Alexander's exploits.'[35] For men like Harlan, Alexander the Great was the north star: a promise that one man could remake the world, and be remembered for ever. A few paces back, balanced unsteadily on his horse and sweating through his old uniform, Masson could not have cared less about ancient history. But he humoured the American and listened as Harlan prattled on.

They took the road north towards Afghanistan, by way of the Indus River. India was joined to the rest of Asia by a dense network of trade and pilgrimage routes. These dusty tracks were the veins of the world. For thousands of years, travellers and merchants had plodded along them, bearing gold and silver, silks and spices, jade and lapis lazuli, inventions and religions. Armies had swept back and forth, leaving new kings and empires in their wake. Now, on the banks of the Indus, Harlan stared up at the distant hills, breathed deeply, and grinned. 'To look for the first time upon the furthest stream that had borne upon its surface the world's victor two thousand years ago. To gaze upon the landscape he had viewed. To tread upon the earth where Alexander bled.'[36] Masson was exhausted and lonely, and not in the mood. As they made their way across the river, he had his eyes fixed not on the horizon, but on a gigantic crocodile, sixteen feet long, immobile on the far bank. Their boat appeared to be heading straight for it. Then the wind changed, and he smelled it: the crocodile was long dead and rotting in the heat. Camped on the far shore of the Indus that night, Masson sat up late 'reflecting on the people and scenes I was about to leave behind. If a feeling of doubt for a moment clouded my mind, one of pride at having penetrated so far removed it, and encouraged me to proceed farther.'[37] Besides, although he didn't say so, Masson hardly had a choice.

Over the next few days, as they followed the Indus north towards the town of Dera Ismail Khan, Harlan talked Masson's ear off about Alexander: the boy from the hills who ruled most of the known world by the time he was twenty-seven. The general who led his army further than the gods dared to go. The dreamer whose dreams came true. Harlan was not interested in the finer points of Alexander's politics, or intrigues between Greeks and Persians, or the oracles of distant gods. He was interested in Alexander's cities: bricks and mortar, gold and swords.

At the height of his power, Alexander built a string of cities across the world, from Egypt and Asia Minor, through the heartland of the Persian Empire, to the plains of Central Asia and the mountains of Afghanistan. All were named for himself: Alexandria. Everyone knows the Alexandria in Egypt, but there were over a dozen more Alexandrias scattered across Alexander's empire. In them, Persians met Afghans, Greek gods turned Indian, and Chinese silks travelled to Rome. Alexander's cities were his greatest legacy.

Harlan, dreaming of an empire of his own, may have been wondering where he should site his first Harlanville (Harlandria? Harlanopolis?). 'The genius displayed by Alexander in the selection of sites for this purpose,' Harlan reflected, made him 'the unrivalled architect of empires'.[38] But, he told Masson, little was left of Alexander's cities today. Almost all of the Alexandrias had disappeared into dust. 'The devastations of two thousand years have not, I believe, left a single architectural monument of the Macedonian conquests in India.'[39]

Masson wasn't so sure about that – and, despite himself, he was beginning to be intrigued by the American's stories.

On the road, Harlan and Masson celebrated a very strange Christmas together. Masson gorged himself on fruit from the orchards of Afghanistan, 'fresh grapes, pears and apples',[40] until he was bloated and happy. It was a long way from the ancient church of St Mary Aldermanbury in London, where he had been baptised and had celebrated Christmas as a child. It was a long way, too, from Harlan's Quaker meeting house in Pennsylvania. By now, the American was seriously jumpy. Every day he was less sure whether he was the predator or the prey. Try as he might, he could not forget an Afghan proverb he had once heard. Other nations, it ran, 'may for a subsistence plough and harrow the earth. We prefer digging into the vitals of our brethren.'[41]

Harlan was also beginning to have doubts about his employer. When he first encountered Shah Shujah in Ludhiana, he had been overawed. He had never met a king before – and the gaunt, quiet Shujah, surrounded by the remnants of his court, made a remarkable impression. 'I saw him,' Harlan remembered, as 'an exiled and legitimate monarch, the victim of treasonable practices, popular in the regard of his subjects.'[42]

But now, recalling his time with Shujah, he couldn't help thinking there had been something deeply odd about it all. The sleepy, dusty streets of Ludhiana were an unlikely place to find royalty, and, for Shujah, keeping up appearances was a full-time job. 'None were allowed to sit in his presence. The Governor General of India would not have been permitted the familiarity of equal pretensions which this privilege implied. Under no circumstances however urgent would his Majesty deviate from the etiquette of the Kabul court,'[43] wrote Harlan. 'Flagellation was a common infliction for trivial delinquencies, and the ear was ever shocked by barbarous threats of mutilation, publicly promulgated through the proclamation of a crier as the award of disobedience.'[44]

When Shujah went for a walk, things got even stranger. He was preceded through the deserted streets of Ludhiana by a phalanx of courtiers, who 'proclaimed the approach of the king, shouting to the lifeless winds and unpeopled highways "Stand afar," as though he was in the middle of obedient subjects. "Stand afar," with the deep and sonorous intonation of self-important command, preceded the awe-inspiring, solemn march of Shujah, where there was none to obey.'[45] Shujah treated his life in Ludhiana as a temporary inconvenience – a brief and unsavoury interlude, like a holiday stay with some disagreeable relatives, to be endured before returning to his throne in Kabul. When Harlan met him, he had been in exile for eighteen years.

For now, Harlan focused on keeping his force together, and Dash well fed. 'Love me, love my dog' was a motto by which he lived.[46] One night, when he and his men rolled into a village, he almost levelled the place in fury after the villagers would not sell him milk for Dash. Finally, Harlan 'directed my valet to buy a sheep which he did at an exorbitant price. A portion of the meat was summarily roasted' for Dash. After the dog had had his fill, Harlan shared out the remaining meat among his followers. 'We luxuriate tonight,' one of them muttered incredulously, 'by the good fortune of a dog!'[47] Many villages were desperately poor. 'We have nothing,' some told Harlan, 'either grain, forage or flour.' But Harlan did not believe in taking no for an answer. He bullied, boomed and threatened violence until, as he put it, 'the people could be induced to comply with our necessary demands'.[48] Masson, his old uniform rapidly disintegrating, was finding Harlan less and less comfortable company. Shaking down farmers was not his idea of a good time.

Harlan's messiah complex was coming along nicely. He often put his rudimentary medical skills to work, treating infections among the villagers. After one procedure, a woman allegedly 'exclaimed "Let me first look upon the face of my deliverer to whom I owe a second creation." She prostrated herself before me with expressions of devout adoration.'[49] Harlan loved every minute of it. By the time his force arrived at Dera Ismail Khan, his doubts were receding, and he was feeling exceedingly pleased with himself.

Masson thought he knew India, but Dera Ismail Khan came as a shock. It was the wickedest little town in Asia, a nest of spies and ne'er-do-wells. You could buy pretty much anything and anyone there. There were horse dealers from Bukhara and Hindu traders from Bombay, saints and sinners (mostly the latter), Afghan pilgrims, descendants of the Prophet, wandering holy men of various degrees of authenticity, trains of heavy-laden camels, and alchemists clutching their books of secrets. Harlan pitched camp on the outskirts of town and unfurled his American flag.[50] Within days, rumours began to circulate that he had Shah Shujah hidden in a box.[51] It was that kind of place.

The nawab, or governor, of Dera Ismail Khan did not like the look of Harlan at all. He thought the American was altogether too slippery and had far too much suspicious-looking baggage. (If Shah Shujah wasn't in Harlan's trunks, then he almost certainly had 'a wonderful missile of violence which could be thrown into the area of a fort by hand, where its explosion would cause the death of the garrison and blow down the walls in an instant'.)[52] The nawab was right to worry. Harlan was scheming at top speed. He had his eye on the nearby fortress of Takht-e-Sulaiman, or the Throne of Solomon – a cold, impossibly steep peak, grey and windswept, commanding the valleys below. He was hoping that a few well-chosen promises and handfuls of money might persuade the garrison to mutiny, and hand the place over to him. When Harlan was wondering how to turn them against their current commander, Sirwa Khan, he had a brainwave: start his own little holy war. 'Remember,' his men said to the garrison, 'Sirwa is a schismatic dog whose blood will purify your orthodox souls, and you shall become hereafter celebrated as ghazis [holy warriors] – go and prosper.'[53] The first American to set foot in modern-day Pakistan and Afghanistan brought with him the first American-sponsored jihad. 'Divide et impera,' Harlan reflected, with satisfaction.[54] Divide and conquer.

Watching the sun set behind his giant flag, Harlan was in an empire-building mood. 'In the midst of that wild landscape,' he wrote, 'the flag of America seemed a dreamy illusion of the imagination, but it was the harbinger of enterprise which distance, space and time had not appalled, for the undaunted sons of Columbia are second to no people in the pursuit of adventure wherever the world is trodden by man.'[55]

The next morning, Harlan awoke to find that most of his army had deserted.

'What? All?' he spluttered.

'With the exception of four men,' replied one of his few remaining servants.[56]

Then Harlan realised that Masson too had disappeared.

'Let everyone retire,' he muttered, 'and leave me to myself.'

Gul Khan and the others backed out slowly, muttering apologies ('How shall I find language to express my upset and indignation – I shall never hold up my head again – I am no better than a dead man . . .').[57]

They came back to tell Harlan that the mutiny at Takht-e-Sulaiman was off as well. The garrison wanted to be paid in advance. This time, Harlan boiled over: 'Traitors and cowards – I offered to enlist them as playfellows? Do you see those mountains before us? Can such wretches who were unable to seize an empty fortress scale those heights and force the fastness in possession of savage robbers? They have proved themselves women in the affairs of war – such retainers I need not. I know their value. The infamous shall receive the award of shame. I discard and abhor them – detestable dogs!'[58]

Seething, Harlan sat beneath his American flag, and adjusted his expectations. Building an empire was going to be harder than he had expected.

While Harlan was stamping his feet, Masson was on the other side of town, having tea with the nawab of Dera Ismail Khan. Sitting in the ancient citadel's flower gardens, taking in the nawab's fantastical court – wrestlers and musicians, monkeys and bears and tough-looking ponies[59] – he barely remembered being James Lewis.

That, then, is the story of how James Lewis became Charles Masson. It's a pretty good story. There's only one problem: like many other stories about Charles Masson, it may not be entirely true.

2

The Illusionists

For almost 200 years people have been searching for the truth about Charles Masson.[1] Was James Lewis his real name, or just another alias?[2] For that matter, was he even British? 'Mr Masson has acquainted me,' reported a British officer, 'that he is from the State of Kentucky in America.'[3] (Masson never set foot in America in his life.) A French scholar went one better and claimed Monsieur Masson for France.[4] (Masson never set foot in France in his life.) Some people believed everything he said. Others decided that he was a real-life Munchausen.[5]

'In the autumn of 1826,' Masson's autobiography begins, 'having traversed the Rajput States of Shekhawati and the kingdom of Bikaner, I entered the desert frontiers of the Khan of Bahawalpur.'[6] That, the very first sentence of his book, is a lie. In the autumn of 1826, Masson was hundreds of miles away, sweating through his uniform in the Bengal Artillery.[7] He did not cross the desert until a year later.

Among Masson's papers there is a little note, ragged around the edges.[8] On it, he drew up his autobiography's fake timeline, where his travels began in 1826. Then, as if with relief, he wrote the true year over each false one: 1826 turned into 1827. Both timelines mark his desertion with the same inky shrug: ~.

Every writer who has taken on Masson has ended up with some embarrassing bruises.[9] One major error on your own first page is the going rate for telling his tale. And the part of his story Masson guarded most carefully was that of how James Lewis became Charles Masson. He never wrote it down. And he only told it to one person.

To find it, you have to go to Philadelphia and catch a little grey train (grey seats, grey floors, grey walls, grey ceiling, grey-haired men in grey suits staring out at grey skies). After nineteen stops, head down the road to West Chester, Pennsylvania, and the Chester County Historical Society. There, in a perfect little town surrounded by faded motels and shopping malls, lies everything that is left of Josiah Harlan: letters, hopes, schemes, a rather splendid document proclaiming him a prince, and the full story of James Lewis's desertion.

Rewind to 4 July 1827 and the Bengal Artillery's camp in Agra. Now, there are two deserters sneaking out, not one – James Lewis and his good friend Richard Potter. Potter was with Lewis all the way, from that first morning in Agra to the crossing of the Thar Desert, the showdown with Harlan and the journey to Dera Ismail Khan. (Potter changed his name too, though, not being the most creative sort, he changed it to John Brown.)[10] Unlike Lewis, Potter stayed with Harlan and would remain at the American's side for years. Potter and Lewis risked their lives together, side by side, in some of the most dangerous places in the world. But not once, afterwards, did Charles Masson mention Potter. Nor did he ever mention his desertion, or his real name. Tracing Masson's footsteps is like following a maze which changes shape as you explore it.

After he left Harlan and Potter behind, Masson sat anxiously in the nawab's gardens in Dera Ismail Khan. The nawab took the measure of his guest. Did Masson, he wondered, know anything about miracles? A traveller had – most unfortunately – recently been murdered nearby, and the nawab just happened to have the dead man's belongings to hand. There were certain British medicines among them, and these medicines claimed to have miraculous properties. Would Masson mind taking a look? It only took a second for Masson to realise that these were the worst kind of quack remedies: chalk pills and brightly coloured water, hawked on the streets of London with promises of fantastic cures. Somehow, they had found their way to the middle of Asia. 'I explained to him the miracles they professed to perform, according to the labels and papers attached to them,' Masson remembered, 'but conjured him to be considerate enough not to employ them.'[11]

Here, Masson realised, the promise of a miracle might go a long way. But if the miracle did not materialise, if the medicine did not cure all ills, it would be unwise for the miracle-worker to be there the next morning to attempt an explanation. One false step and it would all be over for him.

A few days later, Masson scrambled up the rocky slopes outside Dera Ismail Khan to the fortress of Takht-e-Sulaiman. The hill on which it sat was known as the last resting place of Noah's Ark, a story that seemed absurd at the bottom, but became more believable every steep, scrabbling step of the way up. Inside the walls, past smoky, foul-smelling alleys full of belching camels and shouting traders, Masson was led through an ancient door into the governor's private garden. Suddenly, the dust and chaos were gone, and in their place were 'flowers of a thousand hues', lakes reflecting 'orange and pomegranate-trees, with their glowing fruits waving on their margins' and hundreds of spotless white geese floating serenely on the surface. It was the most beautiful thing Masson had ever seen.[12]

The governor's son and vizier, Allahdad Khan, liked Masson's company. And he liked a drink. And when he was drunk, he especially liked Masson's company. Masson became accustomed to the late-night knocks at his door. 'One evening Allahdad Khan returned home so inebriated that it was necessary to hold him on his horse.'[13] Passing Masson's small apartment, the vizier stopped in the middle of the road and demanded that Masson come out and have a drink. The vizier's entire retinue hammered on the door, the windows and the wall, until Masson sleepily emerged, pulling on his clothes and a smile. Before he could get himself quite buttoned up, a cup was thrust into his hand and the party headed for the palace. Wobbling on his horse, talking of poetry and love, Allahdad Khan 'held my hand, and I was on foot, I was in no small dread of being trampled on by his horse's hoofs ... When we gained his apartments the crowd was dismissed, and only two or three persons, with his musicians, remained. He was very elated, and much pressed me to remain with him, to make, as he said, shells, and cross the river and attack the Sikhs. He then produced some pictures, and afterwards sang songs from Hafiz, but for a short time.'[14] Then the wine caught up with him, and Allahdad Khan passed out, happy and dribbling.

It is an old story, and of course Hafiz, the great Sufi poet of desire, tells it best:

Last midnight
He came to me
Beside my bed
Bending close to my ear
Murmuring sadly
'My dearest – my oldest love – do you really sleep?'

Whatever you seek
If you hold this cup as the dawn breaks
And do not feel your heart beat faster
You know nothing of love.

You who wander
You who leave all this behind
Argue not with us
The ones who stay
Until the dregs.

Before the creation of the world
This was our only gift.
We drank full cups
Of the sweet nectar of heaven
And the bitter wine of loss.[15]

Masson tiptoed around the snoring vizier and went home to bed.

Maybe it was the wine. Maybe the governor had started to look at him suspiciously. Maybe he just wanted to keep moving. But whatever the reason, one day Masson 'saw a fakir, who, learning that I wished to go to Kabul, proffered to put me in the way of doing so. I liked the appearance of the man, and my acquaintance telling me I might confide in him, I immediately made up my mind to accompany him.' Fakirs – holy men who relied on the kindness of strangers to survive – were a familiar sight on the roads of India. Masson set out with the fakir that very day, 'trusting all was right'.[16]

And maybe all those songs from Hafiz, sung in the grey light of dawn with the wine in his head, had a little to do with his sudden departure.

> You've thought long enough.
> Now plunge into the sea.
> Let the waves cover your head.
> Afraid of the deep waters?
> Splashing one hair at a time?
> God knows
> You'll never know a thing.[17]

They made an odd pair, Masson and the fakir, on the road from Takht-e-Sulaiman. After years of marching and counter-marching with the East India Company, Masson thought he could outwalk and outlast any half-starved fakir. Within a few hours, he realised how wrong he was. 'My strange friend and guide led me over the country, without troubling himself about a path, pleading the privilege and nonchalance of a fakir; and I was well tired before, late at night, we reached an assemblage of tents, where I was pleased to find my companion well known.' Much to the amusement of the fakir and his friends, Masson collapsed onto the ground, hugging his aching feet. 'We were very well received and entertained, but the people strove to persuade the fakir that he did wrong to encumber himself with me.'[18]

It was not long before Masson realised he had another problem. As they picked their way over the hills, the fakir could rely on the generosity of the pious to put food in his belly. Red-haired strangers could not – especially red-haired strangers who spoke barely a word of any of the local languages. One morning, Masson woke up starving. But it was Ramadan, and all good Muslims (almost everyone, in other words, within a hundred miles) were fasting until dusk. No one had asked Masson's stomach about fasting. So Masson walked a little way off from the camp towards a grove of fruit trees, and 'endeavoured to bring down some of the fruit by casting sticks and stones, when a woman, observing me, pulled a stout stick from a hedge, and without mercy employed it upon me, reviling me as an infidel for breaking my fast. Expostulation seemed but to increase her fury, and I was perplexed how to act.' Meanwhile, the blows were raining down hard. In a combination of Persian and garbled Pashto, he tried to explain: 'Why be angry? I am a Feringhi,' or foreigner. 'Feringhi' got through: the woman 'dropped her weapon, expressed great sorrow at her mistake, and helped me to bring down the fruit, at which she was much more expert than I had been'.[19] Masson limped back, sore but well fed. He was learning respect the hard way. At least, he reflected, it took his mind off his feet.

Soon, those feet were worse: raw, covered with blisters and throbbing constantly. Reduced to a hobble, Masson had to bid farewell to his new friend the fakir. For the next few years, Masson's feet would become a morbid and all-consuming obsession. His diaries linger over blisters, lovingly describe the feeling of blood seeping from his sandals, the cracking of his heels, the horrified looks his lower limbs attracted and the various ways people tried to treat them. He was about to become one of the nineteenth century's greatest travellers, but his was a body made for gentle English country walks and light frosts, not the passes of the Hindu Kush and the winds of an Afghan winter.

Masson was not sure where he was going, or what he was going to do when he got there, but even he knew one thing: travelling alone through the borderlands of Afghanistan was suicidal. Without the fakir, he stood little chance of survival. So relentless were the marauders that people slept on their roofs with the household valuables, drawing up the ladders behind them.[20] He had some small silver coins, hidden in the waistband of his trousers, but nowhere near enough money to get him across the country in safety. He would have to rely on the kindness of strangers to stay alive.

His first attempt to find 'companions for the journey'[21] did not end well. He almost got himself killed. It happened that he met two men on the road. One 'asked me to extend my arm, and, as I thought he did so with a view of assuring his companion [that Masson was not an evil spirit], I complied.' This level of naivety was practically suicidal. What happened next was entirely predictable. 'He seized my wrist, and wrenching it round, brought me, without power of resistance, to the ground. He called upon his friend to come and examine the bundle I carried on my back ... until I roared out that I was the nawab's servant.'[22] Other than carrying around a sign saying 'Rob Me' in half a dozen languages, or going off into the hills with a band of thieves, there was not much more Masson could have done to shorten his life expectancy.

A few days later, he went off into the hills with a band of thieves.

After a few hours in their company, he began to notice that something was amiss. His new friends were behaving rather strangely. 'Many of the party were disposed to be merry, and made motions as if cutting a man's throat, and shooting with arrows, at which I had only to laugh as they did themselves.'[23] Soon, Masson's laughter had become rather forced, and he was clutching his few possessions. The party stopped for the night in a village. The villagers were excessively polite to Masson's comrades, and gave him some strange looks. He slept uneasily, and parted ways with his companions the next day. That was when the villagers broke the news to him. 'The villagers told me they were thieves ... so their civility proceeded from dread ... The villagers inquired how I, as a man of sense, could have accompanied them into the hills.'[24]

Clearly, Masson was not a man of sense. How, you might be wondering, is this poor innocent not dead yet?

After a few weeks on his own, Masson was a physical and mental wreck. He looked terrible and smelled worse. One night, he limped into a village and was lodged at the mosque. But before he slept in their mosque, the villagers insisted he had to wash. 'The village barber was produced, and cut the nails of my fingers and toes, which were deemed to require an operation; and my friends of the village continued their various attentions, shampooing me against my will ... until I signified my wish to take a little rest.'[25]

Slowly, Masson began to notice something. Everyone he met was trying to see through his tricks, but he didn't have any. Once or twice, he had tried to pass himself off as an Afghan, and the results had been disastrous. His table manners were appalling, his prayers were borderline blasphemous and he never did get the hang of smoking a water-pipe: 'I was nearly choked, and spat the contents of my mouth over the machine.'[26] So he always went back to being an innocent travelling Feringhi. But no one believed this for a second.

A Sikh officer, collecting taxes, thought that Masson was an agent of the East India Company. When he travelled with some merchants, the people they met were convinced 'that the property with the party belonged to me: indeed, that my companions were my servants, and that my poverty was assumed, the better to pass through the country'.[27] This was a land of illusionists. Everyone had an act, and everyone was trying to work out what Masson's was. If he wanted to survive much longer, he needed to get one, and it needed to be good. But how? For now, he put the thought out of his mind and kept going.

***

Many miles later, stripped of his money, his belongings and almost all of his clothes, Masson was close to death. A freezing wind was blowing from the mountains, and he could find neither food nor shelter for the night. Half-naked and terrified, shaking with cold and utterly alone, Masson wondered if he would survive until dawn.

His troubles had begun the previous day, in the dusty brown countryside outside Kandahar, when he invited himself to dinner with some men. After the meal, when Masson was complacently settling down for the night, one of the men walked up to him and slapped him across the face. Hoping this was a joke, Masson put on his best awkward smile. Then the man asked for Masson's coat. Masson's smile got a bit more awkward. Of course, this was just high spirits. The next thing he knew, he was flat on the ground, with the men gathered round him, clawing at his clothes, slapping and cursing him. They left him only his shoes and a pair of light pyjamas – nowhere near enough to keep him warm on a freezing night in the mountains – and told him to sleep on the ground, 'cautioning me not to attempt to escape during the night, for I should be certainly seized by the dogs. I stretched myself on my sorrowful bed, and ruminated on my deplorable situation, consoling myself, however, that it did not appear the intention of my friend to despoil me of my pyjamas.'[28]

The next morning, Masson was kicked awake by 'my host, who called me a kafir, or infidel, for not rising to say prayers, which he presently repeated on the very clothes of which he had despoiled me the preceding evening'.[29] Masson's body was stiff from the cold, his face bruised and stinging. Men began to file into the tent. Some were carrying sticks, some whips, others sharp, heavy stones. Masson tried to stop himself shaking. They smiled, they greeted each other, then they fell on him. For a while, everything was a blur of pain. 'I made no doubt but it was intended to destroy me ... At length, the sun being considerably elevated, they dismissed me in the state of nakedness to which they had reduced me.'[30] Bleeding, limping, his head spinning and his stomach a ball of fear, Masson staggered away.

He got perhaps thirty paces before he 'was hailed by a man to return, and eat bread before I went. I was compelled reluctantly to retrace my steps, as a refusal might have involved my destruction, and I again came in contact with the ruffians. Instead of giving me bread, they renewed their consultations concerning me; and I gathered from their discourse that it was in question to bind me, and reduce me to slavery.'[31] The men called in an elder, an Islamic scholar, to ask him a very specific question: 'if it was not lawful, according to the Quran, to detain me as a slave, the singular reason being alleged, that they had performed the rites of hospitality towards me the night before'. Masson held his breath. He knew that the men could do whatever they wanted to him. The only person who could save him was the scholar – which is exactly what he did, telling the men that 'it was neither just nor lawful, nor according to the Quran'[32] for them to enslave Masson. In halting Persian, Masson told him a little of 'how I had been treated. He expressed the greatest regret, and, severely rebuking the offenders, urged them to restore my effects. This they were unwilling to do', but the old man 'seized the robber by his arm, and ordered him to restore the property. His orders were obeyed.'[33]

Unfortunately for Masson, while this was taking place, his trousers, in which he had hidden his money, were slowly disintegrating, revealing the hidden silver. One of the robbers 'wrenched out the webcord from my pyjamas, and, with eyes glittering with delight, unrolled the little money I had'.[34] Masson did not stay to argue. He was happy to escape with his bruises, most of his clothes, the majority of his blood, a little of his money, and his life.

The worst of the day had, surely, to be over. But it was not. That evening, Masson met with some camel drivers on the road, and he barely had time to wish them peace and prosperity before they fell upon him in turn. 'Alas! I was to encounter robbery anew. My clothes and money were now taken, and I was entirely stripped. In return for my pyjamas they gave me a ragged pair, which did not cover my knees; my shoes alone escaped, being either too large or too small for their several feet.' This time, out of a mixture of shame and desperation, Masson tried to put up a fight. The men simply grinned at him and took what they wanted anyway. He pleaded with them – begging them, as men and as Muslims, to take pity on him, 'but this only excited their laughter'.[35]

(Some time later, Masson would lose his shoes, too. At this point, everyone looked like a robber to him. Fleeing one suspicious-looking man, he tumbled straight into the arms of several others. His luck was nothing if not consistent: they were yet more robbers. He was breathlessly pointing out the dubious character on the horizon when he realised his mistake. 'My tattered garments were again explored; and certainly had I possessed anything worth plunder it would have been taken. As it was, the elder of the men remarked, "What could be plundered from you?" and in the same breath asked me to exchange my shoes' for his nasty, sweat-stained sandals. Masson pulled them on, grimacing.)[36]

That night was very cold. Shivering and half-naked, Masson knew he had to find shelter. He sidled up to the camp of a qafela, or caravan of merchants. But by now he cut such a sorry figure that the merchants were suspicious. When Masson asked the leader for food, he 'frankly replied, he would give me none, and further said, I should not accompany the qafela'.[37] Huddled in the open, dressed in nothing but his tattered pyjamas, Masson begged for help at every tent and fire in turn, but each time he was pushed away into the cold. He was shivering, crying out, ready at last to despair.

That night, it was not a trader or a scholar or a prince, but a lowly camel driver who saved Masson's life. 'He kindled his fire, and seated me by it, desiring me on no account to be dejected, that God was merciful, and would provide everything needful.'[38] All night, Masson sat by the camel driver's fire, 'with my knees drawn up to my chin', too cold and too scared to sleep. A little before dawn, a soldier took pity on the hunched, tattered figure sitting next to the embers, and 'came and threw over my shoulders a great-coat made of the skins of large-tailed sheep ... I endeavoured to rise and return thanks, when I found that, what with the heat of the fire in front, and the intensity of the cold behind, my limbs were contracted, and fixed in the cramped position in which I had been so long sitting.'[39] Shaking, smiling, Masson stammered what thanks he could.

When he had deserted, it did not seem likely that James Lewis was about to change history. If the odds against him were long then, they were surely longer now. On nights like this, when he was alone in the world, hundreds of miles from any friends, how did he hold on? What kept him going?

Masson was in the grip of an increasing obsession – not with staying alive, or even escaping from the East India Company, but with Alexander the Great. Almost everyone he met seemed to have a story: a rumour of ancient ruins over the horizon, a battered silver coin worn around a child's neck, a man who claimed Alexander as his ancestor. 'I was now in a part of the country which, there can be no doubt, had been the scene of some of Alexander the Great's exploits,'[40] Masson wrote. Where others saw Alexander as a conquering hero, spreading 'civilisation' to the far corners of the world, Masson saw a lonely man, as far from home as he was, keeping warm by a fire on an Afghan hillside. As he plodded along the roads, swearing at his blistered feet, wondering where his next meal would come from, his mind leaped over mountains and across plains, imagining armies of elephants, Persian archers, Macedonian infantry and Alexander himself on horseback.

Masson was not really following Alexander. He was following a dream. Could he find some trace of Alexander's expedition? For centuries, scholars had wondered about it from the safety of armchairs in Europe. Masson was actually on the spot. But how could he trace a 2,100-year-old journey, which no one had recorded accurately in the first place? How could he even begin, with no books, no maps, no money, no backup – and a death sentence hanging over his head? For now, it was just a mirage, but it kept him warm at night, when it seemed like the whole world was against him. Maybe, just maybe, he could tell Alexander's tale.

Day by day, he was learning the power of stories. On the road, a young man shyly asked him for a love charm 'to secure the affections of a fair maid of whom he was enamoured; or, as he expressed it, to compel her to follow him like a dog'. Awkwardly, Masson declined. But the young man would not take no for an answer. 'I found it necessary to write something on a paper to satisfy him, with which he was so well pleased that he accompanied me two or three miles on the road as I left.'[41] No one had treated Masson so respectfully for weeks (though the young man's feelings when the charm failed to perform may have been different).

With a few scraps of Pashto at his fingertips, more and more people were beginning to mistake Masson for a pilgrim on the Haj. Hajis were often to be found on the roads of India and Afghanistan, and Masson mused, 'their character for sanctity ensures them the best of entertainment, in return for which they give blessings, or, if able to write, scraps of paper, which contain … preservatives, charms, and antidotes against all disasters and diseases'.[42] But one thing was not widely known: many of the men who called themselves Hajis were no more pilgrims than Masson was. They had simply discovered that the surest route to a full stomach and a bed for the night was through other people's piety. Masson had many times envied the Hajis, but he had not dared to pretend to be one himself. Perhaps, he thought, he had simply been too cautious.

One day, Masson 'replied to all I met that I was a Haji'.[43] His meals instantly improved: from stale bread and stolen fruit to warm meats and stews, washed down with cups of sweet tea. Then he tried upgrading himself to a Sayyid, or descendant of the Prophet. This worked even better. Villagers competed to host him for the night. His stomach began to fill out. His ragged clothes were replaced with fine new cotton. One day, in a particularly daring mood, Masson swaggered into a village as a prince of the Afghans. Much to his amazement, even this worked.

After a few weeks of this, he began to look at the world through different eyes. Suddenly, he could see tricks – and tricksters – everywhere. Many travellers had far more elaborate acts than his. One night, Masson was one of three strangers lodging in a village mosque. He found it curious that all three of them – all holy men, or so they claimed – found an excuse to avoid evening prayers. 'I was not asked to pray, as it was said I was a fakir, and fakirs are allowed to be graceless.' That left the other two: a Sayyid and a prince. The prince's act was by far the most transparent: he knew little of the world, and less of Islam. The Sayyid 'gave an account of his travels in a country beyond Tibet, where beggars were fed on golden plates. His frequent mention of Delhi satisfied me as to where he belonged.' 'It must be conceded,' wrote Masson wryly, 'that three imposters were this night trespassing on charity.'[44]

Perhaps, Masson thought, he might find a place in this trickster's world after all.

Masson had learned something important. When you walk into a room full of strangers, there's a precious moment where you can become whoever you want to be: a prince or a beggar, a pilgrim or a scholar, a strong man or a weak one. If you tell your story well enough, you will be believed. The longer Masson spent in Afghanistan, the more he found that he could slip into someone else's skin and see the world through their eyes. He could talk with pilgrims about the hardships of the road and whisper secrets to alchemists. He learned the beggar's song, the prince's greeting, the doctor's touch. He built himself anew, every day, out of stories.

On the road, Masson was 'passed by three Balochi soldiers mounted on camels. One of them said to me in Persian, "Ah! Ah! You are an Uzbek!" I told him I was not, but he maintained that I was ... The mullah who officiated in the principal mosque informed a large company, with an air of great self-satisfaction, that I was a Turk ... At the same place, a woman daily visited me, always bringing me some trifling present of fruit, sweetmeat, etc, and craving my blessing. I could not surmise why she considered me qualified for the task, until I heard her one day tell another woman that I was the idiot from Mastung.'[45]

In Afghanistan, land of illusions, the storyteller's power was very great. And Masson realised that he was a storyteller.

3

The Storyteller

Masson was a long way from safety. No westerner had ever tried to travel through Afghanistan like this before: with no money, no servants and no official protection. Day by day, month by month, James Lewis the ordinary soldier slipped further away, leaving Charles Masson the illusionist in control. Hesitantly, he became a doctor for a while, applying 'cold water, cobwebs, and pressure'[1] and staring intently at a battered copy of *The Edinburgh New Dispensatory*. He spent a rainy season in Ranjit Singh's great capital, Lahore, in the mansion of one of the Maharaja's European mercenaries, Jean-François Allard. Day by day, he would sit in Allard's flower gardens, listening to the rain drumming on the rooftops and wincing at the screams of Allard's prisoners. (Allard's hospitality for his less favoured guests featured thumbscrews and forced labour.)[2] In the distance was the tomb of the great Mughal courtesan Anarkali, a dream-like first draft of the Taj Mahal. It housed the harem of another of the Maharaja's mercenaries, Jean-Baptiste Ventura. If the tomb made Masson think of his days in Agra with the Bengal Artillery, he kept those thoughts to himself.

Every day, Masson wondered how long he could keep his stories up in the air. And the answer the world gave him was always: as long as he wanted to. So, in a particularly rash and homesick moment in 1830, he decided to try his act on the British.

A few weeks later, Major David Wilson, the officer in charge of the British station at Bushehr in the Persian Gulf, noted the arrival

of Mr Masson, a American traveller, 'from which country he had
been absent about ten years'.[3] Day after day, Masson spun out his
tales: the fields of Kentucky, the parties of St Petersburg and the
jewels of Tehran. His accent may have wavered, just occasionally, as
he told tales of countries he had never seen. Masson took advantage
of Wilson's hospitality for months. Never for a moment did the
officer suspect that he was opening his finest wines for Private
James Lewis, late of the Bengal Artillery, wanted deserter.

From Bushehr, Masson made a leisurely circuit of the ancient
cities of the Persian Empire, taking in Tabriz and Baghdad,
entertained by British officers along the way. On the road, he met
another storyteller.

In the village of Soh, just north of Isfahan, under the arches of an
ancient golden caravanserai, he was introduced to the hakim bashi,
or chief physician, of the Shah of Persia. The solemn-looking young
man, reclining under a heap of bedclothes, glanced up sleepily at
Masson. He introduced himself, improbably, as 'Signor Turkoni'
from Milan. 'In course of time the village authorities came with
a breakfast furnished by the village which was spread before the
hakim bashi of the King of Kings.'[4] Signor Turkoni confided to
Masson that 'at Tehran his skill was called upon to devise remedies
for the ailments of the harem beauties',[5] but he was currently on
the run from his Armenian wife, 'whom it appeared, for he took
no care to conceal it, that he had quitted without the ceremony
of taking leave'.[6] At Baghdad, Masson learned that 'the Signor, a
mere boy, had some years since arrived there from Constantinople,
and a physician who resided with the Catholic Bishop had given
him a number of empty phials, telling him that if he had any wit
or genius, he had nothing to do but to fill his phials with variously
coloured liquids and he might make a fortune. Without the least
knowledge of medicine, the youth did as he was recommended.'[7]

In every spare moment, Masson was reading. He devoured the
ancient historians of Alexander: Plutarch and Arrian, Quintus
Curtius Rufus and Diodorus. He had travelled and wondered alone
for so long, and now here were the stories he had been dreaming of.
Masson read like a man possessed, copying out page after laborious

page by hand. He soon saw that everything Harlan had told him about Alexander had only scratched the surface.

There are many stories about Alexander the Great. None of them are entirely true.

The facts are scanty. Alexander was born in 356 BC to Philip II, king of Macedon. He was taught by Aristotle himself. At the age of twenty, Alexander took the throne after his father's assassination. Two years later, he led his army east, crossing into the Persian Empire. In strategic terms, this was like Belgium deciding to invade Russia: not so much foolhardy as suicidal. Persia was the world's superpower, with gigantic armies and a seemingly limitless treasury. But Alexander seized control of it in a series of astonishing campaigns. He won every battle that he fought, no matter the odds. Eventually, he overthrew Darius III, King of Kings, and proclaimed himself Lord of Asia.

Alexander now had more wealth and power than any European in history. But he was not satisfied. He marched his army onwards, east into Afghanistan and India, into battles with elephants and unknown kings, to the edges of the known world and beyond, until his exhausted soldiers laid down their arms on the banks of an Indian river and would go no further. Alexander died in Babylon at the age of thirty-two. His empire was disintegrating before his body was cold.

This is already an incredible story. And so much about it is puzzling: why did Alexander keep going? What was it all for? Historians have been trying to understand Alexander ever since his death. For the most part, they have failed. Who Alexander was, and why he did what he did, remain mysteries. No one, apart from Jesus, has been talked about so much and understood so little. But the more Masson read about Alexander, the more he realised one thing: he wanted to keep us guessing.

Alexander left Greece with an official historian in tow, Callisthenes. Callisthenes was going to write the definitive account of Alexander's expedition. But before he could do that, Alexander had him executed. Callisthenes may have been crucified, though some historians gave him a slightly more pleasant end: after being 'chained up for seven months' he was said to have died from 'obesity and something he caught from a louse'.[8] Alexander hacked giant gaps out of his own story, and dared posterity to fill them.

In the years after Alexander's death, no one could agree on the facts about his life. Weird and magical tales began to be told about him. In Jewish histories, Alexander sacrifices to the God of Israel at the Temple of Jerusalem. (No: Alexander never set foot in Jerusalem.) In Egyptian fables, an exiled pharaoh sneaks into the bedroom of Alexander's mother and is revealed to be Alexander's true father. (Definitely not.) There are Amazons, a journey to the bottom of the sea, and even a voyage to Eden. (No, on all counts.) Alexander became a legend.

Masson wanted to know Alexander. What was he like, before he was Alexander the Great? No one called him that until long after his death. Even then, the title may have been invented by Romans, not Greeks. But where to begin? Alexander left no diaries. He killed his own historian. But there was, Masson realised, one way into Alexander's mind: his lost cities.

Lost cities have hypnotised the world, ever since Plato first told of Atlantis:

> Now, on the island of Atlantis, there was a mighty and wondrous empire. Its power stretched over the whole island, and several others, as well as over much of the mainland. The men of Atlantis had conquered Libya and Egypt, and the lands of the west … But then there came earthquakes and floods. And in one terrible day and one terrible night, all the fighting men sank into the bowels of the earth. And the island of Atlantis disappeared into the depths of the sea.[9]

In the nineteenth century, it was not the loss of Plato's Atlantis, but Alexander's cities, which haunted people's dreams. Alexander founded cities wherever he went: to this day, no one is sure how many Alexandrias there were. The ancient historian Plutarch puts the number as high as seventy, others as low as two dozen. To complicate matters still further: what counts as a city? Obviously a gigantic metropolis like Alexandria in Egypt should make the list, but how about a settlement more like a fortified army camp: a place of safety for soldiers too old, or too badly injured, to keep going? In 1831, two things were generally agreed: almost none of the Alexandrias had been found, and finding one would be a world-changing achievement.

Back in Bushehr, Masson put aside his tales about St Petersburg and Kentucky and spun a very different yarn for Wilson. Drawing on every bit of his new knowledge, he told of how, some years previously, he had stumbled across the site of one of Alexander's lost cities. Alexandria Bucephalia was one of the strangest Alexandrias: it was named in honour of Alexander's horse, Bucephalus, and was founded in May 326 BC, on the banks of a river in present-day Pakistan. To this day, its location remains a mystery.

'I arrived in the Punjab under unfortunate circumstances,' Masson told Wilson, 'having lost all my books and other property some time before, and my memory, although it retained the grand features of Alexander's memorable expedition, failed me as to the minute details which would have been most serviceable in conducting an investigation.'[10]

In the course of my enquiries among the oldest people in a small village near, I learned that there had formerly existed two cities, one on each bank of the river. I repaired to the spot pointed out as the site of one of them, and found abundant vestiges of a once large city, but so complete had been the devastation of time, that no distinct idea of its form or architecture could be gleaned. I set people to work in the ruins, and their exertions were rewarded by the discovery of coins in gold, silver and copper of Alexander the Great, in all twenty-seven, with the same figures and inscriptions, excepting one. On the one side was the bust of Alexander and on the reverse a dismounted lancer with the inscription 'Bucephalia'.[11]

'I now remembered,' Masson went on, 'that in an action of the banks of the Hyphasis, Bucephalus was wounded and died in consequence thereof, and that Alexander in commemoration of his much-prized charger founded two cities which he named after him, at least so writes Plutarch. I therefore had no difficulty in supposing the cities which once stood here to be the ancient cities of Bucephalia.'[12] At this point, Wilson was on the edge of his seat. There was more, Masson told him: a gigantic mound was almost certainly the tomb of Alexander's beloved horse, but he could not find a way into it, 'it being closed on all sides without any appearance or sign of an entrance'.[13]

Wilson was in awe. Did Masson still have those coins? Could he see them? Alas, no. 'Mr Masson's means at that time being small, he could not continue the excavations. Unfortunately he was robbed during a severe illness he had at Multan on his way back to Sind, of such of the coins as had remained in his possession.'[14] With regret, Masson confessed to Wilson that none of his notes, sketches or maps survived.

That was not surprising, since Masson appears to have made the entire story up.[15]

Wilson soon informed Britain's envoy to Persia, John Campbell, of his guest's remarkable discovery. Campbell was just as intoxicated as Wilson had been: he pressed money onto Masson and told him he could count on his support, if he should discover any more of Alexander's cities. Masson was shocked. He had not expected his tale to work so well.

Masson did not realise it, but he had recently stumbled across a genuine lost city. In fact, he had found an entire lost civilisation. A few weeks after he left Lahore, before he set out for Bushehr, he found himself in a corner of the Punjab which no western traveller had visited for over a thousand years. After an exhausting day and 'a long march', Masson was pushing through undergrowth 'of the closest description', with little idea of where he was. Then the trees thinned, the landscape opened out and he found himself staring at the ruins of Harappa. An enormous artificial mound loomed up in one direction, surrounded by weeping fig trees, their trunks cracked and broken with age. 'To the west was an irregular rocky height, crowned with remains of buildings.'[16]

Masson was spellbound. For as long as the light lasted, he searched for clues: what was this place? On the ground, he came across 'two circular perforated stones, affirmed to have been used as bangles, or arm-rings, by a fakir of renown'. But he could find little else but swarms of gnats. Masson was looking at the ruins of a city far more ancient than any Alexandria, a place that would eventually become one of the most significant archaeological sites in Asia. Over 4,000 years ago, Harappa was a vast, thriving metropolis, awash with gold and bronze, fantastical sculptures and delicate seals emblazoned with unicorns. No European had set eyes on it for thousands of years. But that day, Masson could not find a way to tell its story. Try as he might, the ruins remained stubbornly silent. He could not make them speak.

In Bushehr, Masson was in no hurry to move on. But he knew he had to make a decision. What next? The road to London was, if not open to him, then at least relatively clear. He was beyond the East India Company's reach. By a series of miracles, he had stayed alive and out of sight. So why, one day, did he leave the comforts of the British Residency behind, bound not for London, but once more for Kabul?

The answer was simple: Alexander. If Masson made it home to London, he would be returning with nothing. But all those months alone in India and Afghanistan had convinced him of one thing. He could understand Alexander the man – not Alexander the legend – better than anyone ever had. He could tell Alexander's story in a way that no one else ever had. But to make the world listen, he had to find something concrete: not just a story about one of Alexander's lost cities, but an actual Alexandria. And that meant he had to return to Afghanistan.

Bravery did not come naturally to him, but, curled up on one of Wilson's sofas, nibbling on halva, the journey seemed worth the risk. Why not try? His disguise seemed foolproof – and surely, by now, the East India Company must have forgotten about him. This was his chance. Masson knew that for people like him, chances like this came only once in a lifetime.

In April 1831, Masson set out for Kabul once again.

Masson's first journey through Afghanistan had almost killed him. But this time was going to be different – because, this time, Masson was different.

The first people to meet the new Charles Masson were three unlucky soldiers. He took passage across the Persian Gulf, and the soldiers boarded his ship when it was preparing to drop anchor at Karachi. With the lazy confidence of petty officials, they detained Masson and the crew. Days went by. The soldiers would not release them without a hefty bribe, and neither Masson nor the crew would open their purses. 'Two of the three soldiers with me,' Masson remembered, 'were so little inclined to be civil, that I ordered the crew to give them nothing to eat; after enduring hunger for two days, they were constrained to hail a fishing-boat, into which they stepped, and regained the garrison.' That left one soldier. 'Observing my medicine-chest, he would not be satisfied unless I gave him medicine. Judging the opportunity a good one to rid myself of him, I administered a smart dose of jalap', a super-strength laxative. The third soldier was soon in the grip of miserable, uncontrollable diarrhoea. Pale and twitching, doubled over with cramps, 'he was also glad to hail a fishing-boat and to rejoin his companions'.[17] Shortly afterwards, Masson disembarked serenely in Karachi.

Unknown to Masson, he was still a wanted man. The East India Company had a very long memory. In the town of Ludhiana in northern India, a few streets away from the threadbare court of Shah Shujah, a quiet, sinister-looking man was listening to whispers from across the subcontinent. More and more of them were about a deserter who now went by the name of Charles Masson.

From Karachi, Masson headed north up the coast to the town of Sonmiani, hoping to find some merchants heading for Afghanistan. What Masson calls 'my metamorphosis'[18] now became clear. 'I was sitting alone,' he remembered, 'in my hired apartment in the bazaar of Sonmiani, when one of the merchants, a stout well-dressed person, came in front of my abode, evidently with the intent to address me, but after a short gaze, he turned about and went his way. The fact was, I was sitting cross-legged on my

cot, and, according to the fashion here, without a shirt; and not
being in the best humour in the world, my appearance was not
very prepossessing. I guessed the cause of the merchant's abrupt
departure; and to be prepared, in case of another visit, clad myself
in clean white linen, and, preparing coffee, seated myself a little
more gracefully. The beverage I drank from a sparkling tumbler,
in default of china, and before me I had two or three books. In a
short time the Pashtun reappeared, probably without any notion
of accosting me, whom he had rejected as beneath his notice, but
chancing to direct a glance towards me, he seemed astonished at
my metamorphosis; and before he could recover from his surprise
I addressed him with a courteous and sonorous "As-Salaam-
Alaikum" [Peace be upon you]. He, of course, gave the responding
salutation, "Wa-Alaikum-Salaam" [And upon you be peace], and
advanced to me. I invited him to sit down.'[19] The merchant was
heading north that very evening. 'In God's name,' he asked Masson,
'are you going with me?' Masson replied, ' "In God's name, I am,"
when he took my hands, and placing them with his own upon his
eyes, assured me that he would do my kismet on the road.'[20]

Masson had learned the greatest skill of all: how to disappear –
and reappear the next moment, as whoever you wanted him to be.

The Pashtuns say that when God created the world he had
a heap of rocks left over, out of which he made Afghanistan.
Crossing the Afghan borderlands, even in good company, was an
arduous journey. But to Masson, everything seemed strange and
beautiful. Dusty brown plains and wide fertile valleys gave way to
red-gold mountain foothills and snow-covered peaks. Dazed from
lack of sleep, 'I could almost have imagined,' he wrote, 'that I was
travelling in fairyland.'[21] He had fallen in love with this land.

Life on the road was taking its toll on Masson. His clothes began
to disintegrate. His hair began to stick up at all angles. His eyes
became flecked with red. But Masson could now put this persona
to work. He swaggered into the ancient city of Kalat with an air of
ineffability, a slight, crazed-looking man in rags, who could have
been anyone or anything. It was not long before the town came
calling. Din Mohammad Khan, an Afghan nobleman and failed

alchemist, was particularly taken with Masson. 'Din Mohammad,' Masson remembered, 'made two trifling demands of me – to provide him with a son, and to instruct him in the art of making gold.'[22] The alchemist kept a close eye on the comings and goings of travellers, and 'the more unseemly the garb and appearance of the mendicant, the greater he thought the chance of his being in possession of the grand secret'. When Masson arrived in Kalat, Din Mohammad ordered one of his household 'to bring all the limes that could be procured; some bright idea had flashed across his mind that a decisive result could be obtained from lime-juice. At other times he was seeking for seven-years'-old vinegar.'[23] For a few weeks, Masson was a happy alchemist's apprentice. In the land of illusionists, he had become a virtuoso.

The last leg of Masson's journey to Kabul, again in the company of merchants, passed smoothly. When four enterprising Balochi attempted to extract money from the travellers, Masson greeted them warmly and invited them to smoke a pipe together. A few minutes later, the Balochi were unconscious on the ground, 'as if by enchantment'.[24] The pipe had been packed with enough hashish to knock over a tiger.

Few sights in the world could match Kabul, as it was then. From a distance, across the plains, the great stone walls of Dost Mohammad's fortress, the Bala Hissar, loomed up. Before it, the city was laid out: a warren of ancient houses and bazaars, selling iced mulberries sprinkled with rosewater, heaps of sweet-smelling melons, walnuts, figs and pomegranates. Behind the Bala Hissar, snow-capped mountains towered over the city.

The road to Kabul led past groves of fruit trees, which covered the ground in blossoms, and precisely tended formal gardens. Set apart from them, shaded by plane trees, was the tomb of Babur, the great Mughal Emperor. As news of their arrival spread, friends and relatives of the merchants poured out of the city to greet them on the road, 'decked in their holiday garments, and bringing offerings of radishes and lettuce. I had no relatives or friends to welcome my approach, but, as a companion, I was admitted to a share of the delicacies: and my feelings permitted me to participate in the joy of those around me.'[25]

On 9 June 1832, Masson walked through the gates of Kabul, after a journey that had lasted almost five years. 'I saw the country and its inhabitants, in a point of view,' he reflected, 'under which no European is perhaps again likely of having the opportunity to observe them.'[26] Half dazed, he walked up through the streets, marvelling at the richness of the city. 'The day of my arrival was distinguished by the presence in the bazaar of cherries, the first-fruits of the year ... It is scarcely possible that Kabul can be surpassed for the abundance and variety of its fruits, and, perhaps, no city can present, in its season, so beautiful a display.'[27] In the old Armenian quarter, in the shadow of the Bala Hissar, he rented a little room with his remaining silver. Looking out over the city from his new home, drinking a cup of iced buttermilk, he felt, after years of wandering, as if he had come home.

There's an old Afghan proverb: 'First comes one Englishman as a traveller; then come two and make a map; then comes an army and takes the country. Therefore it is better to kill the first Englishman.' He did not know it yet, but Masson is the reason that proverb exists. He was the first Englishman.

4

The Wild East

Joseph Wolff was having a bad day. He was in Afghanistan. He was naked. And he had still not found the Lost Tribes of Israel.[1] 'Oh, if his friends in England could have seen him then, they would have started at him,' Wolff muttered as he trudged towards Kabul. 'Naked like Adam and Eve, and without even an apron of leaves to dress himself.'[2]

A few weeks before Masson reached Kabul, Wolff came lurching out of the mountains towards the city, with only a foot-long red beard[3] to preserve his modesty. He was an exception to the rule that travel broadens the mind. He had spent years wandering through Egypt, Persia and the Crimea, preaching all the way. Every day, he had become grumpier and more dogmatic. After he told some heavily armed Afghans that they were heretics, and would surely burn in hell, there was a long, contemplative silence. 'We will,' one of the men eventually said to him, 'sew you up in a dead donkey, burn you alive, and make sausages of you.'[4] In the end, the Afghans settled for stripping every stitch of clothing from him and turning him loose. Even when fully clothed, Wolff was a remarkable sight. 'His face is very flat, deeply marked with small-pox; his complexion that of dough, and his hair flaxen. His grey eyes roll and start, and fix themselves, at times, most fearfully.'[5] Naked, he quite baffled the thesaurus.

In Kabul, newly supplied with clothes, Wolff attempted to convert the ruler of Afghanistan, Dost Mohammad Khan, to

Christianity. He spent several hours in argument – wild on one side, polite yet perplexed on the other – with an Islamic scholar of the court. 'In this contest,' he wrote, 'Wolff thinks he gained the victory.'[6] Wolff was very interested in questions such as what would happen to all the fish, when the seas dried up during the End Times. ('You may pickle them!')[7] He spoke in a deep, almost incomprehensible German accent, backed up by 'vehement gesticulation'.[8] Occasionally, his voice leaped up the octaves to 'a most curious treble, the effect of which is so startling, one can scarcely refrain from laughter'.[9]

Wolff did not stay long in Kabul. He managed to make it through the Khyber Pass without losing any more clothes, and was soon bearing down on the town of Gujrat, which lay north of Lahore, within the empire of Ranjit Singh. Wolff reached the city well after nightfall, when the markets were deserted and the shops shut up. Not at all daunted, he found his way to the grandest building in town, the palace of Gujrat's governor, and hammered on the door until a bleary-eyed watchman opened it. Wolff demanded to see the governor at once.[10]

The watchman led him through the darkened corridors of the palace. Torchlight flickered on the walls. At first, the only sound was the echo of their footsteps on the floor. But as they approached the heart of the palace, Wolff was sure he could hear singing. The voice was a nasal snuffle. And the song was the very last one Wolff had expected:

Yankee Doodle went to town
A-riding on a pony,
Stuck a feather in his cap
And called it macaroni.

Yankee Doodle keep it up,
Yankee Doodle dandy,
Mind the music and the step,
And with the girls be handy.

Wolff was ushered into the governor's quarters and found Josiah Harlan curled up with a hookah.

Before Wolff could arrange his expression into something other than shock, Harlan languidly introduced himself: 'I am a free citizen of the United States of North America, from the State of Pennsylvania, and the city of Philadelphia. I am the son of a Quaker. My name is Josiah Harlan.'[11]

For the first time in his life, Wolff was at a loss for words.

In the four years since Masson slipped away from him at Dera Ismail Khan, Harlan had been busy. He had, at first, pressed on towards Kabul, still hoping to put Shah Shujah on the throne. His motley little army soon melted away. In order to find shelter on the road, he presented himself as a convert to Islam, who 'only prolonged the operation of circumcision until he should reach Kabul where expert surgeons were to be found'.[12] When Harlan arrived in Kabul, instead of overthrowing Dost Mohammad Khan he moved in with his brother, Jabar Khan. 'He [Harlan] endeavoured to amuse by experiments on quicksilver, and extracting oil from wax, reducing steel to powder, and by other such useless pastimes.'[13] Still dreaming of following in Alexander's footsteps, Harlan tried to persuade Dost Mohammad to let him lead an Afghan raid on India. Instead, Dost Mohammad put him in charge of helping his brother, Amir Mohammad Khan, lose weight. 'This individual was remarkable for extreme obesity – his weight exceeded the strength of any horse to carry. He was obliged to move about in a palanquin borne by eight men and ride upon an elephant when travelling.'[14] Instead of leading an army of Afghans through the Khyber Pass, Harlan found himself in charge of Kabul's first slimming programme.

While in Kabul, Harlan 'once entertained the idea of assuming the disguise of a Greek physician, and as such to pass the countries intervening between Kabul and China. On the frontiers of the latter country he was to remain six months to acquire the Chinese language, which attained he was to repair to Peking, to gain the confidence of the Emperor, to obtain a considerable command in the army and to work a revolution in the country!'[15] ('What might not be affected, thou confident man,' Masson had murmured when he heard the news, 'Was thou but as ready to do, as to plan.')[16]

The world, fortunately, was spared the spectacle of Harlan trying to humbug his way into the Forbidden City. By 1829, he had given up on his dreams of Chinese glory, and had also given up on Shah Shujah, attaching himself instead to Ranjit Singh's court in Lahore. At his first meeting with the Sikh Maharaja, Harlan 'attempted to create an impression that he was a modest, unassuming character, but at the same time possessed of extraordinary talents and acquirements. And by dint of preposterous costume, a hat of enormous dimensions and curious shape, joined to a demure and sanctified appearance, he succeeded.'[17] The Maharaja viewed the gigantic American as a curiosity – rather like an unusual household pet – and added him to his menagerie of foreign mercenaries. 'I will make you Governor of Gujrat, and give you 3,000 rupees a month,' he said to Harlan. 'If you behave well, I will increase your salary; if not, I will cut off your nose.'[18] 'His nose being entire,' Wolff decided, 'was evidence that he had behaved well.'[19]

Harlan, of course, had not been behaving. Rumour had it in Gujrat that he was spending 'his time in his fortress in the practice of alchemy'.[20] In fact, he was counterfeiting money. In public, Harlan appeared as a fakir, 'suffered his hair to grow to a great length, which hangs on his shoulders ... sits on a leopard's skin, and has in one hand a long wand, and with the other sets in motion the beads of a rosary which is long enough to hang the stoutest rogue in the Punjab, while he gravely mutters or makes a motion with his lips as if repeating "Bismillah" [In God's name]'.[21] Even after so many years, some things had not changed: he was still furious at Masson.[22] And he had still not been circumcised.

In Kabul, Masson settled into sleepy domesticity. He found that he was free to come and go as he pleased. Hardly anyone noticed the slight, ragged stranger wandering the markets and haggling for fruit. There was, in fact, very little about Masson to notice: he 'had with him two or three books in a foreign character, a compass, a map and an astrolabe. He was shabbily dressed, and his outward appearance denoted distress. He had neither servant, horse, nor mule to carry his baggage.'[23] To the few who asked his business, Masson described 'himself as an Englishman, by name Masson, and of the sect of priests. He had been absent from his country twelve years, during which time he had been travelling.'[24]

'Oppressed with laziness infernal, till now I never kept a journal,' Masson wrote, a few weeks after his arrival in Kabul, 'but now resolve to do so truly, from this the eleventh day of July.'[25] Old habits died hard: his first entry was full of blanks.

Masson soon learned that he was not the only traveller to have passed this way recently. As well as the well-ventilated Revd Wolff, two British travellers, Alexander Burnes and Dr James Gerard, had spent several weeks in Kabul, leaving a few days before Masson arrived. They were heading north and east, bound for Bukhara, the ancient Silk Road metropolis hidden in the deserts of Uzbekistan. Burnes insisted that he was not a spy, though no one believed him.[26] He was as obsessed with Alexander the Great as Masson, and had taken to calling himself 'the second Alexander'.[27]

Towards the end of the summer, Masson received an invitation. North-west of Kabul, about 150 miles from the city, lay Bamiyan. So steep were the mountain passes that the region enjoyed almost complete independence from the capital. For years, the Hazara people of Bamiyan had answered Dost Mohammad's tax demands 'according to an old Hazara custom … a stone or a goat; that is, they held a goat in one hand and a stone in the other, saying, if the Afghans are willing to accept the goat in place of a sheep we will give tribute, if unwilling, they shall have stones'.[28]

Dost Mohammad wanted to change that. He put one of his most fearsome commanders, the 'very influential and powerful'[29] Haji Khan Kakur, in charge of collecting Bamiyan's back taxes. This had the added benefit of getting Haji Khan out of Kabul. 'The whole political deportment of Haji Khan was calculated to excite the mistrust of a chief.'[30] He had spent the last few months quietly building up a private army.[31] Most prominent Afghans were in his debt. 'On more than one occasion' he had even saved Dost Mohammad 'from being blinded, if not put to death, by his brother'.[32]

If there was a plot in Afghanistan, Haji Khan wanted to be at the centre of it. Now, he invited Masson to accompany him to Bamiyan.

Masson had been hearing stories about Bamiyan for years. Only a handful of western travellers had ever set eyes on it, but they brought back tales of impossible things: a ruined city, perched atop a hill. Gigantic statues, carved into the cliffs, faceless and ancient. No one knew who had built them, or what they represented: could they be gods, or long-lost kings?[33] What else might be hiding there? Perhaps – just perhaps – Bamiyan was the site of one of Alexander's cities.

Masson knew he had to see Bamiyan for himself. The road was dangerous, even by Afghan standards, so Haji Khan's invitation seemed like a godsend. He hired a patient pony for a few rupees and, on 10 September 1832, rode out of the city towards Haji Khan's camp. Masson had not lived in Kabul for long, so he did not know much about Haji Khan. He had no idea what he was getting himself into.[34]

The journey proved to be an education. Some of Haji Khan's men soon caught up with him. The road was crammed with sheep being driven down towards Kabul,[35] and by nightfall everyone was dreaming of roast mutton. Masson was used to life as a solitary traveller: food and shelter were luxuries. His companions had a different approach. When they halted for the night, camp was pitched and food was demanded from the local villagers. The villagers refused. The guests drew their swords. The reluctant hosts reconsidered. Some 'cakes of pea and barley-flour' and 'large bowls of boiled milk' were offered.[36] 'Their hospitable offices were indignantly refused,' wrote Masson. 'It was ridiculous enough to behold five hungry Afghans refusing to satisfy their appetites; but the fact was, they were now employing stratagem. A sheep had been exhibited, and although in the first instance scornfully rejected, it was not intended that it should escape slaughter.' Masson's companions prepared for bed, all the while loudly cursing their hosts 'as inhospitable infidels'.[37] Everything in Afghanistan was a negotiation.

By morning, 'the stratagem of the Afghans had succeeded; an entire sheep had been roasted during the night'. But Haji Khan's men still held out: it was only after much 'supplication, weeping and kissing their feet, that they consented, as a matter of especial favour, to sit down to a magnificent breakfast of a fine hot roasted sheep, bowls of curds, and warm bread-cakes'.[38]

Masson felt so guilty about his part in it all that he tracked down the owner of the sheep and pressed 'its value in money'[39] into his hands.

Haji Khan's camp, on the banks of the Helmand River, was a jumble of tents and hungry-looking soldiers, horses, cooking fires and an overworked elephant. There were also several professional mysterious strangers – a father-and-son apothecary team, who fiercely guarded their enormous boxes of drugs, and a couple of dubious-looking holy men. Masson, to his slight chagrin, was put in their tent.

That evening, before dinner, Haji Khan sent for Masson. He 'was profuse in expressions of satisfaction at seeing me, and said that when at Kabul, from the pressure of his affairs, he was prevented from showing me the attentions he wished; now we should be constant companions'.[40] To Masson's surprise, he 'was placed by the Khan by his side, which on all occasions after was my seat'.[41] If he had known his host better, Masson would have been alarmed. But he assumed, complacently, that Haji Khan was just pleased to see him.

Over dinner – heaps of pilau rice and stewed meats – Haji Khan showed his hand. Dost Mohammad, he grumbled, had promised him five times as many troops as had actually turned up.[42] 'A mutual distrust had for some time existed' between the two men.[43] Dost Mohammad, Haji Khan knew, would not be terribly upset if a stray bullet happened to hit him somewhere along the road to Bamiyan. Haji Khan 'was essentially the child of circumstances: his grand object was to preserve himself'.[44] As the evening wore on, he turned the conversation to history, 'remarking that anyone who had read the histories of Genghis Khan . . . or any other great man who had become padshah [king], would see the necessity of disregarding family ties; that it was by the slaughter of kinsmen they had reached the summit of power; and he who would be, like them, fortunate, must be, like them, cruel'.[45] His men roared their approval, and Masson shifted uncomfortably in his seat.

The prospect of bloodshed put his host in an excellent mood. 'Here,' bellowed Haji Khan, grabbing Masson by the hand, 'is a Feringhi, shall I allow him to tell his countrymen that Haji Khan marched from Kabul with a fine force of gallant cavalry, and guns, and elephants, and returned without striking a blow? Forbid it, heaven!'[46] Masson finally realised what everyone else in the tent already knew: Haji Khan did not intend to return to Kabul. He was on his way to Bamiyan to seize power. Masson had planned a small archaeological adventure. He was now stuck with one of Asia's most ruthless warlords and was in the middle of an attempted coup.

A few days later, the travellers camped out next to a dragon.

The Hazara people tell of how, once upon a time, a monstrous dragon lived in a valley near Bamiyan. It spread fear far and wide. It burned houses to the ground, leaving entire villages in ashes. It devoured farmers and their animals, gulping down sheep and spitting out the bones. Then, one day, Hazrat Ali, the son-in-law of the Prophet Muhammad, rode into the valley to do battle with the dragon. He found it sleeping at the far end of the valley, and shot an arrow into its eye, killing it instantly.

Masson was shown the dragon's remains: its body, now turned to stone, stretching out across the valley floor; its mane, stinking of sulphur; its head, still leaking brains, 'which trickle down in small lucid currents … rippling over a surface of variously coloured red, yellow and white rock'.[47] 'The vivid red rock which is found about the head is imagined to be tinged with the blood of the dragon.'[48]

That night, after everyone else had gone to sleep, Haji Khan sent for Masson.[49] In the darkest hours of the night, they sat together by the fire and told one another their dreams. 'The Khan explained that he was favoured by visions, and had been instructed in them that he was to become a great man; that the country, whether Afghan or Uzbek, was bi-sahib, or without a master; and he proposed that he and I should benefit by such a state of things, and turn ourselves into padshah and vizier.'⁵⁰ Dost Mohammad 'could not assail' them at Bamiyan: they would be their own masters.⁵¹ Then, when Masson's mind was still reeling from the idea, the Khan pulled off his signet ring and offered it to him. This was power: the power of a king, there for the taking.

Masson had no wish to be a king. Nor had he any wish to offend Haji Khan. He smiled and very carefully refused Haji Khan's ring, 'assuring him that it could be in no better custody than his own'.⁵²

Masson walked back to his tent in a daze. The hours before dawn were cold and clear.⁵³ He tried to sleep. The world, he reflected, kept getting stranger. When he woke the next morning, the previous night seemed as distant as a dream. 'I forget,' he wrote, 'which of us was to have been the padshah.'⁵⁴

Nothing Masson had seen in all his travels prepared him for his first sight of Bamiyan. The path into the valley was narrow and treacherous: on one side, the slopes were too steep to imagine climbing, while, on the other, the ground dropped away into nothingness. Alexander Burnes, who had come this way a few months earlier, had tiptoed his way in. 'Frightful precipices hung over us; and many a fragment beneath informed us of their instability. For about a mile it was impossible to proceed on horseback, and we advanced on foot, with a gulf beneath us.'⁵⁵ Then the valley opened out, lined by steep hills 'on either side, alternating in shade from deep red to bluish grey, and forming here and there long lines of perpendicular cliff.'⁵⁶ At the end of the valley, perched atop a hill so sheer it seemed almost vertical, lay the ruined city of Gholghola.

Then, looking almost like a mirage, an even larger cliff-face, honeycombed with caves, came into view. Two vast, faceless figures, carved into its rock walls, looked serenely down at Masson: the Buddhas of Bamiyan. Above them, snow-capped and impossibly high, hung the peaks of the Koh-i-Baba, the Father of Mountains.

The valley was hushed and covered with snow. 'The winter had set in prematurely, and the sheaves of grain were lying untrodden under snow. The oldest inhabitants did not remember such an occurrence.'⁵⁷ The banks of the Kunduz River, which wound its way down the valley floor, were 'clad with vast icicles'.⁵⁸

Masson was awestruck. Standing at the foot of the cliffs, looking up at the Buddhas, he could only stare. 'If the eye should fall upon them from a distance,' the Persian traveller Yahyā ibn Khālid had written, over a thousand years earlier, 'a man would be obliged to lower his eyes, overawed by them. If he is lacking in attention or careless when he sees them, it is necessary for him to return to a place from which he cannot view them and then to approach them, seeking them as an object for his attention with reverence for them.'[59]

Haji Khan and his men set up camp at the Buddhas' feet.[60] 'The Khan, profuse in the distribution of presents, had long since exhausted the stock he brought from Kabul.' In consequence, when local dignitaries came to call on him – expecting to be greeted with gifts, as was the custom – his attendants had to scramble for a solution. The one they devised was a very Afghan answer to the parable of the endless loaves and fishes: as each dignitary left Haji Khan's tent, bearing his gift, he was intercepted by the Khan's servants. The gift was repurchased, then taken back into the tent surreptitiously, so that Haji Khan could 'confer [it] upon another'.[61]

Haji Khan had not marched all the way to Bamiyan to give people presents. Having settled into camp, he began 'a general system of seizure and spoliation'.[62] Anything portable was liable to be appropriated: not just money and jewellery, but livestock and furniture. When some of his men needed shelter, he took over an old fortress, leading to 'the ejection of about eighty families in the midst of winter, and depriving them of fuel, and provender for their cattle, turning a deaf ear to the prayers of the aged women of the castle, who appeared before him, each with a Quran in her hands, exhorting him to look in the face of God, and be merciful.'[63] The Hazara people of Bamiyan had endured repression and discrimination for centuries, but the cruelty made Masson sick. He promised himself that, in future, he would travel alone. 'Later,' as a Hazara proverb runs, 'may it be better!'

Masson slipped away from camp to explore the abandoned city, which loomed over the valley of Bamiyan. It was known as Gholghola, City of Screams. In spite of the cold, he sat in its snow-covered ruins for hours on end, listening to the howling of the wind as it blew through the empty streets. 'The winds, as they whistle in their passage through its pinnacles and towers, impart shrill lugubrious tones which impress with sensations of surprise the most indifferent being. So remarkable is this feature, that often while strolling near it, the mournful melody of the breeze irresistibly riveting my attention, would compel me involuntarily to direct my eyes upward to the eminence, and frequently would I sit for a long time together, expecting the occasional repetition of the singular cadences.'[64] The people of Bamiyan 'consider these mournful and unearthly sounds as the music of departed souls'.[65]

The city was in ruins for one simple reason: Genghis Khan. When the Mongol army reached Bamiyan in 1221, the people of the city 'issued forth in hostility and resistance, and on both sides hands were laid to arrows and catapults'. That was unwise. But according to the Persian historian Ata-Malik Juvayni, the city's fate was sealed by what happened next:

Suddenly, by the thumb of Fate, who was the destroyer of all that people, an arrow, which gave no respite, was discharged from the town and hit ... the favourite grandchild of Genghis Khan. The Mongols made the greater haste to capture the town, and when it was taken Genghis Khan gave orders that every living creature, from mankind down to the brute beasts, should be killed; that no prisoner should be taken; and that not even the child in its mother's womb should be spared; and that henceforth no living creature should dwell therein. He gave it the name of 'Ma'u-Baligh,' which means in Persian 'Bad Town.' And to this very day no living creature has taken up abode therein.[66]

From the heights of Gholghola, Masson could see the entire valley. Lost 'in deep reflection and wonder',[67] he tried to make sense of the landscape spread out before him. And the more he looked, the more he realised that he did not have the first idea what he was looking at.

No one at the time knew that the Buddhas of Bamiyan were actually Buddhas. Afghanistan had been one of the greatest centres of Buddhist worship and culture in the world: monasteries clung to its mountainsides and its plains were dotted with stupas, sites of prayer and meditation. More than a thousand monks had once lived and worshipped in Bamiyan, some in monasteries along the valley floor, and others living as hermits in the cliffs. So many hermits converged on Bamiyan that their caves – 'called samootch by the people'[68] – stacked up, one on top of another, in the cliff-faces.

The gigantic Buddhas were almost 1,500 years old. The smaller Buddha, 115 feet tall, was constructed in the middle of the sixth century AD. The larger Buddha, which stood even taller, at 174 feet, joined it around half a century later. The Buddhas did not mark a serene pilgrimage site on the edges of the known world: Bamiyan was, at the time, a riotous stop on the Silk Road. The Buddhas were painted in wild, vivid colours: incandescent red for the larger and blinding white for the smaller. So richly and brightly were they decorated that the Chinese traveller Xuanzang thought one of them was made entirely of brass.

But Buddhism had been swept out of Afghanistan in the wake of the Islamic conquest of the region. Not even the stories remained.

Imagine wandering the streets of Rome and seeing the churches on almost every corner, but not knowing what they were, or what religion they belonged to. Bamiyan was the most wondrous place Masson had ever seen, but, for the first time in his life, 'mystery and awe'[69] were not enough. He wanted answers: looking up at the enormous, broken statues, he wanted to know the truth about this place. He realised that whatever Bamiyan was, it was not one of Alexander's lost cities.[70] But other than that, he did not know where to begin. He felt like a fool.

He was standing in front of one of the wonders of the world, one of the few westerners to pass this way for centuries. He had no idea what he was doing. And he only had one sheet of paper. 'The stock I had brought with me from Kabul was exhausted,' Masson recalled ruefully, 'chiefly in enabling the soldiers of the camp to write to their friends, a fresh supply I had sent for from Kabul never reached me, our communications with that city having been closed, in the general way, by snow. From Haji Khan's secretary, who was much in the same dilemma as myself with respect to paper, I obtained as a great favour a single sheet, which I was obliged to employ with care, and only on such objects as seemed to me the most deserving. It was most wretched paper, but I was obliged both to make it serve and be thankful for it.'[71]

Standing at the foot of the smaller Buddha, Masson spotted a flight of stairs ascending into the rock walls. He followed them uncertainly. The passageway was narrow and dark, carved out of the red stone of the cliffs. The walls and ceiling seemed to press in on him. Masson climbed higher and higher. The only light came from narrow slits cut in the rock.[72] Through them, he caught glimpses of the Buddha: a fold of drapery, a gigantic arm, a pendulous earlobe. Outside, the world was hushed and still. A few plumes of black smoke rose on the wind.

Then Masson emerged into the light above the Buddha's head and saw a world more beautiful, and stranger, than he had ever dared to imagine. Outside, the winter sun shone on clear, bright drifts of snow. Close to the top of the cliff-face, within the caves, lapis lazuli and gold shimmered in shafts of sunlight.[73] Everywhere Masson looked there were domes, intricate carvings and impossibly beautiful paintings.[74] This was no footnote in history: this was an entire lost civilisation, unknown to western scholarship. It was like seeing colour for the first time: he realised that here in Afghanistan, there was a whole world of wonders waiting to be discovered.

Masson was dizzy with awe. Even his sketches, after years of sober black and white, suddenly spring into full colour. At that moment, looking down on Bamiyan, he knew that he wanted to tell the story of Afghanistan. He had no idea how: he knew that he was 'standing only on the threshold of discovery'.[75] But, inside, his heart was dancing. 'Inveni portum,' he scribbled on a pencil sketch of the caves. 'Spes et Fortuna valete.'[76] 'I have reached safe harbour. Farewell, hope and fortune. You have played your games with me: now, play them with others.'

That night, the sky was full of falling stars.[77]

Several weeks later, Masson staggered through the gates of Kabul. His journey back, in company with some of Haji Khan's men, had been horrific. Snowdrifts reached up to his chest and threatened to swallow him whole.[78] Some nights, he was driven away from shelter with stones and curses, and slept on the ground, rolled up in his cloak.[79] By the time he reached Kabul, he was frozen and frostbitten. His clothes were in tatters. His feet were blistered. He had almost been blinded by snowstorms.[80] But the world seemed like a gift.

It was Christmas Day.[81]

In 1924, two French archaeologists clambered cautiously down the cliff-face of Bamiyan. They were aiming for a cave which disappeared into the sheer rock wall, high above the head of the tallest Buddha. Sliding and scrambling into the cave mouth, they caught their breath and looked around triumphantly. It was hard to imagine a more inaccessible spot: it was possible that no one else had stepped inside it for centuries. It took a few moments for their eyes to adjust to the darkness, but they looked around eagerly: unimaginable treasures could be waiting for them.

Then – and his heart must have sunk – one of the archaeologists noticed two rude lines of verse, scratched on the rock wall, in front of their very noses:

If any fool this high samootch explore,
Know Charles Masson has been here before.[82]

5

The City Beneath the Mountains

In the winter months the people of Kabul retreated indoors and wrapped themselves in heavy sheepskins. Wine froze, and 'copper vessels burst during the night'.[1] In spite of the bitter cold, Masson was happy. No one knew whether he was a traveller, a spy or a madman, and no one cared. 'There are few places where a stranger so soon feels himself at home, and becomes familiar with all classes, as at Kabul. There can be none where all', he wrote, 'so much exert themselves to promote his satisfaction and amusement. He must not be unhappy. To avow himself so would be, he is told, a reproach upon the hospitality of his hosts and entertainers. I had not been a month in Kabul before I had become acquainted with I know not how many people; and become a visitor at their houses.'[2] Muslims, Christians, Jews and Hindus lived side by side: eating together, celebrating together, and walking in one another's funeral processions.[3] 'They mutually attended each other's weddings, and participated in the little matters which spring up in society.'[4] A Christian would offer gifts to his Muslim neighbours on Nowruz, the Islamic new year, and, in turn, 'he received them on his own Christmas day'.[5] Almost nothing is left of that Afghanistan today. The old city is in ruins. The old ways of life are barely remembered. But Kabul, in 1833, was one of the most tolerant cities in the world.

(Kabul was almost aggressively tolerant. Whenever any of the city's Christians sought to convert to Islam, they used to be interrogated by the vizier, who would ask the unfortunate convert 'what they had discovered of evil in their own faiths, that they were anxious to change them, and would upbraid them as worthless unprincipled fellows'.)[6]

Masson spent his days wandering Kabul. The city's bazaar was one of the wonders of Asia. Mohan Lal, an Indian scholar who travelled with Alexander Burnes (and kept him from being killed more than a few times), was not easily impressed: he had grown up in Delhi. But Kabul's bazaar left him awestruck. 'The parts of the bazaar which are arched over exceed anything the imagination can picture. The shops rise over each other, in steps glittering in tinsel splendour, till, from the effect of elevation, the whole fades into a confused and twinkling mass, like stars shining through clouds.'[7] As Masson worked his way from one stall to another, examining the winter displays of 'wild ducks and sparrows',[8] he had no idea that he was being watched.

The East India Company had a spy hard at work in Kabul, and he kept a very close eye on the comings and goings of strangers. Soon after Masson returned from Bamiyan, the spy reported that 'whilst seated in a shop in the bazaar, a man passed by me, who had the appearance of a European, grey eyes, red beard, with the hair of his head close cut. He had no stockings nor shoes, a green cap was on his head, and a fakir or dervish drinking cup over his shoulder. He did not, however, resemble a dervish much, and appeared to be staring at everything with the curiosity of a stranger. I observed to the owner of the shop, who had been in Russia, that the man was a Russian; he replied, "Yes, and all who have seen him say so; but he is an Afghan." The man was then lost in the crowd, but a few days later I saw him again, and accosted him, but got no answer, and he walked away very fast.'[9]

The spy's report was soon on its way over the mountains to India. He resolved not to let the red-haired stranger slip away so easily the next time they met.

Masson, meanwhile, spent his evenings reading and sketching out Alexander's route. Deciding to find a lost city is easy but, Masson was realising, knowing where to begin was much harder.

In 1812, when he was looking for Petra, Johann Ludwig Burckhardt simply asked for directions.

Burckhardt wandered through the Middle East in disguise, calling himself Sheikh Ibrahim Ibn Abdallah, and asking everyone he met about Petra, the ancient trading city in the mountains of Jordan. Eventually, he was told about a path leading into a deep, hidden valley, near a tomb said to be that of the Prophet Aaron. Burckhardt followed the path. Sandstone cliffs rose higher and higher on either side. The dust clung to his clothes. Then, at last, Petra opened up before him:

> It seems no work of Man's creative hand,
> by labour wrought as wavering fancy planned;
> But from the rock as if by magic grown,
> eternal, silent, beautiful, alone ...
> A rose-red city half as old as time.[10]

When he returned to Europe, Burckhardt's discovery of Petra made him a household name. In Jordan, it was met with bemusement: Burckhardt's 'discovery' had been common knowledge for centuries. Sultan Baibars of Egypt had visited Petra in the thirteenth century, over 500 years earlier.

Masson knew that finding one of Alexander's lost cities would not be so straightforward. Most of the Alexandrias are truly lost: even today, our best guesses for their locations are little more than pins stuck in a map. 'In most cases the vital factors which would enable us to identify this or that ancient site with a modern locality simply do not exist, and to debate the preference,' Peter Fraser recently wrote, 'is fruitless. In almost every case any attempt to be more precise than the ancient source leads to a dead end.'[11] But, sitting by the fire in Kabul, wrapped up in a sheepskin, Masson soon knew which Alexandria he was looking for.

In 329 BC, Alexander stood at the foot of the Hindu Kush mountains, looking east into an unknown world. He and his army had travelled further than any Greeks before them. They had won greater victories than the heroes of old. The ends of the earth were close at hand. 'Alexander led his army towards Mount Caucasus,' wrote Arrian, 'and there, he founded a city, and named it Alexandria. Then, after offering sacrifices to all of the gods he was accustomed to sacrifice to, he led his army across Mount Caucasus.'[12] Three thousand of his men settled there: soldiers too old or too sick to carry on. Like Masson, they found a new home in a strange land.

After Alexander's death, Alexandria beneath the Mountains,[13] as the city came to be known, thrived for centuries. At the edge of Alexander's empire, it was left to govern itself. A thousand years after Alexander's death, a Chinese traveller wrote fondly of it. Nestled beneath the Hindu Kush, rich in fruit trees, it still inspired awe.[14] Then, it slowly faded from memory.

Masson knew that Alexandria beneath the Mountains might have been a city of wonder. Alexandria in Egypt, the most famous of Alexander's cities, was one of the glories of the ancient world: a cultural and intellectual crossroads like no other, where scholars, traders, artists and writers developed new ways of understanding the world. In Afghanistan, might there be ancient theatres lying hidden? Temples to strange gods? Palaces of unknown kings? Anything was possible. Not all lost cities are real (no one is about to find Atlantis), but this one was. Somewhere in Afghanistan, hidden by time, by dust and snow, lay the remains of a fabulous city.

For over 1,000 years, Afghanistan had been a blank space in western knowledge. In 1833, scholars thought Alexandria beneath the Mountains was underneath modern-day Kandahar, around 300 miles from Kabul. Masson knew they were wrong: that relied on Alexander's army crossing Afghanistan from north to south, on foot, in only ten days.[15] Every blister on his feet told him this was impossible. The city had to be much closer to Kabul. But where?

The ancient historians of Alexander were no help: a more untrustworthy crew has rarely been assembled. The most reliable of them, Arrian, never set foot in Afghanistan. His narrative is full of weird portents and dubious anecdotes (if his battles seem less than exciting, perhaps he might offer an interlude with

Alexander and the Amazons?).[16] He devotes only a few lines to the foundation of Alexandria beneath the Mountains. He spends much longer on the story of an Afghan city which it would be brave to seek: Nysa.

When Alexander's army appeared before the walls of Nysa, Arrian says, the people sent a delegation out to meet him, dressed in their finest clothes. 'When they entered Alexander's tent, they found him sitting there, covered in dust and weary from travel. He was still in his armour: a helmet was on his head, and a spear was in his hand. For a moment, no one spoke, then the people of Nysa fell on their faces before him.' They told Alexander their story. Their city had been built by none other than Dionysus, the Greek god of wine and misrule himself. 'On his way home from India, he founded this city as a memorial of his long journey, and his many victories. The men he settled here were those of his companions, and his priests, who could go no further. He and you are alike: for, after all, you have founded Alexandria beneath the Mountains and Alexandria in Egypt, and many other cities too. And you will go on to found still more. Soon, indeed, you will have accomplished more than Dionysus himself.'[17]

This was the only evidence Masson had to work with. It was not enough.

***

Kabul was a city of storytellers. Even in the depths of winter, 'in the most crowded parts of the city there are storytellers amusing the idlers, or dervishes proclaiming the glories and deeds of the Prophet. If a baker makes his appearance before these worthies, they demand a cake in the name of some prophet; and, to judge by the number who follow their occupation, it must be a profitable one.'[18]

The stories they told were wild, filthy, hilarious things. Often, they were about the misadventures of Mulla Nasrudin. Nasrudin was a thirteenth-century Sufi satirist and philosopher: the perfect wise man and the perfect fool. The storytellers of Afghanistan still hold their audiences spellbound with tales of his misadventures: someone, somewhere, is telling a Mulla Nasrudin story right now.

One day, Nasrudin was hungry, so he crept into a garden and began filling his sack with vegetables. Soon the owner noticed and came running over.

'What exactly,' said the owner to Nasrudin, 'do you think you are doing in my garden?'

'I'm terribly sorry,' said Nasrudin. 'It was an awful accident: I was blown here by the wind.'

'Then,' said the owner, 'why have all my vegetables been pulled out of the ground?'

'That,' said Nasrudin, 'should be obvious. I was trying to stop myself getting blown away again. I had to grab hold of something.'

'Fair enough,' said the owner. 'But tell me this: how did all those vegetables end up in your sack?'

'You know,' said Nasrudin, 'I've been wondering that myself.'[19]

Masson listened to the storytellers, hoping for clues to the location of Alexandria.[20] And in between the mother-in-law jokes and the yarns about Mulla Nasrudin and his donkey, he heard some very curious things: 'strange stories of the innumerable coins and other relics found on the soil' on the plain of Bagram, around forty miles from Kabul.[21] The presence of ancient coins and artefacts on the surface could mean that far more substantial structures were hidden just below ground: possibly even an entire city. Masson wondered: could tales from the bazaar point him towards a place no scholar could find?

Spring was coming. Soon, Masson would be able to find out for himself. As the snow melted, 'in consequence of the mud walls of the buildings having become completely saturated with moisture, their foundations yielded to the pressure of the weight above them, and very many houses fell in. Each accident was announced by a tremendous crash.'[22] In the fields around Kabul, Masson saw the grass starting to grow back, and 'a small flower with six white petals'[23] poking out of the sodden ground. The markets began to fill with spinach and spring vegetables.[24] Frogs, or 'the nightingale of the waters' as the Afghans ruefully called them, became loud, lewd and abundant.[25]

Meanwhile, the East India Company's spy had been keeping an eye out for the red-haired dervish. And he had learned something interesting. One day, in the bazaar, a man took Masson aside and begged him to help heal his sick son. Reluctantly, Masson agreed to visit his house and, 'seeing his son, said he had not his medicine with him, or he would cure him. The man asked him to write down the medicine and he would get it; whereupon the dervish said it was not procurable in India. He then asked a spell of the dervish, who, after muttering to himself, produced a small pen and ink, wrote something on a paper', as holy men were accustomed to write down charms, 'which he threw into the fire, and said: "Your son will recover."' Then the dervish melted back into the crowds.[26]

Despite not being able to help the man, Masson thought he had at least stayed in character. He did not realise that he had made one fatal mistake. When he wrote down the charm for the sick child, he wrote it instinctively from left to right, in the western manner, rather than right to left.[27] When the spy heard that, he smiled: this dervish was no Afghan. In his head, he was already composing his next report.

Masson was increasingly convinced that Bagram was the site of Alexander's lost city. But if he turned up unannounced with a shovel, even if he was successful, he would end up in the position of Mulla Nasrudin in the tale: holding a sack full of finds on someone else's land, vainly trying to explain himself.

He decided to start small.

One of his friends owned some land on the outskirts of Kabul. The fields surrounding the city were dotted with artificial mounds: some of them huge and imposing, others relatively modest. Masson did not have the resources to excavate one of the 'massive' ones, 'where considerable expense was required; still, the inferior indications of the olden time might repay the labour bestowed upon them, and by testing the feeling which my excavations created I might smooth the way for the time when I should be in condition to undertake the superior monuments. Without asking permission of any one I commenced an operation upon a mound.'[28] Some of Masson's Afghan acquaintances agreed to help. He had no idea what the mound was, or when it dated from: it was 'composed of two stages, the lower and superior [larger] one being garnished with caves',[29] but it could have been two hundred years old, or two thousand.

Masson began with the caves. 'The entrances are small so that it is necessary to crawl in, but the interiors of some of them are spacious. At the closed entrance of one of them, observing some fragments of earth which had been painted over with a coat of white and the blue of lapis lazuli, we were inclined to clear away the earth, and found an arched entrance, on the side of which was affixed an image of earth, painted with white and red lead.'[30] After a few days of digging, Masson found a way into the heart of the mound: inside, there was an 'arched recess, ornamentally carved, and supported by two slender pillars. In it we found the remains of several earthen images; the heads of the two larger ones only were sufficiently entire to bear removal.'[31] After the wonders of Bamiyan, finding only a few fragments of sculpture was an anticlimax. Yet in this damp, faded space, there were still glimpses of riches and astonishing colours. 'We could yet from slight traces ascertain that the figures had been originally covered with layers of red and white paint, and that over the latter had been placed a surface of gold leaf. The hair of the heads, tastefully arranged in curls, had been painted with an azure colour. The recess also had been embellished with gold leaf and lapis lazuli.'[32] Just as at Bamiyan, he had found traces of a vanished civilisation: the mound probably held the remains of an ancient Buddhist hermitage. But now Masson was thinking like an archaeologist, not a traveller. He was no longer satisfied with seeing the world. He wanted to discover what lay beneath the surface. He wanted to know its secrets.

When Masson's friends heard about what he was doing, they were horrified. Rumours travelled fast in Kabul, and 'my researches became the subject of conversation in the city'. 'My friends prayed me to desist from such labours in future, urging that the country was bad, as were the people, and that I should probably get into trouble. I smiled as I essayed to console my friends, and to point out that little notice would be taken of me so long as broken idols were the fruits of my proceedings.'[33]

When Akbar Khan, Dost Mohammad's son, summoned Masson to the palace a few days later, he realised just how wrong he had been. Wrapping up his finds as carefully as he could, Masson climbed up the winding streets of Kabul towards Dost Mohammad's citadel, the Bala Hissar. It stood, high and cold and isolated, on a rocky outcrop at the top of the city. As he walked through its great arched gates, Masson wondered what was waiting for him inside. He had counted on remaining inconspicuous. That, clearly, had been a bad plan.

Masson had no reason to worry: Akbar Khan was delighted by the shabby little stranger with his bag full of ancient sculptures. He insisted on seeing Masson's discoveries. That afternoon, the deserter and the prince sat together for hours, turning over one piece after another, lingering on a curl of hair, or a perfectly sculpted eye. Neither of them knew what Masson had found, but both knew beauty when they saw it. Akbar Khan 'was enraptured with two female heads, and lamented that the ideal beauties of the sculpture could not be realized in nature'.[34] When one of his attendants muttered that Masson was helping himself to things that did not belong to him, 'he remarked to those about him, who suggested that I might be seeking treasure, that my only purpose was to advance science, which would lead to my credit on my return to my native country'. Masson had made a very unexpected, and very valuable friend. 'From this time on a kind of acquaintance subsisted between us. I became a pretty constant visitor at his tea-table.'[35]

Hesitantly, Masson mentioned his grander ambitions to Akbar Khan: the stories he had heard of Bagram and his wish to excavate there. To his shock and delight, he soon found himself holding a sheaf of letters from Dost Mohammad's son, addressed to the local chiefs and tribal leaders in the areas around Kabul. They all said one thing: give this man what he wants.[36]

Spring had now given way to summer. The markets were crammed again: fruits, vegetables and delicate sweets filled the stalls. They rested on 'square crystallized heaps' of fresh snow, which sparkled in the sunlight.[37] 'Quantities are brought from the elevated heights of the Caucasus by donkey drivers and individual carriers, who never refuse a drink of ice water to the sweltering beggar who asks.'[38]

One summer day, when the flowers were in full bloom, Masson rode out of Kabul. After months of planning, he was ready to see if Bagram really could be the site of one of Alexander's lost cities. 'A primary object of my rambles,' he wrote, 'was to ascertain if any vestiges existed which I might venture to refer to Alexandria … the site of which, I felt assured, ought to be looked for at the skirts of the Hindu Kush.'[39] Crowds were pouring out of the city, making for the shade of the gardens which surrounded it. 'Bird fanciers carry out in covered cages their larks and nightingales', while in the gardens, 'crowds gather around professional storytellers', their faces 'excited' and full of wonder.[40] 'The serious pursuit of a Kabuli', as Harlan realised during his time in the city, 'is to devise and enjoy the pleasures of life, exclaiming with gusto: "Each moment's pleasure is a blessing – live whilst we live, for tomorrow we die." '[41]

When he reached the plains of Bagram, Masson fell in love. 'The winding courses of its rivers, the picturesque appearance of its castles and gardens, the verdure of its pastures, the bold and varied aspect of its hills, crowned by the snowy summits of the Caucasus, form a landscape whose beauty can scarcely be conceived.'[42]

On the way, Masson had been told the story of Mohammad Shah Khan, a local weaver, 'who rose one morning and fancied himself destined to be padshah of Delhi. Grasping his musket, he left the house alone, shot the two or three first men he met, to show that he was in earnest, and took the road to Kabul.' Soon, 'crowds began to flock in to him. At the head of four or five thousand men he entered Kabul.'[43] The weaver was said to have ruled Kabul for a whole winter, until a sufficiently large army could be collected to dislodge him. In Afghanistan, with luck on your side, anything was possible.

Luck, however, did not appear to be on Masson's side. In one of the first villages he reached at Bagram, the locals 'were inclined to be merry at my expense, and in walking the bazaar I incurred the hazard of being mobbed, one rogue passing the word to the other that a "strange bird" had come'.[44] Masson did not mind the jokes: he knew he looked odd, even at the best of times. But jokes were all he was able to collect. Everyone he asked, in one village after another, told him the same thing: the stories were not true. No ancient coins had ever been found nearby. At one village, 'there were seven considerable Hindu traders,' Masson wrote, 'but we applied to them for coins in vain'.[45] Masson circled the plain, fruitlessly. Again and again he was told that the stories were only stories, nothing more.

Masson gave up. He set out, sadly, back towards Kabul.

Then, in a village a few miles from Bagram, he began to hear the stories again. 'We heard fresh tales of Bagram, and the treasures found there, and my curiosity was so intensely excited, that I determined to revisit it.'[46]

Masson rode back towards the plain, trailed by some very perplexed Afghan horsemen, who had been sent by a local chief to look after the 'strange bird'. At the first village he reached, Masson tried again. Initially, the response was the same: no one had any coins, and no one had ever found any. Masson was ready to admit defeat.

Then an old man brought out a single, ancient copper coin.[47]

Masson held it up to the light. Battered, defaced and impossibly old, it was like a message from another world. The face of an unknown king, and letters in an ancient script stared back at him. That coin told him the stories might be true. He pressed money into the old man's hand, far more than the coin was worth.

Immediately, everything changed. Once the villagers realised that Masson intended to pay for the coins, one after the other they quietly slipped away and reappeared clutching bags bulging with ancient coins. Famine became feast: Masson dived into the bags like a starving man who has just had a banquet set before him. He could not afford to buy many of them, but he lovingly picked out the best examples, 'as suited my purpose. I had the satisfaction to obtain in this manner some eighty coins, of types which led me to anticipate bright results from the future.'[48]

The villagers had feared that, if they revealed their hoards to Masson, he would simply take them by force. Still worse, they might be compelled to act as 'forced labourers, to scour the plain in search of antique relics, on which account it had been determined to conceal from me, if possible, their existence. I afterwards learned from a goldsmith that at the time I applied to him he had ... about fifteen pounds in weight of old coins by him, which his companions deterred him from exhibiting.'[49]

After a few hours of happy haggling, 'the report had spread that a Feringhi had come to engage soldiers, and crowds came from the neighbouring castles to ascertain the truth, and what pay was given. I now thought it better to leave.'[50]

Masson rode back to Kabul with his head spinning, and his pockets full of the past. The stories about Bagram – those tales he had been told in the marketplace of Kabul, along with the yarns of Mulla Nasrudin – had been true all along.

Had he actually found Alexandria beneath the Mountains?

He knew that he was close: he could be riding over the ruins of Alexander's walls at that very moment. But a few coins proved nothing. They were so battered as to be almost indecipherable, and none of them seemed to depict Alexander himself. Even then, finding a single coin with Alexander on it would not prove that this was the site of Alexander's city. 'The presence of mounds, the casual discovery of coins and other antiques, are generally supposed to indicate the site of a city, whereas they may only point out that of its burial-grounds.'[51] Masson needed something much more substantial.

He had work to do.

On the way back to Kabul it occurred to him, rather later than it should have done, that he had just spent all of his money.

6

The Golden Casket

The kingdom of Kutch lay in the far west of India, on the edge of the great white deserts, about 750 miles from Kabul. It was a wild, salt-baked country, blasted by winds and boiled by the summer heat. Kutch was ruled from a crumbling palace in the little town of Bhuj by Maharaja Deshalji II, who made up for his lack of power with a superabundance of titles, and of everything else he could lay his hands on. Maharajadhiraj Mirza Maharao Shri Deshalji II Sahib Bahadur turned his desert capital into the most flamboyant little kingdom in India. His palace was stuffed with Venetian chandeliers, fountains which ran with multicoloured water, intricate clocks, palanquins, stained glass and a morose, taxidermied hippopotamus. On the walls, fleshy portraits of European ladies hung next to a print entitled, laconically, *Revelling with Harlots*. From the battlements of his palace, the Maharaja could look down over the town to the green lawns and white walls of the British Residency, home to perhaps the angriest man in India, the East India Company's Resident in Bhuj, Henry Pottinger.

Think back to the most easily irritated person you have ever met. Double their sensitivity. You might now be coming close to Pottinger. If you left him alone in a room for a few minutes, he would probably be nursing a lifelong grudge against the sofa and two of the floorboards by the time you returned. Even in his official portrait, he looks as if he is about to put down his papers and punch the artist: his moustaches are bristling, and his cheeks are flushed

furious red. His ability to get offended was exceeded only by his
ability to get ill. In its finite wisdom, the East India Company put
him in charge of one of the toughest and most sensitive districts
in India. (Even today, Kutch is not a place to be trifled with. The
closer you get to the border with Pakistan, the more pointed the
signs lining the road become: 'Trespassers will be shot.')

Pottinger was not suited to pulling the strings of the Maharaja's
golden, tumbledown kingdom. In the summer, the heat dried up
his mouth and his eyes, until it felt like his eyeballs were about to
seize up in their sockets. Most mornings, he would wake up and
not know what to be angry about first: the bandits, the Maharaja,
his incompetent subordinates, his incompetent superiors, the
weather, his enemies, or everything at once. He generally chose
everything at once.

One day in 1833, a few months before Masson set out for Bagram,
Pottinger was not angry. He was curious. He had just received
an unexpected letter from Kabul. It was written on blue Russian
paper, with the anxiety of a stranger trying to make a good first
impression. It was full of gossip about Dost Mohammad's court
and the schemes of Haji Khan. But the writer was much more
interested in the past than in the present. 'My particular object
in these countries is to capture their antiquities,' he wrote. 'I have
not been unsuccessful.' Would Pottinger, he asked, be interested in
hearing more about his finds? If so, 'I shall be in Kabul at least for
the next six or eight months, and any communication will reach
me, by being simply addressed to Masson, Feringhi, in the quarter
called Bala Hissar.'[1]

'I may need to be pardoned,' Masson wrote, 'for addressing you,
to whom I am personally unknown.'[2] That was not all Masson
needed to be pardoned for. Pottinger had no idea that his new
correspondent was a wanted deserter. Masson's letter had been
eagerly revealing of everything but himself. Even by Masson's
standards, it was reckless to open a correspondence with an officer
of the East India Company, someone who would have arrested him
on sight had he known the full story. But, when Masson was in
Persia, he had heard about Pottinger: the only thing that matched

his irritability, he was told, was his obsession with the past. To Masson, that sounded wonderful. And Masson needed friends.

You can cross a mountain on your own. It might not be advisable – indeed, it might be foolhardy in the extreme – but it has been done. You cannot excavate a lost city on your own. It has never been done. If you were equipped with a shovel and a sufficient supply of determination, you might, over a few weeks, be able to dig a single trench and uncover a single wall. But even then, assuming that, by miraculous good fortune, you happened to dig in exactly the right place on your first attempt, how could you lift blocks of masonry single-handedly? And, Masson knew, there were the real problems. If he succeeded – if, against the odds, he did manage to find something more than 'broken idols'[3] – what then? How could his finds be carried back to Kabul? How could he pay for them to be transported to India, let alone to Britain? Who would take care of them on the journey, and who would be there to receive them on the other end? (It would, unfortunately, be many years before archaeologists realised that carrying away a country's heritage without the consent of its population, and stripping the sites of their discoveries bare, were deeply destructive practices.) Masson was hoping that Pottinger might help.

When Masson returned to Kabul, still dazed from his discoveries at Bagram, it was high summer. The markets were full of lettuces and unripe plums, apricots, radishes and cucumbers. In the gardens surrounding the city walls, the roses were in full bloom and their scent hung in the air through the long summer twilight.[4] Masson sat in the ruined pleasure gardens of Babur, the first Mughal Emperor – its pavilions untended, its lawns overgrown, its paths choked with weeds, its fruit trees abundant – and watched the sun set. Young men and women gathered there from all over Kabul, the men tumbling over each other in chaotic games of leapfrog, the women singing and playing tambourines.[5] 'All is,' he wrote, 'going to decay.'[6] Yet it was utterly 'delightful'.[7]

Masson had good reason to be cheerful. A letter from Pottinger had been waiting for him when he returned to the city. Pottinger had not just replied very warmly, he had also sent Masson some money to fund his excavations. Masson was grateful beyond words. 'For this token of goodness, I beg you will accept my best thanks,' he wrote to Pottinger. 'It has been my misfortune to have spent a good deal of very unprofitable time in Kabul, being unable to move, from immediate restraint. Your kindness has now delivered me ... I have it much at heart to allocate the several places enumerated in Alexander the Great's Indian expedition, and in many I hope to be successful.'[8]

Masson had another frequent visitor that summer: Karamat Ali, the East India Company's spy in Kabul. Karamat Ali had not been having a good year. 'He had wished to preserve his incognito; but a letter, destined for Herat, having been intercepted, his existence, and the nature of his employment, became revealed, and he was consigned to the prison of Dost Mohammad Khan.'[9] Dost Mohammad's brother, Jabar Khan, got the not-so-secret agent out of jail once he promised not to write a word about Dost Mohammad in future. After that, Karamat Ali decided that creeping around Kabul for the East India Company was a wildly overrated occupation and moved in with Jabar Khan instead.

One day during Ramadan he turned up on Masson's doorstep. He introduced himself, rather grandly, as an 'agent of the Supreme Government of India', and invited himself to lunch.[10] Karamat Ali did not enjoy fasting, and Masson's little house in the Armenian quarter was one of the few places in Kabul where he could break his fast discreetly. Masson 'had much of his company'[11] for the rest of Ramadan. The spy ate very well and said nothing more about Masson to the East India Company.

Sitting in Babur's garden, Masson tried to make sense of what he had found at Bagram. He stared at the coins he had bought, hoping to see some detail, some word, which might help him understand what he was looking at. The faces of unknown kings stared back at him. Were these the kings of Alexandria? Masson had almost no books, so he had no idea 'what is known and what is unknown to the European world'.[12] But even if he had had the greatest libraries of the world at his disposal, he would not have been able to solve that puzzle. 'When Alexander marched away,' as one recent historian put it, 'darkness swallowed the land.'[13] If he wanted to find Alexandria, Masson had to answer a question no one had been able to solve for a thousand years: what happened after Alexander left Afghanistan?

Pottinger's letter was not the only surprise awaiting Masson when he returned from Bagram. A few miles from the city walls, he came upon a treasure-hunting Transylvanian, Johann Martin Honigberger, 'engaged in demolishing' a structure Masson had been eyeing up for months: 'one of those numerous ancient buildings'[14] which surrounded the city. Honigberger liked quoting Cicero, practising homeopathy and smashing things. He had spent the last four years at Ranjit Singh's court in Lahore, and 'by the practice of physic and the manufacture of gunpowder he would appear to have realized something handsome, and he is now proceeding to Europe'.[15] Honigberger had been responsible for making Ranjit Singh's favourite cocktail: 'hotter than any whisky, it actually burns like fire. This he [Ranjit Singh] especially gave to English travellers to drink, in order that he might extract news from them.'[16]

To Honigberger, Afghanistan's ancient sites looked like money. Through the summer months, Masson watched him pickaxe his way through one ruin after another, looking for valuables. 'I could have wished to have been the first to have opened them – that I have been anticipated is entirely owing to my straitened means,' he wrote, sadly. 'I have endeavoured to raise money in Kabul, and can do so, but under such tremendous loss, that as matters stand, I can only remain quiet.'[17] Honigberger gloated over his finds to Masson, showing him a 'superb gold medal' which he had dug up near Kabul. He told Masson cheerfully that he was 'not versed in ancient history' and had no idea what his discoveries were, 'but they were valuable'.[18]

(Masson's own excavation techniques, of course, would cause any modern archaeologist to blanch in horror. Pickaxes and hope have long since been displaced by ground-penetrating radar and tweezers. But compared to many nineteenth-century archaeologists,

Masson was meticulous. When Heinrich Schliemann excavated the site of ancient Troy decades later, he did so with dynamite.)

Hoping to distract Honigberger, Masson suggested that they ride out of Kabul together, and spend a few days in the countryside. 'Our objects are different,' Masson wrote, hopefully, 'the doctor directing his attention to objects of natural history and myself to those of antiquities and the geography of the country.'[19] Honigberger turned up with a mule, a secretary mounted 'on a vicious pony of the Punjab'[20] and a number of very large empty bags. He 'collected every plant that came within his observation', pulling them out of the earth and mashing them into a thick black book. With appalled fascination, Masson watched his fingers working busily away, sticky with sap, grubbing and crushing.[21]

In the autumn, two more travellers reached Kabul. Dr James Gerard and Mohan Lal had passed through the city in 1832 with Alexander Burnes, 'the second Alexander'.[22] Now, they were on their way back to India. Gerard was almost as fascinated by Afghanistan's ancient history as Masson. He fell hard for the shy, ragged storyteller. 'Masson's life has been vagrant and full of vicissitudes,' he wrote. 'It will not be unobserved that as a traveller, I am prejudiced in favour of Mr Masson … but he has merits of no common order':[23]

> His subsequent researches, part of which I am acquainted with, furnish a type of intelligence and industry, to which a parallel is rarely to be found … His latest discoveries embrace antiquities in Afghanistan, of which Bamiyan and Bagram are objects of great interest: the former is known for its gigantic idols, but of which all our information is confined to that meagre fact. Mr Masson, by ascending the mountains, found numerous images, legends and inscriptions. The latter place [Bagram] is likely to answer to Alexandria … Highly educated, and much superior to the general level of social acquisitions, he directs his attention to everything around him.[24]

There was something about the singularity of Masson's obsession, and his willingness to bet everything on it every day, which made him intoxicating company. Gerard could not remember the last time he had met someone so fiercely alive.

Behind closed doors, life in Kabul was wild. Babur used to call the city 'the very best place in the world to drink wine in'.[25] After years of drinking his courtiers under the table, Dost Mohammad had recently 'renounced wine, and under the severest penalties, commands that his subjects should be equally abstemious'.[26] His prohibition was as successful as prohibitions generally are: 'a single rupee' still bought 'forty bottles of wine or ten of brandy'.[27] During his time in Kabul, Harlan had been caught up in one particularly rowdy night where 'the chief musician got drunk and abused the nawab [Jabar Khan] in the free language of a mad bacchanal, at all of which his highness laughed most heartily, and with unaffected forbearance. A mullah, having undertaken a long draught of strong brandy, was taken in the midst of his genuflections, unable to rise from his knees. But whatever passed did so in confidence amongst the Afghans, who never betray each other, in these illicit orgies, to the austere and exemplary of the community.'[28] The city's parties left Masson breathless.

For years, Masson had lived one day, one footstep, at a time. Now he was beginning to imagine what the future might hold.

His finds were multiplying. 'The discovery of so interesting a locality as that of Bagram imposed upon me new, agreeable, and I should hope, not unprofitable employment. I availed myself of every opportunity to visit it,' Masson wrote. 'Before the commencement of winter, when the plain, covered with snow, is of course closed to research, I had accumulated one thousand eight hundred and sixty five copper coins, besides a few silver ones, and many rings, signets, and other relics.'[29] Masson had come a long way: from forging his own diaries, to carefully listing hundreds of coins; from his earliest faint sketches, to notebooks from Bagram full of painstaking detail.

And, for the first time in a long time, Masson had friends. Pottinger and Gerard – two men who would never have looked twice at Private James Lewis – were both in awe of Charles Masson. Masson's first shy letter to Pottinger began a correspondence which grew warm, then gossipy, then gleeful, so rapidly it took both men by surprise. Gerard was left 'with an impression of the highest respect for his abilities, his enterprise, and indefatigable industry, in researches so interesting and useful'.[30]

But Masson's new life was built on the shallowest foundations. Pottinger's rupees had vanished in a few weeks: 'of the 164 rupees I received here at Kabul, after clearing myself of obligations contracted during the winter but 80 remained to me, and these I have now exhausted.'[31] Desperate to continue his excavations, Masson was running up debts all over Kabul. He had no idea how he would repay them.

There was one piece of good news: having filled his bags, 'Honigberger was now making preparations for his departure to Bukhara, and then through Russia to Germany,' Gerard wrote, 'after having ransacked and destroyed a vast number of mausolea ... in the spirit of a precipitate zeal to outstrip his less fortunate but more deserving contemporary [Masson], and to his [Masson's] laudable and interesting discoveries adding much actual mischief, from his inability or disinclination to pursue enquiry beyond the mere collection of the remains, which I imagine are designed to be put up to the highest bidder among the eminent literati of his country. Mr Masson's objects were of a higher order, and embraced the identification of ancient sites, and their connection with historical records, in which research much curious information may be expected, but the penury of resources has left him far behind his more favoured competitor.'[32]

But, in spite of his poverty and the difficulties he faced, Masson found that, slowly, ancient Afghanistan was giving up its secrets.

Masson showed Gerard and Mohan Lal the mound on the outskirts of Kabul where he had made his first discoveries.[33] 'On the 7th of November 1833,' wrote Mohan Lal, 'we hurried down to the above place, and hired nine men to dig.' After several days, 'they opened in a large and beautiful roofed square; it must have remained long in such a state of preservation that one might suppose that it was freshly plastered with lime. The cell was handsomely gilt and coloured by lapis lazuli.'[34] To someone with a hammer, everything looks like a nail – and to someone looking for Alexander, everything looks Greek: Masson had wondered if the mound had been constructed 'immediately subsequent to the expedition of Alexander the Great'.³⁵ Once Mohan Lal stepped inside, it took him barely a second to realise what they were all looking at: this was a Buddhist place of worship, and so were the dozens of mounds like it in the countryside around Kabul.³⁶

Meanwhile, the coins from Bagram began to reveal themselves. Masson spread out some of the best-preserved ones, and, as he copied their inscriptions, one faded character at a time, he realised that he was reading ancient Greek. Coin after coin had the same words stamped onto it: 'Basileus Basileon', 'King of Kings'. Masson now had two pieces of his puzzle: at some point after Alexander's expedition, the rulers of Afghanistan had written in ancient Greek – and at some point, Afghanistan was a Buddhist country. What the rest of the picture looked like was, for now, a mystery.

Every time he returned to Bagram, in one village after another, handfuls of ancient coins were offered to Masson. That meant one thing: he had not found the site of an unimportant town, but an ancient city 'of immense extent', which once stretched across the plains, 'if we judge from its vestiges, which cover an extent of soil perhaps thirty miles in circumference. That these were flourishing in the period of the Greek sovereignty, I presume from the coins found there.'³⁷ The scale of the site was dizzying.

Whether this was Alexandria or not, Masson needed money more than ever. He estimated that '1500 rupees would enable me to carry on operations here for a twelvemonth or perhaps more'.³⁸ This was not an enormous sum: approximately £15,000 or $18,750 today. But Masson knew that he could not ask Pottinger for so much. That left just one option: the East India Company itself. 'Should you consider the matter of sufficient importance, I have no objection that you should propose to the government of Bombay to supply me with funds to carry on the operation of excavating,' he wrote to Pottinger. 'And in return everything that is elicited, I shall place at their disposal.' By the end of the letter, Masson had thought better of it, and scribbled a quick postscript: 'I think upon reflection it will be better to omit making any proposals at Bombay – even such sums as will enable me to do much and keep me on my legs … It would be mortifying to meet with a refusal, and I know not why, for so small a sum that is required here, I should place myself in dependence.'[39] However desperate he was, he did not want the East India Company's clerks making any enquiries into Mr Charles Masson.

There was, at least, no further danger from Karamat Ali, the East India Company's spy. By the end of 1833, Karamat Ali had stopped reporting on almost everything, apart from how wonderful he (Karamat Ali) was. And how unappreciated he was. And how his expenses were overdue. 'What use is it to me if I get no reward, nor mere thanks for what I have done,' he complained. 'O God, forbid anyone should have a master wanting in generosity – although among the wise it is considered highly discreditable to sing one's own praises, yet without any exaggeration, I have written the plain truth, that none of my services have been hitherto properly acknowledged.'[40]

When pressed to keep the East India Company informed about subjects other than Karamat Ali, he began to spin wild tales about his exploits in Kabul. Instead of admitting that he had been locked up by Dost Mohammad, he told the British that Afghanistan's elite were nothing more than his puppets. 'I am become quite necessary to them,' he wrote. 'They are in my power and I not in theirs. Do not alarm yourself, I wish only that you should know that I have gained the confidence of all, and on this account they are guided by my advice.'[41] 'They have not, therefore, a secret which they do not trust to me, and in no one do they put so much confidence as in me.'[42]

A good spy should be unpredictable: when you look left, he goes right. Karamat Ali used to be a good spy. But he was now a very bad spy: when you look left, he goes left, then tries to go right, then trips over his feet, then falls flat on his face. With little actual intelligence to pass on, his fantasies became more and more elaborate. Towards the end of 1833, he reported that Dost Mohammad and his brothers had met the previous night and decided 'to deliver over their country to the English'.[43]

Karamat Ali sketched the scene: an inner sanctum of the palace, and a secret meeting of the most powerful men in Afghanistan. Jabar Khan had made an impassioned speech: 'I who am your eldest brother say to you,' he had told Dost Mohammad, 'if you do not follow my advice, you must not place your hope in me, for I shall follow my own cause.' 'It has been his desire,' Karamat Ali wrote about the man who had got him out of jail, 'from the first day of my arrival that the English should become possessed of the country.' Dost Mohammad and his brothers therefore 'propose that some sahib should come here, that the government of the country should be given to the English, on a provision being made for themselves of six or seven annas in the rupee, or whatever might be agreed by both parties, and they would retire into private life . . . Those whose language was at first full of threat I have made so soft, that you may mould them as you will,' he concluded. 'It is my humble opinion that the sooner the British government take into consideration the affairs of this country, the better.'[44]

Munchausen would have blushed to tell such a story. But Karamat Ali was rather attached to it, despite not a word being true. He was outraged when the East India Company's spymaster did not believe him and (as the spymaster wearily recorded in his own report) 'laments that he should not be believed in all that he writes, whereas if a sahib filled his situation, everything he wrote would be received as Gospel'.[45]

Karamat Ali's rapid downward spiral had an unexpected side effect. Masson's gossipy letters to Pottinger became the best intelligence the East India Company had coming out of Afghanistan.

Early 1834 found Masson in Bimaran, a tiny, tumbledown village of twenty houses built on an ancient trading route, about ninety miles from Kabul.[46] Five gigantic artificial mounds towered over the village. Masson now knew that they were Buddhist sites. In fact, the mounds were ruined stupas: huge domes, built of brick and earth, which contained sacred relics. For centuries, when Afghanistan was a Buddhist country, the stupas were sites of devotion. Pilgrims would garland them with flowers and circle them in prayer. Every stupa had a treasure at its heart: sometimes simple votive offerings, sometimes prayers written on thin rolls of paper, and sometimes gold and precious jewels.

At Bimaran, Masson was waiting, with his heart in his mouth, for the workmen he had hired to reach the centre of one of the stupas. 'After clearing round its summit, I proceeded to open it, and soon beheld flattering omens,' he wrote. 'To my joy, the workmen fell upon an apartment formed by slates, but which, on being opened, yielded nothing more than a little loose mould, in which, after the most minute inspection, and subsequent dissolution in water, no fragment of bone or any other debris could be found.' Masson felt deflated. After several days of work, all he had found was a little dust and a solitary spider, which had spun its web inside the stupa, 'and sallied forth from his long-concealed retreat when our profane hands had violated the privacy of his asylum and caused the admission of light'.[47]

There was another stupa nearby. It had been the subject of one of Honigberger's smash-and-grab raids, but the Transylvanian had not managed to extract anything from it and had retired empty-handed. Masson had a hunch that something might still be buried deep inside. With the last of his funds, he set the workmen digging again, half expecting to find nothing but another spider.

In the heart of the stupa, the workmen uncovered, once again, 'a small apartment formed as usual from squares of slate'. But this one was not empty. A container of heavy grey soapstone sat on the ground, next to some coins inscribed with the same familiar words: 'Basileus Basileon', 'King of Kings'. Masson had eyes only for the container. Slowly, carefully, he lifted the lid. Inside, the light shimmered and glinted on metal and jewels. The stone container was full of 'burnt pearls, beads of sapphire' and precious gems. 'In the centre was standing a casket of pure gold.'[48]

Masson lifted it out, awestruck. It was six and a half centimetres high, inset with garnets the colour of old red wine, and was almost 2,000 years old. At some point in the first century AD, one of the master craftsmen of Afghanistan had beaten and worked a sheet of gold until it held eight perfectly defined miniature figures. In the centre was the Buddha. His clothing hung in folds, like the waves of a Greek tunic, and his pose was straight out of ancient Athens or Renaissance Florence: contrapposto, with one knee bent and most of his weight resting on one foot. He was flanked by two Hindu gods, Brahma and Indra.

Images of the Buddha are ubiquitous today: millions are produced each year, and tens of millions can be found in every corner of the world. But Buddhists initially resisted portraying the Buddha in human form. Early Buddhist art is symbolic: it might depict a Bodhi tree, or the Buddha's footprints. Masson was holding the very earliest dateable image of the Buddha which has ever been found. It was a world-changing discovery: equivalent to finding the earliest known depiction of Jesus. Posed like a Greek, flanked by Hindu gods, the Buddha's hands are held in a mudra, a gesture with a simple message: all are welcome; be at peace.

7

Pothos

Wherever Alexander went, he left stories behind him. In Egypt, he was worshipped as a god: in the western desert, in the oasis of Qasr el-Miqisba, a temple to Alexander has been uncovered. In Greece, he was damned as a barbarian. 'He is no Greek,' said the Athenian orator Demosthenes of Alexander's father Philip, and by extension his son. 'He is nothing like a Greek. He is not even a decent barbarian. He's a virus. He's from Macedon. You can't even buy a decent slave from Macedon.'[1]

Alexander travelled far. But stories about him have travelled even further. There is an Icelandic *Alexander Saga* and an Armenian epic, a Balinese poem and a French romance. And over more than 2,000 years, the tales have grown taller, and history has slipped into legend. In medieval Europe, Alexander flies to the stars, carried by griffins. He finds his way into the Quran (as 'the two-horned one'), and into Iraqi Jewish folktales, where he also has horns, but is so self-conscious that he grows his hair long to cover them up, and keeps killing his barbers. In Ethiopia, Alexander discovers a magical city in the middle of the desert, full of dancing robots. In the *Thousand and One Nights*, he builds a magical city instead: the City of Brass, 'located in the Andalusian desert' and 'inaccessible due to a cordon of enchantments'.[2] Alexander is the king of stories. For over 2,000 years he has been a universal translator. A historian called him 'a bottle which could be filled with any wine'.[3]

But there was one place where, for a long time, Alexander's story was almost impossible to tell: Persia.

When Alexander crossed into Asia in 334 BC, the Persian Empire was ruled by Darius III, King of Kings. To the Greeks, Darius's empire and wealth seemed infinite. But Alexander took his power to pieces, in a few brief years of campaigning. Egypt fell. Babylon opened its gates. The royal armies were broken in battle. Soon, Darius's power had melted away: his cities had been captured, his armies had fled and his advisers were turning on him. By 330 BC, Alexander himself was in pursuit of Darius, and was gaining on him. The Greek historian Arrian recorded the last moments of the King of Kings:

> Alexander caught up with the Persians just before dawn. Their discipline had been forgotten and their weapons had been lost. Only a few of them put up a fight: most, once they caught sight of Alexander, fled for their lives before a blow had been struck ... When Alexander had almost drawn level with them, two courtiers, Nabarzanes and Barsaëntes, stabbed Darius and left him by the roadside. Then, with the last six hundred horsemen, they too fled. Darius died of his wounds almost immediately, before Alexander reached him.[4]

Alexander was now King of Kings. For the Persians, the world had been turned upside down: being ruled by Alexander was as mind-bending as the idea of Darius as monarch of Greece would have been to the Greeks. Alexander's conquest was a moment of profound national humiliation. For a long time, in Persia, it was the story that could not be told.

Then, around AD 1000, the Persian poet Firdausi wrote his *Shahnameh*. The *Shahnameh*, or *Book of Kings*, was the story of Persia: all the way from the earliest legends to the age of history. Not many books maintain their popularity for a thousand years. The *Shahnameh* is the exception. Today in Iran, Firdausi's work is as celebrated as Shakespeare's is in the English-speaking world.

At the heart of the *Shahnameh* is one of history's greatest pieces of cultural appropriation. Firdausi tells the story of Alexander, or

Sikandar. Initially, it looks familiar. Sikandar leads an army against Persia, ruled by Darius, or Dara in Firdausi. Sikandar puts Dara to flight and catches up with him just after he has been stabbed by his courtiers. But then the story changes. When Sikandar reaches Dara, he realises that the king is still alive:

> Swift as the desert wind, Sikandar rested on his lap
> The dying king,
> And waited, barely breathing,
> For Dara to speak.
> He touched Dara's face, and said:
>
> 'All shall be well.
> You and I, together,
> We shall break your enemies' hearts.
> Come, try to stand –
> Here is a golden litter to bring you home.
> If you have the strength,
> Here is your horse, ready for you.
> All the doctors of the East,
> All the doctors of the West
> Shall be brought to you.
> For every one of your tears
> I will shed one of blood.
> The country is yours.
> The throne is yours.'

Dara heard this, and spoke:

> 'May wisdom walk beside you forever.
> God will reward you for your words, I know it.
> Iran is yours.
> But take care. Never say:
> "I conquered this land of legends,
> I conquered this people
> With my own strength."

All joy comes from God.
All sorrow comes from God.
Every day that He gives you in the light
Be thankful.'[5]

Alexander is no longer a usurper; he is the chosen successor
of the dying king. But Firdausi goes further: in the *Shahnameh*,
Alexander's father is not Philip of Macedon. Instead, Alexander
is the secret son of Darab, king of Persia (in Firdausi's account)
before Darius. Alexander was a Persian all along. He is Darius's
half-brother, and the rightful heir to the Persian throne. When he
leads his army against Persia, he is reclaiming his kingdom.

Persia was not destroyed by Alexander. Persia could be proud of
her Alexander – her Sikandar.

In the sixteenth century, the Emperor Babur sat in his gardens
in Kabul – where, centuries later, Masson would spend his
summer evenings – and listened to recitations of Firdausi. Babur
treasured his *Shahnameh*: he carried it with him for his entire adult
life, from his days of exile to his days of glory, and bequeathed
it with his treasures to his successor.[6] In the nineteenth century,
Firdausi's Alexander was still everywhere you looked in India and
Afghanistan. Ranjit Singh commissioned a spectacular new copy of
the *Shahnameh* for himself and his court.[7] In Kashmir, the scribes
had two bestsellers. 'They transcribe the Quran or the *Shahnameh*,
and a very small number of other books, that are the objects of a
small but regular trade. The best are paid one rupee per thousand
couplets of the *Shahnameh*.'[8]

For Islamic writers, Alexander did not want to conquer the
world, he wanted to understand it. He was driven not by greed, or
by bloodlust, but by an insatiable curiosity. His world was not just
one of battles, alliances, marriages and the clamour of a victorious
army. It was full of giant creatures, magic and wonder, and journeys
to impossible places. Alexander was the great explorer. He went
further, and he saw stranger things, than anyone ever had before.

This Alexander was defined not by his strength, but by his
intelligence.[9] He could solve every riddle. He came up with a new

invention every day (red-hot statues! trained mice! automata!).
Once, Alexander even found a way to explore the most unknowable
place on earth, the world beneath the waves. After he returned from
the depths, he told the story of his adventures:

> I made an iron cage, and inside it I put an enormous jar, two
> feet wide and made of glass. I had a hole made in the bottom
> of the jar, just big enough for a man's head. I had a plan: I
> was going to be lowered down, and find out for myself what
> was on the seabed ... Then I had a huge chain made, almost
> two thousand feet long. I attached one end to the cage,
> and told my men not to pull me up until the chain started
> shaking.
>
> 'When I reach the bottom of the sea,' I told them, 'I will
> shake the jar. Then, bring me back up to the surface.'
>
> Everything was prepared. I climbed into the glass jar, ready to
> attempt the impossible.[10]

Today, in the high, faded galleries of the Indian Museum in
Calcutta, fossils and dinosaurs lurk in dark wooden cabinets,
mummies leer out from glass cases and unmentionable things in
jars huddle in the shadows. The Museum is one of the world's
greatest and weirdest treasure houses, a Victorian fantasia of green
lawns, colonnades and molluscs, washed by the monsoon rains.
Here, too, Firdausi's Alexander has a place of honour: in one
vivid Mughal painting after another, in shades of gold and green
and indigo, Alexander's fascination with the world plays out, as
he witnesses the invention of mirrors and watches the debates of
Indian philosophers.

But in Firdausi, Alexander's unquenchable thirst for knowledge
slowly tears him apart. His obsession with discovering every secret,
finding every lost treasure and seeing every corner of the world can
never be satisfied. There is a word for this kind of quest in ancient
Greek: pothos. It means a longing so great that it bursts your
heart. A desire for the impossible. For the Greeks, if you wanted
to understand Alexander you had to understand his pothos: what

drove him to do one impossible thing after another, to follow his dreams, to the ends of the earth and beyond.

For the Greeks, pothos was not just an obsession: it was an obsession that would, inevitably, go too far. It was desire, longing and regret. Firdausi's Alexander eventually realises that he is only human: though his dreams are infinite, his strength and his time are not.

***

On 30 April 1834, the world began to pay attention to Charles Masson's own quest.

Calcutta, city of books, lies in the far east of India, on the Hooghly River in Bengal. For centuries, Bengal has been one of the intellectual centres of the world. While British clerks sweated and grumbled in the halls of Fort William and the elephantine Writers' Building, a life less ordinary unfurled in the nearby bookshops of Bowbazar. Bengali scholars who spent their days translating for the British gathered in the evenings to discuss poetry and philosophy, history and legend. One of the few places where the Bengali and British worlds met was in a low, white-painted building on Park Street, next to the rolling lawns of the Maidan, Calcutta's enormous central park. This was the Asiatic Society of Bengal, Calcutta's house of curiosity.

If the protagonists of a Victorian comic novel had decided to start a learned society, it might have resembled the Asiatic Society of Bengal. In April 1834, the Society was trying to solve the problem of a stranded mummy. It had been donated by Lieutenant Archbold, a British army officer. But getting it from Egypt to Calcutta proved problematic. Such was its state of decomposition that the first ship Archbold attempted to load it on to refused to carry it, leaving him and his unfortunate cargo stranded on the docks. Eventually, a British warship agreed to transport the mummy as far as Bombay, after which it had to make its own way to Calcutta. All the while, heat and humidity were hard at work on the mummy. After almost 4,000 years, the smell was unspeakable. (Today, the treasures of the Asiatic Society form the heart of Calcutta's Indian Museum. When, recently, the Museum's air conditioning failed, the mummy began to rot again: the *Times of India* reported that 'visitors are forced to cover their noses to keep the stench out'.)[11]

Once the mummy's travel arrangements had been dealt with, silence fell. Dr James Gerard, the British traveller who met Masson in Kabul, had sent the Society a letter from Masson. Masson spoke, hesitantly, of his first discoveries. 'I was,' he wrote apologetically, 'but ill situated to undertake such an enquiry, being wholly unprovided with those authors to whom it would have been profitable to refer, and was compelled therefore to draw upon memory for the vestiges of the information it had treasured up of the reading of early days, when I had little expected that the events of my future life would ever cause me to revert to it.'[12] Yet when he spoke of his finds from Bagram, the pride in his words was unmistakable. 'The coins were of such a type and description, as naturally increased my ardour in their research; and, succeeding in allaying the mistrusts of the finders, I obtained successive parcels, until up to this time (November 28th 1833), I have accumulated 1,865 copper coins and fourteen gold and silver ones.'[13]

Extrapolating from what he had seen, Masson estimated that 'no less a number than thirty thousand coins, probably a much larger number, are found annually on the plain of Bagram'. Whether or not Bagram was Alexandria, he wrote, it was a place of wonders waiting to give up its secrets, 'a second Babylon'.[14] From hundreds of miles away, he spoke to a room full of people he had never met, and he spoke straight from the heart: 'For the last six or seven years, I have directed my attention to the antiquities of Central Asia … In spite of conflicting circumstances, I have made many discoveries, which one day, by the favour of the Almighty, I shall make public. I shall not remit my labours: notwithstanding the inevitable casualties of time.'[15]

The applause was so loud it might almost have been heard in Kabul.

In early 1834, life in Kabul was becoming less peaceful. Shah Shujah, the long-exiled king of Afghanistan, was on the move. The previous year, he had set out from Ludhiana in northern India, hoping once again to retake his throne. 'Kabul,' Masson wrote, 'is agitated by a thousand rumours relative to the advance of Shah Shujah.'[16] Letters from Shujah were being passed from hand to hand in the city. Even Harlan, hundreds of miles away, was involved: one of his servants carried 'six or seven' letters back and forth between Shujah and Haji Khan.[17]

The further Shujah went, the larger his army became. And the larger his army became, the angrier his letters got. 'Execrable dogs, do you prescribe terms to your master? God willing, I will give you such a blow that you shall be an example to the whole world,' he wrote. 'The only way to treat a rabid dog is to put a rope round its neck. Are you coming to attack me? By all means come, I am ready to receive you and do not fear you. God is the disposer of events, the country shall belong to the conqueror.'[18]

Officially, the East India Company had nothing to do with Shah Shujah's expedition. Each of his previous attempts to reclaim his throne had been accompanied by an official shrug from Calcutta. 'With regard to the belief, which it is evident Shah Shujah is desirous of encouraging,' wrote one official in 1816, 'that the British government is disposed to espouse his cause, His Lordship in Council conceives it may be necessary to guard against whatever may have the tendency of countenancing such reports.'[19] 'I hear that he [Shujah] has also succeeded in instilling an impression into the minds of all classes that he is secretly supported by the British government of India,' Pottinger now wrote to Masson, 'but which I have myself no reason to credit.'[20]

Unofficially, Captain Claude Wade, the Company's frontier spymaster, was neck-deep in Shujah's schemes. 'When the sun enters the sign Libra and the season becomes moderate,' Shujah wrote to Wade, 'I shall prosecute my journey towards the place of my destination, and through the blessing of God, I hope soon to obtain my object and to gain possession of Kandahar, which will then become a dwelling of my friends (the Honourable Company), since concord and union always exist between us.'[21] 'I have no doubt of a continuance of his good fortune,' Wade wrote, 'and that he will meet the exigences of his situation with that prudence and sagacity which long tried adversity, and the intimate knowledge which he has acquired of our institutions, have conferred on him.'[22]

In May 1834, Shujah's plans unravelled when Dost Mohammad swatted him away from Kandahar. The Shah, quite forgetting his earlier bloodthirsty threats, fled for his life before the battle was half over. His army promptly disintegrated. 'Shah Shujah has become a wanderer in the wilderness of adversity,' Dost Mohammad exulted after the battle. 'The whole property belonging to him has been captured by our victorious troops.'[23] The Shah was soon back in Ludhiana, working on yet another plan to reclaim his kingdom.

Masson was careful to keep his distance from the scheming, but Karamat Ali, the East India Company's spy in Kabul, was not so lucky. His life was going from bad to worse. Just when the Company needed his intelligence network most, it was disintegrating. Hari Singh, the new Sikh military governor of Peshawar, did not enjoy sharing the city with British spies. He made his feelings known by confiscating the house of one of Karamat Ali's 'newswriters', fining another 700 rupees, and finally ordering Karamat Ali's letters to India to be intercepted and 'torn to pieces'.[24] When Karamat Ali's reports did get through, the East India Company did not know what to trust least: his news from Kabul or his expenses. 'It is not the custom of accurate accountants,' the spy was told, 'to send in accounts in the loose manner which you have done.'[25] Masson was quietly amused by it all. 'Hari Singh has no objection to me,' he remarked. His letters to India were allowed 'to pass unopened'.[26]

Masson had no time for plots. He was lost in a world of gods and demons.

One and a half thousand years ago, Hadda, 100 miles east of Kabul, was a Buddhist wonderland. Stupas, monasteries and chapels dotted the hills and valleys. Each one was richer and wilder than the last: hideous spirits leered out at Masson with huge eyes and splayed teeth. A delicately carved man removed his own head and held it suspended above his neck. There were sculptures by the thousand in every direction. And the closer Masson looked, the more surprising some of them became.

Atlas, the legendary Titan of Greek myth, condemned to hold up the sky for all eternity, here held up a Buddhist temple. A musclebound figure next to the Buddha looked almost exactly like Hercules, complete with club and lion skin, but was actually Vajrapani, one of the Buddha's followers. On the walls, wine flowed from Greek amphorae and a young man with a basket full of flowers attended the Buddha. He had been sculpted using techniques honed in the workshops of Alexandria, Egypt.

Masson was deliriously happy. For once, he did not even have to worry about money. A letter from Pottinger had arrived a few weeks earlier, with a lifeline. In return for his future finds, and the coins he had already collected from Bagram,[27] the East India Company had agreed to fund Masson's excavations. 'The Bombay government,' Pottinger wrote, 'has authorized me to place fifteen hundred rupees at your disposal, and made me its agent to receive any communications or relics of antiquity, which you may hereafter wish to send.'[28] Masson could barely believe it. 'I need scarcely intimate how much I appreciate the favour you have conferred upon me,' he wrote, 'and I rejoice that information reached me here, as I was on the point of making a sacrifice of some very interesting relics to enable me to prosecute further researches.'[29] He promised Pottinger that the money would be well spent.

Masson also noted, with a slight inward lurch, that Pottinger had described him to the East India Company as 'an American gentleman I believe, who is perhaps not unknown by name to the Right Honourable the Governor in Council'.[30] But, he told himself, the true identity of Charles Masson had to be 'unknown' to the Company: after so many years, and so many miles, surely they had no idea who he really was.

In Hadda's largest stupa, close to the foundations, Masson found a battered copper vessel, half full of fluid. Within the copper vessel was a smaller, silver casket, full of shimmering coins and a rich blue stone. Hiding underneath it was 'a mass of crystal' and a final casket, made of pure gold and inlaid with precious gems. It contained 'a colourless limpid fluid of the most delightful musk fragrance', but no sooner had Masson caught its scent than it 'evaporated'.[31]

In the copper vessel, Masson found a handful of gold coins, almost perfectly preserved, bearing the portraits of three different rulers, 'Theodosius, Marcian and Leo'. This was the kind of clue he had been hoping for: if he could find out when each of them held power, that would give him a good idea when the stupa was constructed. But however hard he racked his brains, he could not place any of the three. At a loss, he wrote to Pottinger, asking for help.[32]

Hundreds of miles, and many weeks' dangerous travel, from any library which might have helped him,[33] Masson was painfully aware that 'I had no authority to consult but memory'.[34] He begged Pottinger for books, any books, 'common school books indeed, but which might be useful to me here, Lemprière's *Classical Dictionary*, Potter's *Grecian Antiquities*, Moor's *Hindu Pantheon*, Greek Grammar by any author, and a dictionary – while I shall be very glad for any of these, I beg no great trouble may be taken about them'.[35] Also, if it would not be too much trouble, some pencils, a volume of Alexander Pope[36] and some opium.[37]

When he received Masson's letter about the three gold coins, Pottinger spent hours combing through every book he could get his hands on, until he finally realised where to look. Grabbing his copy of Gibbon's *The History of the Decline and Fall of the Roman Empire*, he sent Masson 'a short memorandum of the eras of Theodosius, Marcian and Leo, extracted from Gibbon, by which you will see that they all flourished within the 5th century of our date'.[38] All three were Roman emperors, but emperors of the East, who ruled from Constantinople. Theodosius II was the youngest emperor in history: in AD 402, when he was less than one year old, he was proclaimed ruler of much of the known world. Once he could walk and talk, he governed uneasily, buying off everyone he could not fight, until his death in AD 450. Masson's coin had been forged in the imperial mints of Constantinople, and had somehow found its way to the middle of Afghanistan. 'Our lord Theodosius, prosperous and happy', read the Latin. Masson had his first clear date: if Theodosius II ruled between AD 402 and 450, then the stupa was probably around 1,500 years old.

Through miniature pieces of knowledge, passed from hand to hand, carried by caravans of camels across the passes of Afghanistan, Masson began to understand the world he was unearthing. Years earlier, he had obsessively erased every detail of his own past. Now what he wanted, above all, was to tell a true story.

East of Kabul, in a valley between the city and Bagram, is the stupa of Topdara. For Masson, it was 'perhaps the most complete and beautiful monument of the kind in these countries':[39] an enormous drum, thirty metres tall, that looms over the surrounding countryside. Masson had first dug there in 1833. Now he returned, notebook in hand. The local villagers were used to the comings and goings of the 'strange bird',[40] and made him welcome. 'I had succeeded in forming acquaintances at all the stage villages,' he wrote, 'and was certain whenever I dropped in at any of them to be received with civility.'[41] Hour after hour, Masson sat sketching beside a stream that ran down the nearby hillside, lingering over every detail of the brickwork and the reliefs. He was meticulous. Years later, when Topdara came to be restored by an Afghan archaeological team in 2016, they relied on Masson's smudged, faded, fiercely accurate sketches to reconstruct it.

The world was opening up to Masson. 'If I can be the medium of making your most interesting discoveries known to the world,' Pottinger wrote to him, 'my sole object will be obtained.'

> On the subject of your manuscripts, I told you in my last, that if you would entrust them to me, I would undertake that they should be published either under the auspices of the Bombay government, or by one of the learned societies of Great Britain, any of which would gladly snatch at such a prize ... I would even offer to conduct it (to use a technical phrase) through the press myself, but my pursuits through life, having come to India as a boy of fourteen years of age, do not permit me to venture on such an undertaking, and I should regret that you had any cause for disappointment in the manner of it being brought out.[42]

The storyteller of Kabul found that his stories were coming true. Every morning, he woke up with a huge grin, and went to work.

Then, one day in early 1835, Masson received a letter. He read it and felt the ground drop away beneath his feet.

It was from the East India Company's spymaster, Claude Wade. Wade knew everything. He knew that Charles Masson was Private James Lewis of the Bengal Artillery. He knew that he was a deserter. He knew that he had been on the run for almost a decade. And he had a simple message for Masson: you belong to me now.

8

Our Man in Kabul

'You are looking for something,' Rumi once wrote. 'Something is looking for you.'

Claude Wade had been looking for Private James Lewis ever since he ran away from the East India Company in 1827.

Wade was a squat, perpetually hungry man, with a dimpled chin, a scrubby moustache and the look of a sleepy spider.[1] Every piece of intelligence from Afghanistan went through him: the French traveller Victor Jacquemont called him 'the king of the frontier'.[2] Money was his pleasure – his love of a bribe gave him the nickname 'baksheesh sahib', or 'Mr Payoff'[3] – but information was his passion. From an unmarked house in dusty Ludhiana – a town so sleepy that today cows ruminate in the middle of its gleaming new highways, and tractors rumble past abandoned mansions – he spun his webs and whispered in the ears of kings. By the time you realised that you wanted something, Wade would already have it locked away.

In the autumn of 1827 Wade had received a report about two deserters from the Bengal Artillery, James Lewis and Richard Potter. At the time, Josiah Harlan was in Ludhiana. The American was trying to persuade Shah Shujah that he could restore him to his throne in Kabul. Wade showed Harlan the report and told him to keep an eye out for the two men. When Harlan did stumble across Masson in Ahmedpur several weeks later, thanks to the dispatch 'received by the government official at Ludhiana a short time before my departure', he had no doubt who the ragged stranger really was. 'I concluded these men were probably the individuals alluded to in that document. Subsequently my inference was verified.'[4]

Harlan told Masson that he 'had no connection with the British government, and consequently neither interest nor duty could induce me to betray him now or hereafter'.[5] But, as with most things to do with Josiah Harlan, that was not strictly correct. Harlan had been in Wade's pocket ever since he had left Ludhiana. When the American reached Kabul, he set about recruiting informants for the East India Company. He even approached Dost Mohammad's brother, Jabar Khan, and 'recommended him to address a friendly epistle to the British agent at Ludhiana'.[6] After he abandoned Shah Shujah's cause and decamped to the court of Ranjit Singh, Harlan kept the East India Company informed on everything down to Ranjit Singh's bowel movements. 'Since my arrival here in Lahore,' he wrote, the Maharaja had 'a slight diarrhoea. The report you mention of the Maharaja's serious relapse is not true.'[7] When Wade received a report from Kabul in 1833 about a Mr Masson who had arrived in the city, claiming to have 'been absent from his country twelve years, during which time he had been travelling',[8] he had a good idea who this mysterious stranger really was: 'a deserter from our artillery'.[9]

While Masson settled happily into life in Kabul, Wade began to build a file on him. When Masson rode out to Bamiyan to join Haji Khan, Wade knew where he was going, what he was doing and how much he had paid to hire his pony. When Masson wrote to his friends in Kabul, asking for 'some tea and wine, some writing paper, and a few articles of apparel', Wade knew about it.[10] But he did not yet have enough evidence to act.

The final piece of the puzzle was supplied by Dr James Gerard, the British traveller. Gerard had been delighted with Masson's company in Kabul, 'and though still in doubt regarding one whose situation and pursuits seemed so mysterious, I sought not to satisfy my curiosity at the expense of his feelings, nor was there any disposition on his part to unmask his character'. But the more time Gerard spent with Masson, and the more he heard about his discoveries, the 'more anxious' he became 'to ascertain the secret of his history'.[11]

On his way back to India, Gerard passed through Lahore. Ranjit Singh's foreign mercenaries were obsessed with ancient history, so Gerard entertained them with tales of the shy 'explorer' he had met in Kabul, his 'merits of no common order' and 'the light which his interesting researches are likely to throw in the history, antiquities, and present state of Afghanistan'. As Gerard unfurled his tale, there was a spluttering sound from a corner of the room. Josiah Harlan was coming to the boil. And then, as Gerard put it, 'the veil was lifted'.[12]

Harlan told Gerard the full story. The man the doctor so admired was 'a fugitive servant of the Honourable Company's Artillery, who had thrown off his fidelity at Bharatpur (after the capture of that place, however) in alliance with a fellow soldier named Potter, his own (I presume feigned) name at that time being Lewis. It appears that he had at first travelled with Dr Harlan (now in Ranjit Singh's service), but disliking that gentleman's impetuous and foolhardy conduct, as it appeared to him, he secretly escaped (according to Dr Harlan, deserted him), when he was preparing to make an attempt upon a fortified place in favour of Shah Shujah's authority.' Aware that he might be condemning his new friend to a very painful death, Gerard added limply, in his letter to Wade, 'my subsequent knowledge of the above individual's history, though of an unpleasant nature, has not weakened my own regard for him, nor prejudiced me against his talents'.[13]

After years of tracking Masson, Wade now had everything he needed. 'Mr Masson,' he wrote, triumphantly, 'was formerly a private soldier in the Bengal Artillery, and his real name is Lewis. He attracted the particular notice of Major General Hardwick when he was the commander of that corps, and was employed by him in arranging and depicting his zoological specimens. At the time of his desertion, he was a trooper in the 3rd Troop 1st Brigade of Horse Artillery commanded by Captain Hyde, and served in it during the siege of Bharatpur. Shortly after that event, he and a man named Potter, belonging to the same troop, deserted from

Agra, and went to the Punjab. Potter is now in the service of Rajah Gulab Singh of Jammu.'[14]

Now that he knew who Masson was, Wade wondered what to do with him. Gerard's report had some intriguing details. 'Mr Masson's diffident deportment ensures him security and respect. The haughty ruler of Kabul scarcely stoops to notice him, and only on one occasion evinced any suspicion of his objects,' he told Wade.[15] Gerard admired Masson, and thought the East India Company should blackmail him into becoming a spy. 'The political condition of the Afghan state is awaiting illustration through his ability,' he wrote. 'Nothing would so much precipitate our process [the expansion of British influence], as a previous acquaintance with the country by means of such an individual as Mr Masson, whose own peculiar pursuits, hitherto chequered and cramped by poverty, would be too deeply dependent upon the source that offered its hand of amnesty and aid, not to be eager to fulfil whatever considerations might be suggested......' Wade looked at the long, suggestive ellipsis, and smiled.

Wade was in desperate need of a new spy in Kabul. The luckless Karamat Ali was driving him to distraction. Masson, he mused, would be perfect for the job. 'His long residence in Afghanistan has not only enabled him to acquire a complete geographical and statistical knowledge of that country, but living as he has been like a native of it, on terms of intimacy and familiarity with its inhabitants, he has enjoyed opportunities of making his observations which no other European travellers have hitherto possessed. In the course of his journeys he has visited various parts of Afghanistan which they have never seen. They have kept to the beaten track and been favoured guests of its chiefs. He has entered the recesses of the country.'[16]

Slowly, Wade began to spin his web.

In early 1834, he composed a syrupy letter to Masson, careful to drop no hints that he knew his secret. 'The singular discoveries which you have been engaged in making,' he wrote, 'are of deep interest to the literary and scientific world ... It will afford me real satisfaction if you can avail yourself in any way of my humble services for their prosecution. If at any time you should be in want of funds, I hope you will draw on me to the extent of your wants ... and hope that you will confide in the sincerity with which my profession of good offices is made.'[17]

A few days later, Wade wrote to the East India Company in Calcutta, laying out his plan. 'Desertion is a crime which is viewed I believe by our government with a degree of rigour that scarcely ever admits of pardon,' he wrote, 'but if the severity of our laws is such as to preclude the extension of His Lordship's clemency to him, I still hope that I shall be excused for the correspondence which I have opened with Mr Masson ... The observations which he has made, and the information which he has collected, on the government and resources of a country which is of daily increasing interest to the British government cannot be an object of indifference.' As for the awkwardness of employing a wanted deserter, 'the circumstances of Mr Masson's having assumed a new name may in some measure be allowed to remove the embarrassment of recognizing him in his present situation'.[18]

When he received Wade's first letter – which was followed by another and another, each more unctuous than the last – Masson was left with an uneasy feeling that something was amiss. Gerard had told him about Wade. 'His Political Highness,' he wrote to Masson, 'is very ready to improve upon suggestions, or follow up the footsteps of others, in objects of which he had before been wholly oblivious ... He cares little for such researches as yours, except it be to oppose another's pursuits in rivalry.'[19] But, 'as I have no reason to doubt the sincerity of his professions, I answered him in a correspondent manner,' Masson wrote to Pottinger. 'I know not, to what my correspondence with Captain Wade may lead, or that it may lead to anything, but thought it right to note to yourself as much of its nature as I have now detailed, and in confidence – if confidence be necessary.'[20]

In Calcutta, Wade's report on Masson was read with incredulity by William Macnaghten, Secretary to the Government of India. Macnaghten surveyed the world from behind a pair of huge blue spectacles, and did not blink before it. 'He speaks Persian rather more fluently than English; Arabic better than Persian; but for familiar conversation rather prefers Sanskrit.'[21] While Wade was sweat-stained and acquisitive, Macnaghten was cold and bureaucratic – as dry and pitiless as the deserts of Kutch. A few weeks earlier, he had joined the crowds in the Asiatic Society's building on Park Street to listen, transported, to Masson's notes from Kabul. He was more than a little surprised to hear of Charles Masson again. Macnaghten did not like being surprised. He thought Masson would make an excellent spy, but, unlike Wade, he was not inclined to blackmail him into taking the job – at least, not yet. 'It is not deemed necessary at present that Mr Masson should be recognized by government,' he wrote. 'To secure his zealous services it will probably be enough that you afford him encouragement to maintain the communication.'[22] Wade had other ideas.

Early in 1835, on one of the first bright days of spring, Masson was staying at Jabar Khan's country house, nestled into a curve of the Kabul River a few miles from the capital, when a packet of letters from Wade arrived. Moments later, Masson's life had changed for ever.

'Government has at my recommendation been pleased to appoint you our Agent in Kabul for communicating intelligence of the state of affairs in that quarter,' Wade wrote.[23] His head spinning, Masson read on. Now, Wade showed his hand. He advised Masson to 'give strong assurance of your desire to regain through its [the East India Company's] favour, that station in society which you have had the misfortune to lose'. 'In the event of your continued efforts to serve the government, and fulfil the expectations which are now entertained of you', Masson might, in time, hope to be pardoned. 'The offence which you have unfortunately committed is, in a military point of view, undoubtedly a grievous one, but it will, I hope, be deemed susceptible of extenuation.'[24] Work hard, Wade told his new spy, because your life depends on it.

And if Masson refused? He did not have to be reminded of the consequences. The words had been at the back of his mind for years. 'If any person shall … desert the said Company's service', whether in the 'territories which are or may be under the government of the said Company, or in foreign parts, upon land or upon the sea, within or without the limits of the charter of the said united Company', that person 'shall suffer death, transportation, or such other punishment as by a court-martial shall be awarded'.[25]

If anything happened to Masson, few people would hear about it, and even fewer would care. A few months earlier, Dr John Gilchrist, a Scottish surgeon who had devoted his life to the study of Hindustani, had confronted the Company's Court of Directors in London about their record of atrocities. He had been laughed out of the room:

> He [Gilchrist] had seen reports in the papers of horrible butcheries having been committed recently in India – of men having been blown from the mouths of cannon for certain offences. Now he wished to know whether the Court of Directors had received any accounts of these transactions; or was it a mere matter of rumour, without foundation.
>
> The Chairman: I have no hesitation in saying, that not one syllable of such accounts has reached us ...
>
> Dr Gilchrist: If such barbarities were allowed, to a certainty they [the East India Company] would not be long in possession of India. The very idea of blowing men away from the mouths of cannon made one's flesh shudder. Gentlemen might laugh; but it was no laughing matter to those unhappy wretches, whose flesh continued to be torn by the cat [o'nine tails] in Madras and Bombay. Gentlemen behind the bar might laugh; though, in his opinion, they ought to set a very different example.[26]

The Company's denial was, of course, a lie. Just a few weeks earlier, a military court in Calcutta had matter-of-factly sentenced 'the said Tippoo, havildar [sergeant] and drill havildar; Budderodeen, private; Shaikh Ismail, havildar; and Kullunder Beg, private, to suffer death by being blown away from a gun ... at such time and place as His Excellency the Commander-in-Chief may be pleased to direct'.[27] The men's fate was recorded in a brief paragraph in an obscure journal. Masson would be just as quickly forgotten. 'I was therefore led to believe,' Masson wrote, 'I had no option.'[28]

Masson sat with the letter, looking out over the Kabul River and the hills covered in mulberry trees. His hands shook. He knew that nothing would ever be the same again.

What now? Should he run? He could slip into one of a dozen disguises, leave Afghanistan at once, and disappear into the back roads of Asia. Wade would never catch up with him. But he would lose his chance to find Alexandria. If he stayed, he would be at the mercy of Wade and the East India Company, but he might just find Alexander's city. He had to make a choice.

Masson stayed. For the sake of his dream, he became a spy for the people he despised most in the world.

In Kabul there were few secrets and it was soon well known that Masson was working for the East India Company. Old friends began to keep their distance. Some treated him with 'marked rudeness',[29] or claimed to be 'confined by a dysentery and even talked of dying'[30] when he called on them. Masson was now about as welcome in Kabul as explosive diarrhoea.

For years, he had been able to keep the city's politics, its plots and counter-plots, at arm's length. His new employment dropped him right into the middle of them.

Dost Mohammad Khan had been in power for almost ten years. He was, Masson reflected, 'beloved'[31] by the Afghan people. 'He was fair and impartial, and free from haughtiness; and accessible to all classes. Vigilant in the administration of the country, crimes became few. People ceased to commit them, conscious they should be called to account.'[32] Alexander Burnes, the British traveller, had been equally impressed. 'No one better merits the high character which he has obtained,' he wrote. 'The merchant may travel, without guard or protection, from one frontier to another – an unheard of circumstance in the time of the kings.'[33]

Dost Mohammad's justice was proverbial. Decades later, Afghans were still asking one another: 'Is Dost Mohammad dead, that there is no justice?'[34] Dost Mohammad's capacity for violence was equally proverbial. 'He has killed many chiefs of the country,' wrote Mohan Lal, the Indian scholar who travelled with Burnes, 'after having sworn seven times by the holy soul of Muhammad, and even upon the Quran' that he would not harm them. His intended victims would then relax: no good Muslim would break an oath on the Quran. Just before taking the oath, however, Dost Mohammad would swap his Quran for a 'common book' in an identical binding.[35] His victims never noticed. It was a very deadly, very Afghan version of three-card monte.

The ruler of Afghanistan was an enigma, and he worked hard to keep it that way. He 'dealt a good deal in sarcasm, and was ever ready to trump his adversary's trick'.[36] Whenever he and his lawyer played chess, Dost Mohammad always won. No one was sure if the lawyer let him win – or if Dost Mohammad let the lawyer think he was letting him win.[37] Lal confessed that 'I might be able to delineate him in Persian', but it was not possible 'to do his character justice'[38] in English.

In 1835, Afghanistan was a small, poor country surrounded by large, hungry ones. In the east, Ranjit Singh had recently helped himself to the Afghan city of Peshawar, which commanded the ancient Silk Road route through the Khyber Pass. He had evicted one of Dost Mohammad's brothers, Sultan Mohammad Khan, from the city and moved in his own forces. Beyond Ranjit Singh's empire, the East India Company watched and waited. In the west, the Shah of Persia's armies were within striking distance of the border city of Herat. To the north, Russian agents were fanning out across the steppes of Central Asia. Just in case Dost Mohammad needed any more reasons to sleep with one eye open, there was also Shah Shujah: the former king was still in Ludhiana and was still determined to recover his throne.

Dost Mohammad knew that most of the people around him wanted him dead. He trusted no one: 'Dost Mohammad Khan might have an accomplice, he could never have a friend.'[39] His brother, Jabar Khan, was the sole exception. 'Never was a man more modest, and more beloved,' Alexander Burnes wrote. 'He will permit but a single attendant to follow him; and the people on the high- and by-ways stop to bless him.'[40] Masson had always thought Jabar Khan was mild mannered to a fault. Then, soon after he received Wade's letter, Dost Mohammad's brother summoned him, and dropped the mask.

'I became for the first time acquainted with the fact that the nawab [Jabar Khan] had been concerned in almost nefarious transactions with Karamat Ali,'[41] Masson wrote, incredulously. This cheerful, white-bearded old man, who looked as if he would not hurt a fly, had been plotting against his own brother for almost a decade. In 1828, he had taken Harlan aside and told the American that he would happily depose Dost Mohammad and put Shah Shujah back on the throne, for the right price. 'His Majesty will find myself an able and devoted servant,' Jabar Khan had said. 'But mark! without that assistance, no domestic feud shall induce me to sacrifice my family interests.'[42] 'I was,' Masson confessed, 'entirely ignorant of the nature of his intrigues.'[43]

Meanwhile, it took Wade's former spy, Karamat Ali, some time to realise that he had been fired. He did not take the news well. 'Listen to my grievances and award me justice,' he wrote furiously to the East India Company's Governor General in Calcutta. 'I am not aware of what fault I am guilty, but I know that I never committed the least fault. I have served the Honourable Company, and not Captain Wade.'[44]

In the spring, as the snows melted on the slopes of the Hindu Kush mountains, and the wildflowers began to bloom, Masson rode uncomfortably out of Kabul. He had spent the winter happily making plans to hunt down Alexander's city at Bagram. But now, he was on his way to Peshawar. Dost Mohammad – who had recently crowned himself Amir of Afghanistan, in a notably threadbare ceremony – was leading an army to retake the city. The East India Company had ordered Masson to keep an eye on the expedition.

'Joined by all our brothers, and attended by our triumphant troops, and artillery scattering thunder, we shall,' Dost Mohammad wrote to Ranjit Singh, 'settle such points with you as require explanation.'[45] In camp, 'he exclaimed audibly, of course that he might be heard by those around, that he was a weak fly, about to encounter a huge elephant; that, if it pleased God, the fly could overcome the elephant, and he implored God to grant him victory'.[46] In fact, the last thing the new Amir wanted was a war.

Dost Mohammad was broke. His commanders were 'destitute' and could barely afford to feed themselves. Haji Khan had to pawn a sword 'to procure 20 rupees, and the shifts he (as well as others) is obliged to resort to, to raise the wind, are considered remarkable'.[47] Dost Mohammad was hoping that the British would ally with him against Ranjit Singh, or at least persuade the Maharaja to step back from his frontiers, before he was obliged to fight a battle. 'In the critical situation in which the Amir stands,' Masson wrote to Wade, 'he [Dost Mohammad] would gladly be enabled to extricate himself without risking a conflict, but he feels that one must be ventured upon, if the Sikhs insist upon the retention of Peshawar'.[48]

He would appear to have entertained great hopes of British mediation, and that he still does, is manifest from the anxiety he expresses, as well as all others here, on the receipt of any intelligence from India.

Perhaps an occasion of interposing British mediation with so good a grace as at the present moment, may never again present itself – and if any objections be made thereto, on the plea of the Sadozai interests [the family of Shah Shujah], it may be observed that the sun of that dynasty appears to have set. In the recent efforts of Shah Shujah, there is little doubt, but that a single British officer accompanied him, not as an ally or assistant, but was a mere reporter of proceedings to his government, the Shah would have been established, but as such was not the case, there is little hope from his personal unaided attempts. It will have been seen that the Shah's cause was not a popular one – as no persons of any distinction or note joined or espoused it.[49]

'Afghanistan,' Masson wrote, 'is the natural ally of the British.'[50] But from Calcutta, there came no reply.

On the way to Peshawar, a report arrived which cheered everyone up immensely. Ranjit Singh had pulled Harlan out of his palace in Gujrat and sent him to negotiate with Dost Mohammad's brother, Sultan Mohammad Khan. Sultan Mohammad informed his brother 'of Mr Harlan's arrival, and that he had been put to death, while his elephants and property had been made booty. This news created a sensation in the camp, and the multitude exulted ... The brothers had become one, and had wiped away their enmities in Feringhi blood.'[51]

When Dost Mohammad's army reached Peshawar, Ranjit Singh's troops were waiting for them. The Maharaja himself, however, was still some distance away, and had ordered his commanders 'to avoid a general action, and await his arrival. In consequence of such orders, the Sikhs resumed negotiations to amuse the Amir.'[52] Into Dost Mohammad's camp swaggered a tall, sallow man, with a 'large head and gaunt face over it', dressed 'like a mountebank' in all the colours of the rainbow.[53] Reports of Josiah Harlan's death had been greatly exaggerated.

Harlan thought he was negotiating the fate of nations. He was actually there to waste time. Ranjit Singh needed a few hours to move his armies into position, so he sent the biggest braggart in the Punjab to distract Dost Mohammad. Harlan talked and talked and talked. 'I spoke in an exalted strain of the efficiency of the Sikh army,' he wrote, 'and displayed the wealth and military force of Ranjit.' But, Masson noted, 'Mr Harlan did not find the Amir so facile as his brother, and was upbraided for his interference in matters which could not concern him ... Mr Harlan found it necessary to send the Amir a Quran, and to make many promises.'[54] Dost Mohammad looked at Harlan sourly. 'When Sikandar (Alexander) visited this country,' he told the American, 'he sent a confidential agent to the prince hereabout, and the mountaineers murdered Sikandar's ambassador.'[55] The history lesson was interrupted when Dost Mohammad realised that his camp had just been surrounded on three sides by Ranjit Singh.

The battle was over before it began. Dost Mohammad knew that 'but one of two alternatives remained to him, to fight, or to retreat without loss of time. He was confounded for the moment.'[56] After a half-hearted attempt at kidnapping Harlan, he decided to retreat. He 'had too much experience in Afghan camps not to know that an orderly retreat is almost an impossibility'[57] and, sure enough, as soon as the retreat was sounded, half of his army began plundering the other half. He had stationed some troops on the road to Kabul, 'with orders to turn back any fugitives from the army seeking to reach Kabul. The first strong body that arrived . . . overpowered the guard, and plundered it of horses, arms and accoutrements. The Amir, in disgust, made no further attempt to restrain the flight of his men, and eventually reached Kabul privately by night.'[58] He had even less money, and was in an even worse mood, than when he set out.

When Masson returned to Kabul, he found that his former peaceful life was a distant memory. The retreating Afghan army had brought chaos in its wake, and 'the streets were the theatres of constant conflicts and slaughters, of which no one seemed to take notice, and the city appeared on the verge of delapsing into anarchy'.[59] Masson began to look over his shoulder more frequently. Even Bagram had changed. What Masson delicately called 'disturbances' were becoming more common, as local chiefs and bands of robbers fought for control.[60] On more than one occasion he was compelled to abandon half-finished excavations 'owing to the agitated state of the country'. 'The plain of Bagram,' he wrote to Pottinger, 'is a dangerous site, but I trust my precautions for the safety of my labourers will be effectual.'[61]

His new life as a spy weighed heavily on Masson. There were days when 'my affairs took so awkward a turn, that my mind was too fully occupied with them, to allow me to follow my former researches with pleasure'.[62] But he was not about to give up. Wade had promised him a small salary, which Masson planned to divert straight to his excavations. He still had many friends. And he still had a trick or two up his sleeve.

Soon after his return to Kabul, Masson and some men began excavating a stupa near Bagram. 'For a day or two, operations were uninterrupted, but one morning a man ... called my friend, named Baloch Khan, telling him someone at the village below wished to speak with him.' When Baloch Khan reached the village, he found it occupied by one of the local gangs:

They expressed that it was a great blessing on their soul they had learned that he was present, for having been appraised that a Feringhi was extracting treasure ... they had, to the number of sixty, taken oaths with each other to attack him, and had now come, determined to first fire a volley and then to have rushed on with their knives, but, they asked: 'What do you here Baloch Khan? Why do you bring the Feringhi here?' Baloch Khan replied that he was a friend with the Feringhi, and anxious to oblige him, that treasure was out of the question, a few pice [hundredths of a rupee] was all that would be found, and much more in the same style.[63]

The robbers 'rejoined, that if such was the case, as well as on his account, they would not interrupt the work . . . Further, they engaged if the other [local] gang should be inclined to interfere, that they would protect the party against them.'[64]

Whatever happened, Masson told himself, whatever the world might throw at him, he had his dream. He had his pothos. He had Alexandria. 'If you work on what is in your hands at this moment, following the path of truth and reason seriously, calmly, and with every ounce of your strength, not allowing anything else to distract you,' the Roman emperor Marcus Aurelius wrote in his *Meditations*, 'if you hold onto this, expecting nothing, fearing nothing, but finding satisfaction in what you are doing right now, with truth and courage behind every word you speak, you will live happily. And no man in the world can prevent this.'[65]

9

Stranger than Fiction

Masson's identity was now an open secret. One by one, people who had known him when he was still James Lewis heard that their old friend was still very much alive. In 1835, Charles Brownlow, who had served with Masson in the Bengal Artillery, sat in the hushed cool of St Andrew's Library in Calcutta and wondered how he should begin his letter to 'my dear Lewis'.

> Though nearly thirteen years have elapsed since I last saw you, and though probably since that time, I have seldom crossed your memory, I cannot resist the temptation I feel to address you a few lines. I am aware of recent documents that have passed through the hands of the Bengal government. They restore to the land of the living one whom all his friends had years since consigned to the grave. I know not if you are aware of the fact, but a report was widely circulated and believed that you had destroyed yourself [committed suicide] shortly after you quitted the service of the East India Company. I congratulate you that the rumour is not true, and that you yet live to build a name for yourself. I am a member of the Asiatic Society, and have derived much pleasure from the perusal of your antiquarian papers in the *Journal of the Asiatic Society*. Little did I dream, however, that I was indebted for them to one so long and so intimately known to me.[1]

Brownlow passed on greetings from another of Masson's old friends, George Jephson. Jephson had recently seen Masson's old commanding officer, and the two 'had a long conversation about you, not deeming you in the land of the living'. 'You must,' wrote Brownlow, 'have had a curious game to play.'[2]

The game was getting curiouser. In the summer of 1835, Masson was adjusting to his new life as a spy. He hated it. 'Its invidious nature, its tendency to compromise me with the people with whom I had long and creditably resided, the check it imposed on the antiquarian researches in which I had been engaged, the loss of independence and freedom to move where I pleased, were amongst my causes for dissatisfaction,' he wrote sadly.[3] But unfortunately for him, he was an exceedingly good spy.

Within a few months, Masson had rebuilt Karamat Ali's shattered intelligence operation. He soon had all the gossip of Kabul at his fingertips. Dost Mohammad and his advisors were furious about the ignominious retreat from Peshawar. 'If I tell you,' Haji Khan had fumed to the Amir, 'that you went with twenty thousand men, and placed yourself in front of seventy thousand Sikhs, that you discharged your guns upon them, that you fought them, and brought their heads into your camp – then you are angry. If I tell you, that you went and showed them your nakedness, and sneaked off – then you are angry; there is no saying anything to please you.'[4] Many blamed the British: if the East India Company had not ignored their pleas for support, muttered Dost Mohammad's chief minister Sami Khan, things might have turned out very differently.[5]

By the end of the summer, Masson's networks had spread out across Central Asia. His travels had left him with friends in almost every town and city, not to mention among the merchants whose caravans of camels plodded back and forth across the mountains, laden with silks and spices. When a suspicious-looking character calling himself Mirza Jafar arrived in the great Silk Road metropolis of Bukhara, hundreds of miles away, Masson knew about it. While Mirza Jafar was saying his prayers at the central mosque, Masson's agents were shadowing him. He spoke, Masson noted, 'Arabic, Persian and Turkish', and occasionally claimed to be a Frenchman.

Rumour had it that the Russian governor of Orenburg had 'brought Mirza Jafar' from St Petersburg[6] and sent him across the frontier to gather intelligence.

Wade could barely believe 'the extent and accuracy of the information' coming from Kabul.[7] He thanked Masson 'for the zealous attention which you continue to evince in the discharge of the duties that have been imposed on you'.[8] Soon, Masson's reports were making their way to Calcutta. He became 'an authority greatly relied on by the Indian government'.[9]

Wade was also anxious. Macnaghten had told him to stop referring to Masson as 'our Agent' in Kabul,[10] since it implied Masson had been given an official appointment. 'I have avoided giving any other designations to Mr Masson than that he was "connected with my office,"' Wade promised, insincerely.[11] He hoped Masson would not read between the lines. Above all, he hoped Masson would not realise that he had already been pardoned.

In early 1835, Wade's report on Masson reached London. It landed on the desk of Lord Ellenborough, the President of the East India Company's Board of Control. Ellenborough was rather smitten by the story of Masson's adventures. Wade had intended to dangle the possibility of a pardon in front of Masson indefinitely. He did not care whether the pardon was granted or not.[12] It was the leverage that mattered. Ellenborough had other ideas. He wrote to the King, 'requesting that a pardon may be granted to James Lewis, alias Charles Masson'[13] immediately, not because of his work as a spy, but because of his archaeological discoveries:

He has assumed the name of Charles Masson. He is possessed of much science and ability. He has acquired and communicated much useful information respecting the condition of the people and territories bordering on the Indus, and is now engaged in prosecuting his enquiries, more of a scientific than a political nature ...

Under all the circumstances, Lord Ellenborough humbly advises your Majesty to grant the pardon which the Governor General of India has solicited for this person, whose private character appears to be unimpeached, except as regards the crime of desertion, and who seems disposed to atone as far as he can for that crime by useful contributions to the ancient history, and to our present knowledge, of the nations in the vicinity of the Indus.[14]

Three days later, a pardon from King William IV was signed, sealed and ready to send to India.[15] Masson did not know it, but Alexandria had set him free.

When the pardon reached Ludhiana, Wade was not pleased. He could not avoid sending the news to Kabul, but, he told Masson, the East India Company would be holding on to the pardon itself, 'for reasons that you may be able to appreciate',[16] and had decided that it would remain secret. That left Masson guessing: why had he been pardoned, and were there any conditions? He had no idea 'whether or not I was a free agent',[17] but he knew that if he guessed wrong it could cost him his life.

For years, Masson had told stories to survive. Now, he was caught in Wade's web, and day by day, he was being pulled further in. After almost ten years on the run, a part of him had never stopped being afraid. He feared that he had only been pardoned because of his work as a spy, and that his pardon could be revoked at any time. Neither of those things were true. But as Masson was discovering, becoming a spy is easy. Stopping is much harder.

Masson was increasingly tied to Kabul. 'The official appointment as Agent,' he wrote sadly to Pottinger, 'you will easily imagine by charging me with new duties, and restricting, as it were, my residence to Kabul, has prevented me from following up the more agreeable antiquarian researches which I was engaged in.'[18] But he trusted his Afghan assistants. They were now operating independently for much of the year, buying up coins in Bagram and running excavations. 'One of them, by name Hassan, is a young man who has been with me ever since I have been at Kabul, of which he is a native, and has attached himself to me under all circumstances and fortune with remarkable fidelity. He has been of the greatest service to me in my various operations, being fully to be depended upon, and having the wit to make himself agreeable wherever he goes, which is no trivial thing.'[19]

It was slow, expensive work. But every rupee Wade doled out went straight to Masson's excavations, and Pottinger continued to send funds whenever he could. Along with the typical expenses of an excavation – 'sharpening implements etc.' – Masson had to spend a fortune on bribes. Each local official had his weakness: one 'drove off my workmen with an armed party. On an explanation, he was amused by some medicines he requested, and I kept him in good humour during the operations by occasional small presents of fruits.' And each of 'the numerous persons necessary to conciliate' had to be paid off separately. 'Should any of the items be considered objectionable,' Masson wrote apologetically to Pottinger, when he sent on his accounts, 'I beg they may be expunged.'[20]

In Bagram, the outlines of a city were taking shape. 'In many places,' Masson wrote, 'it has been proved that by digging about a yard in depth, lines of cement, seeming to denote the outlines of structures and their apartments, may be found.'[21] And Hassan's finds were piling up. In every room of Masson's tiny house, there were bags of coins, heaps of jewellery and caskets propped in the corners. An unknown world was coming into focus. 'Not only was great light about to be cast on the obscurity which had involved so many ages and nations, but many theories which had previously gained the assent of the learned world, were about to be displaced.'[22]

Masson knew that if he wanted to tell the story of ancient Afghanistan, he had to move quickly.[23] After years of painstaking work, others might anticipate him.

Thousands of miles away, Johann Martin Honigberger, the Transylvanian treasure-hunter, was composing a letter to the British Museum. 'During my sojourn at Kabul (more than four months),' Honigberger wrote, he had excavated the stupas 'of the town and its environs, as far as Jalalabad. I opened them all.'

Encouraged by the zeal for the promotion of science, and with the sole intention of being enabled to offer the British Museum hidden treasures hitherto unknown in Europe, at the same time calculating out the reward of my services ... It would be utterly impossible for me to fix any particular value on objects of such great and invaluable importance. But allowing me to direct your special attention to the immense expense of nearly £1200 I incurred of making the overland journey from Lahore to London, and to the dangers to which I was exposed, the precautions I adopted, the fatigue I underwent, and the difficulties I had to overcome, for the sole purpose of seeing these treasures safely lodged in England, will enable you to an adequate idea of the remuneration I deserve.[24]

When Edward Hawkins, the Museum's Keeper of Antiquities, saw Honigberger's finds from Afghanistan, it was lust at first sight. 'The Museum must, yes must, buy them even if it pawns something to raise the money,' he wrote.[25] But £1,200 was an enormous sum: £120,000 or $150,000 today. Honigberger soon dropped his price to £700. The Museum's curators muttered about his 'apparent humbug',[26] and tried to scrape together enough cash to make him an offer. 'Do not on any account,' Hawkins pleaded, 'omit securing some part of the abominable German's treasures.'[27]

The golden, jewel-encrusted Bimaran Casket, a more important find than all of Honigberger's collection put together, cost the East India Company a total of five rupees:[28] £50 or $62 today. Masson thought the Company was doing very well out of their deal. Once, he unwisely said so to Wade.

In the autumn of 1835, out of the blue, Masson received a furious letter from Pottinger. Wade had told him that Masson resented their partnership, and the money he had offered. 'You can hardly blame him,' Wade wrote, 'for preferring my offer of employment when you consider its vital importance to his future happiness.'[29] Masson had said nothing of the sort, but Pottinger took the bait. He told Masson, icily, that he would not get a single rupee more for his excavations from him. He never wanted to hear from Masson again.[30]

Masson was devastated. He wrote three long, miserable letters to Pottinger, asking him to 'hold me guiltless of matters which I did not prompt or suggest'.[31] 'It is not mere regret I feel, that the smooth and agreeable course of the correspondence, subsisting between yourself and me, should have been ruffled, and that attempts have been made, not only to dissolve a connection which I valued, but to excite unpleasant feelings in your breast and to cast reproach upon myself.' Wade had twisted his words beyond all recognition, and 'though he may pretend friendship and disinterestedness, I certainly very much question the one and the other'.[32]

Wade needed his spy helpless, alone and entirely dependent on him. Now, he turned the screws. Masson's finds were held up indefinitely in Ludhiana.[33] Any letters about his excavations had to be approved first. 'I considered it objectionable,' Wade wrote, 'that you should communicate on the subject of them through any other channel than that of my office.'[34] Masson's salary went unpaid. 'He must have been sensible that I had no means of meeting my expenses, but of incurring debts at Kabul,' Masson wrote. 'I suspect his object was to keep my hands tied up, in which in some measure he succeeded.'[35] But Wade had underestimated Masson.

In the evenings, as the lamps were lit, and the call to prayer echoed across Kabul, Masson spread out his finds from Bagram and tried to understand them. Was this Alexander's city, or not? Coins were battered and defaced. Inscriptions, written on ancient leaves of bark, were so fragile that they often fell to pieces before he could copy them. He still had almost no books. 'Some eighteen months' after he first promised to help, 'Captain Wade did forward some dozen English works, amongst which were Robertson's *Histories* [of Scotland and America] and Young's *Algebra* … with the view, I presume, of enlightening me upon the history of ancient Bactria [Central Asia].'[36] But one day, turning over a coin for perhaps the hundredth time, Masson suddenly realised what he was looking at.

On one side of the coin there was a portrait of a king, and an inscription in ancient Greek. On the other side, there were symbols in an unknown script. Neither Masson nor anyone else in the world knew how to read it. For years, Masson had wondered if he would ever find a way to decipher the symbols. Then he realised that the secret had been staring right at him all along.

'Basileus', the Greek inscription on the front of the coin always began: 'King'. On the other side of the coin, Masson realised, the inscription also began with the same series of symbols every time. The coins were bilingual: the unknown script on the back said the same thing as the Greek on the front. If Masson could read the Greek, he could also decipher the lost language. Each coin was a miniature Rosetta Stone.

The unknown script was called Kharoshthi. It was introduced around 100 years after Alexander's expedition, and spread through modern-day Afghanistan and Pakistan, along the Silk Road into China. By the fourth century AD it had fallen out of use in Afghanistan, and by the seventh century it had died out completely. No one had been able to read it for over a thousand years.

In 150 BC, it had been used by King Menander I. Menander was born on the plains of Bagram, in a tiny village near Alexandria.[37] He had ruled a kingdom centred on Afghanistan, stretching south to the plains of the Punjab. Masson had found over 100 of his coins. 'Basileus Soteros Menandrou' read the front of the coins: 'King Menander the saviour'. 'Maharajasa tratarasa Menamdrasa' read the words in Kharoshthi on the reverse, which Masson had wondered about for so long: 'King Menander the saviour'.

The more Masson understood about his discoveries, the more puzzling they became.

In 1835, almost every British history book told the same story: there could be no common ground between East and West. Alexander's expedition, just like the history of the East India Company, marked the triumph of 'the discipline and intrepidity of the Greeks and Macedonians ... over barbarian craft and desultory fury'.[38] Alexander's empire was brought down by 'his disposition to abandon the character of a Greek as contradistinguished from a barbarian'.[39] And after his death, in India and Afghanistan, 'the barbarians ... at last obliterated all the traces of European civilisation left there by Alexander'.[40]

The story Masson was uncovering had none of those parts. It was a story about Alexander the Great, but, unlike every other one, it

The Bimaran Casket

A unicorn seal from Harappa,
2600 BC–1900 BC

An attendant of the Buddha, from Hadda

The golden clue: a coin of the Roman emperor
Theodosius II, found by Masson at Hadda

The miniature Rosetta Stone: a bilingual coin
of Menander I, found by Masson

Augustus and the emperor of Afghanistan: a
coin of Kujula Kadphises, found by Masson

Medallion of a young man, from Bagram

The Bala Hissar, Kabul

The city of Kabul

The Buddhas of Bamiyan in 1832

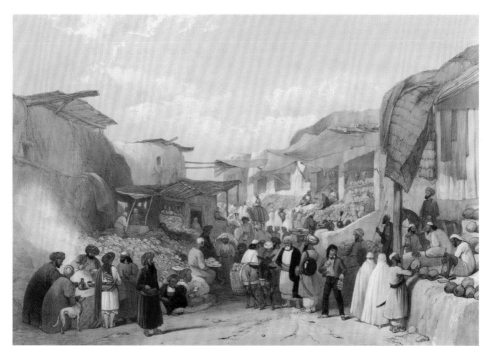

The bazaars of Kabul

The plains of Bagram

The gardens of Babur, Kabul

The court of Dost Mohammad Khan

The wonders of Bamiyan: one of Masson's sketches

Sikandar and the Brahmins

Alexander's flying machine

Alexander is lowered
beneath the waves

was also about Buddhist art and Chinese travellers. It was a story
about the Greeks in Asia, but, unlike every other one, it was not a
story of the West's triumph over the East. Every day Masson spent
in Afghanistan, every new discovery, cast doubt on the ideas he had
grown up with. The cool, grey certainties of Britain, of empire, of
western superiority, were fading away.

Masson could not decide whether to trust his material, or to
fit his ideas around the old dusty models. 'I fear to write,' he
confessed.[41] 'The want of authorities for reference and comparison,
which has sorely been felt by me in all my enquiries, especially as
many of them were directed upon subjects unexpected and novel,
should perhaps have made me hesitate.'[42] Yet Masson could not
hold back his excitement. Sitting in his house in the Armenian
quarter, looking out over the rooftops of Kabul, he spread out
his new finds and picked up his pen. He was so caught up in his
work that when one of Dost Mohammad's confidants 'hinted that
I knew too much of the affairs at Kabul', he did not pay as much
attention as he should have done.[43]

When Masson's notes reached Calcutta, James Prinsep, the
Secretary of the Asiatic Society, could barely believe what he was
reading. If Masson was right about the unknown script, then it
would soon be possible 'to unravel' the entire lost language.[44] In
Calcutta, holding onto the past was almost impossible. The air was
heavy with sweat and decay. Freshly painted buildings sprouted
mould. Stuffed animals rotted. Paintings warped and cracked. In
Park Street Cemetery, just down the road from the Asiatic Society,
vines crept inexorably over the pillars and porticos of British
tombs, and thick green moss covered their epitaphs. Every day,
India reminded the British that nothing lasts for ever.

However hard the Asiatic Society fought to preserve the past,
it was trapped in a losing battle with inevitability. The East India
Company was no help. When Prinsep asked for its support
publishing the masterpieces of Sanskrit literature, the Company
replied that it had no wish 'to accumulate stores of waste paper'
and that its funds would be 'employed in imparting to the native
population a knowledge of English literature'.[45] (When he heard

this, Macnaghten, resplendent in his blue spectacles, began shouting furiously in Latin.)[46] So Masson's promise that the lost language of the coins might be understood again was a dream come true. Reading Masson's letter from Kabul was the most 'seductive' moment Prinsep could remember.[47]

Masson realised that the city he had found at Bagram changed everything. These Greeks had not wanted to wipe out other cultures. They had wanted to learn from them. In the centuries after Alexander's death, the blood and chaos of his campaign had mostly been forgotten. Curiosity endured.

In Islamic legend, Sikandar 'set out to the land of the Brahmins, to learn something of their ancient wisdom',[48] and challenged the wisest man in India to a battle of wits:

> To make trial of the wise master, Sikandar sent him a cup full of oil to anoint him therewith; the sage cast it into a thousand needles and set it back to Sikandar, who had a ring formed out of them which he sent to the master, who polished it bright as a mirror and sent it back ... Sikandar had intended to say, 'I am wiser than all the philosophers;' the Indian had replied, 'Sikandar and his knowledge are transitory;' the king had sent the ring to signify his power; the sage had set a mirror before him that he might see himself.[49]

Menander I, the king born in the shadow of Alexandria, stamped his coins with Athena, Greek goddess of wisdom, but many argue that he also converted to Buddhism. An ancient Buddhist text, the *Questions of King Milinda*, records a dialogue between Menander and a Buddhist monk. 'When,' the monk told Menander, 'someone brings a lamp into a dark house, the light of the lamp dispels the darkness, casts light in every direction, and illuminates the rooms. Such, my king, is the work of wisdom. When it is inside us, it dispels the darkness of our ignorance and casts the light of insight. It lights the spark of knowledge, and illuminates all that is true.'[50]

During Menander's reign, a great Buddhist pilgrimage set out from Alexandria beneath the Mountains. The pilgrims wound their way through the passes and covered the entire length of India, before crossing the sea to Sri Lanka. At the dedication of the Buddhist stupa in the Sri Lankan city of Anuradhapura, according to an ancient chronicle, 'from Alexandria, the city of the Greeks, came the elder Greek Mahadhammarakkhita with thirty thousand monks'.[51] Indian rulers were equally intrigued by the Greeks: one king dispatched ambassadors to Alexander's successors, asking for 'sweet wine, dried figs and a philosopher'. (The wine and figs were duly sent but, the reply came, 'our philosophers are not for sale'.)[52]

The civilisation Masson had found was neither Greek nor Afghan. It was neither pagan nor Buddhist. It was all of those things. This was a culture that did not fit any model in the history books. Alexander's cities had not been isolated bastions of Greek culture in a distant land. Though many had been founded as grim military garrisons, they had become outposts of curiosity. Seen from Alexandria beneath the Mountains, East and West were not opposed, but had been living side by side, and learning from one another, for over 2,000 years.[53] Masson realised that just like the two sides of his coins, the story of the world was interconnected: Greek and Buddhist, Alexander and Sikandar.

Masson had found the story he had been chasing for years. It was about Alexander, but it was also about himself: about strangers who find a home in a strange land.

'Truth is strange,' Brownlow wrote to Masson, 'stranger than fiction. Your history is a romance! And so notwithstanding the ample indulgence you have already afforded to your rambling propensities, the tendency is still as strong upon you as ever – growing by what it feeds upon.' He felt sure that his old friend was on the brink of 'the elucidation of a history which has been a standing enigma for two thousand years'.[54]

Then the assassins came for Masson.

One night, a sudden noise pulled him from sleep. He blinked awake and stumbled to the door. Men with knives were running up the stairs.[55]

10

The Age of Everything

It took Masson a moment to realise what was happening. The men's faces were 'muffled' and their knives were gripped tightly in their hands.[1] They were making straight for him.

Masson was no brawler. His preferred survival skills were talking and running. The men were not interested in a conversation, and he had nowhere to run. He barricaded the door of his room, and yelled as loudly as he could for help. Fortunately, the men did not wait around to find out if any would be coming. They disappeared into the alleys of Kabul as quickly as they had arrived.

The next night, they were back.[2]

From that point on, Masson slept uneasily, when he could sleep at all.[3] Every few weeks, desperate to keep Wade happy, he dispatched another report to Ludhiana. As he wrote, he cursed the spymaster under his breath. 'I do not venture upon [writing] his name, for I have been so accustomed at Kabul to hear it coupled with the epithet "dog," that I fear I might make a mistake and put it too.'[4] Every time Masson picked up his pen to write to Wade, he itched to begin: 'Dear Dog'.

Masson's dispatches were Britain's only window into Afghanistan, and they were read with increasing interest not just by Wade, but by the men who ran the East India Company from Calcutta. Their eyes were turning covetously towards Afghanistan. 'The policy of the frontier where you are cannot remain long pacific,' Brownlow warned Masson, 'and when the blow is struck – which it will be, when Ranjit closes his eye – there will be no need of divination to decide what will be the result: the extension of our boundary.'[5]

Early in 1836, Masson climbed the steep path up to the Bala Hissar, to Dost Mohammad's court. He slipped into the back of the crowd, watching and listening. Then, at the sound of a familiar nasal voice, he looked up sharply. A tall, heavily bearded man was holding forth, 'dressed in a light, shining, pea-green satin jacket, maroon-coloured silk small-clothes, buff boots, a silver-lace girdle fastened with a large square buckle bigger than a soldier's breast-plate, and on his head a white cat-skin foraging cap, with a glittering gold band and tassels.'[6] Josiah Harlan had returned.

Harlan had outstayed his welcome in the Punjab. Ranjit Singh discovered his counterfeiting operation,[7] and summoned the giant American to explain himself. By way of apology, Harlan 'constructed a talisman' for the Maharaja, and showed it to his chief adviser, Fakir Azizuddin. As the court chronicle recorded, his plan went downhill from there. Azizuddin, 'who was a learned and capable man, felt surprised at the sight of a gold chain round a pig representing the talisman of life, and gave an account of it to the Maharaja, who said that he must give an idea of handsome reward to Harlan sahib, making him expectant of great favours on the recovery of the Maharaja. The aforesaid person [Harlan] demanded 100,000 rupees [£1,000,000 or $1,250,000 today] before he undertook to treat the Maharaja', and 'began to talk nonsense and rubbish'. Ranjit Singh's courtiers 'explained the details of his stupid behaviour to the Maharaja, who flew into a rage and ordered that he should be turned out of the town bare-footed'.[8]

Swiftly, Harlan claimed that he had been misunderstood. He did not want 100,000 rupees for his pig charm. Instead, he wanted to construct 'a galvanic battery' and hook Ranjit Singh up to it. 'His plan of galvanizing the Maharaja met with a ready consent on the part of the latter',[9] until Harlan mentioned the cost. The materials, he told Ranjit Singh, would come to exactly 100,000 rupees.

Wade, hoping to keep his informant in Lahore, wrote to Ranjit Singh that 'Harlan sahib was a very wise and intelligent person, and that the talisman prepared by him was quite accurate and exact, and eulogised him a great deal'.[10] But it was too late. Ranjit Singh 'threatened to wreak his vengeance on Dr Harlan if he did not speedily leave his dominions. Dr Harlan, well knowing the character of the man he had to deal with, lost no time in making his escape to Ludhiana.'[11]

By the time he reached Ludhiana, Harlan was almost penniless. He took the road to Kabul, muttering furiously. Wade's deputy watched him go. 'His declared intention is to bring down an army to avenge himself on his former master [Ranjit Singh] for the injuries he had received (he says) at his hands. He is an eccentric, and undoubtedly an enterprising man; but that he has a talent to gain such an ascendancy over the ruler at Kabul as will enable him to carry out his threat, is, in my opinion, more than doubtful.'[12]

When he arrived in Kabul, Harlan was on his best behaviour. He had written Dost Mohammad a poem. 'Thou stand'st a warrior in the midst of war! / Here to find a throne, or fill a hero's grave,' he boomed, 'For God, the Prophet, and thy deeds of fame, / A martyr's paradise, or victor's name.'[13] Like most things about Harlan, it sounded impressive, but did not bear close examination. Dost Mohammad put him in charge of a handful of soldiers 'as a temporary measure'.[14] Harlan began introducing himself 'as counsellor of state, aide-de-camp, and General of the Staff of Dost Mohammad Khan, Amir of Kabul'.[15]

In Bhuj, Henry Pottinger was even angrier than usual. Having cut off his correspondence with Masson months earlier, he had just received a heartbroken series of letters from Kabul. Reading them, he realised that Wade had made a fool out of him. 'I had,' he wrote to a friend, 'the unfeigned gratification of receiving a very large packet of letters from Mr Masson in which he affords me the fullest explanation of his share in the business, and clearly proves that Captain Wade, for reasons best known to himself, had made use of an extract of a private letter written now nearly two years ago, to sow dissentions between Mr Masson and myself, and to break off our further correspondence. To say that Mr Masson's letter has given me pleasure conveys but a very faint idea of my feelings on the subject.'[16] To Masson he wrote, 'as my friendship is valuable to you, you have it with all sincerity'.[17] 'Of Captain Wade's conduct,' he added, 'I must not trust myself to speak.'[18] (Pottinger soon reconsidered this: letters sufficient 'to fill a volume' began to pour out of Bhuj towards Wade, Wade's superiors and the authorities in Bombay and Calcutta. 'I would not,' one of Pottinger's acquaintances remarked, 'be Captain Wade for the world.')[19] Masson and Pottinger picked up the threads of their friendship. 'I rejoice,' Masson wrote.[20]

But Masson had little else to lift his heart. In 1836, a new Governor General, Lord Auckland, had been appointed to India. Both Masson and Dost Mohammad hoped for a new beginning. 'The arrival of Lord Auckland again excites hopes, and if the intercourse between India and Kabul be not promoted, it will not be from the objections of the Amir Dost Mohammad, who continually complains that no duly authorized person has been sent to confer with him,'[21] Masson noted. 'The field of my hopes,' Dost Mohammad wrote to Auckland, 'which has before been chilled by the cold blast of the times, has, by the happy tidings of your Lordship's arrival, become the envy of the garden of Paradise.'[22] But Dost Mohammad's letters went unanswered, and the Amir took his frustration out on Masson.[23] Meanwhile, Masson's debts were piling up again. And life in Kabul was changing faster than ever.

One day, walking near the city with a friend, Masson saw 'a man running, with a musket in his hand'. He was shouting, 'Is the Feringhi gone?' Someone pointed out Masson in the distance, and the man knelt down, settled his gun on the ground beside a stream and carefully took aim. 'That fellow,' Masson murmured, 'means to fire.' 'No,' his friend replied, 'he can hardly mean it.' 'Heavens, he does!' No sooner had 'the words passed my mouth the shot came, striking about a foot beneath us'.[24]

Masson wondered, grimly, how long his luck would hold: sooner or later a knife or a bullet was bound to get through. He sent his papers to 'a place of security' with Pottinger.[25] 'I shall be happy to be enabled to dispatch by degrees the whole of my manuscripts,' he wrote, 'as I shall be less fearful of any accident eventually happening to myself in these countries, and be careless about it, should it happen.'²⁶ 'I will,' Pottinger replied, 'consider them a sacred charge.'²⁷ 'On some future and happier day,' Masson wrote wistfully, 'I may at my leisure prepare them.'²⁸ He was exhausted, and edging ever closer to a breakdown.

Spying for the East India Company had been awful even before people began shooting at him. Now, life as Wade's puppet, his 'tool and his fool', was unspeakable. 'If I measure his iniquity by the misery he has occasioned me,' reflected Masson, 'it is great indeed.'²⁹ From Calcutta, Brownlow advised him to keep his head down and keep quiet: 'I am much concerned to learn that there has been a rupture between yourself and Captain Wade, for he possesses vast influence and has everything in his power, either to make or to mar your fortunes.'³⁰ But Masson was tired of keeping quiet. 'I know not if I improperly attach a value to independence,' he wrote, 'and doing so whether my horror at dependence be justifiable or not, but I think any honest man will allow that the individual was a luckless one, whose fate was at the disposal of a secretarial letter.'³¹ He had a pardon. It was time, he thought, to find out if it had any strings attached.

Masson sent a letter directly to Calcutta, 'taking the desperate chance of resigning the appointment of Agent at Kabul',³² since 'I had been brought to consider the patronage of the supreme government a curse'.³³ 'I did not resolve upon this step until I had suffered some five or six months of the most severe mental agony I ever before endured,' he ended. 'I have little to confide in for the future, but God and my own resources.'³⁴ Sealing the letter, Masson's hands shook. Watching his courier ride away through the gates of Kabul, following the road to India, he knew that he might be condemning himself to death.

Masson's letter never made it to Calcutta. When it reached Ludhiana, Wade intercepted it, opened it, read it and kept it. He dispatched a silky warning back to Kabul:

> I beg that you will first consider your own interests … You have contracted obligations which are deserving of particular reflection, before you forfeit the consideration that has been extended to you.

A sacrifice of personal advantages may be a matter of no importance in your mind, but I am loath to believe that you are equally indifferent to the claims which a generous government appears to me to have established on your gratitude and devotion to its service, when you have thoroughly considered the extent of them.

I hope you will appreciate the motives which have induced me not to forward your letter to the secretary of government without affording you another opportunity of exercising your judgment, trusting that it will dispose you to weigh the subject in its relation to the government as well as its effects on your future prospects in life.[35]

Wade, of course, was bluffing: Masson could have walked away from it all, a free man. But the letter seemed to confirm Masson's worst fears. He had 'contracted obligations' with the East India Company, and his 'future prospects in life' would be very different if he ignored them. His pardon had strings attached. He would have to be a spy. There was no way out.

***

In the summer of 1836, Godfrey Vigne, an English traveller in an enormous white hat, rode up to the ancient city of Ghazni, about 100 miles south of Kabul. Hassan, Masson's Afghan friend, was excavating a stupa nearby. Vigne rode over to introduce himself and was somewhat surprised by what happened next. Hassan and his workmen 'were emptying the well which is usually found in the centre of these buildings'. Vigne told Hassan 'that I should shortly become acquainted with Mr Masson, and that I was sure that gentleman would have no objection to my seeing the well opened. The man set himself down immediately on the top of the well, struck it with his trowel, and, with a good-natured look, affirmed that it was impossible.'[36]

'Hassan,' as Masson put it with satisfaction, 'gave him to understand he would not be allowed to interfere in his operations, and he passed on to Kabul, baffled.'[37] Masson and Jabar Khan met Vigne outside the city. 'By their advice,' Vigne wrote, 'I had doffed my English shooting-jacket and broad-brimmed white hat, in favour of a handsome Multan silk turban and a native dress of English printed calico, which were presented to me, ready-made, by the nawab.'³⁸

Masson took the freshly made-over Vigne out for dinner with Dost Mohammad's chief minister, Sami Khan. After the meal there were, as always, songs. Vigne, who knew 'scarcely a syllable' of Persian, did not understand why Masson kept shooting him 'a very significant glance from time to time'.³⁹ 'Do you not hear what he sings?' Sami Khan finally asked his guests. ' "If we don't get an answer from one city, we will from another! My heart is filled with affliction, and how long are my hopes to be delayed?" It is surprising,' he added, 'how soon they learn anything from my teaching. When they go out elsewhere, they sing the songs of Hafiz; but, when they come to my house, they find other themes for their songs.' It was Sami Khan's way of reminding Masson that news of 'the intentions of the Indian government towards Kabul' was long overdue.⁴⁰

Vigne smiled and blundered his way through life in Kabul. 'I well remember meeting a mule laden with grass, that was just entering a narrow street as I was coming out of it. I could only turn my horse with the greatest difficulty, and motioned to the driver to go back. He did so, but exclaimed aloud, "Is Dost Mohammad dead, that there is no justice?" '⁴¹ Sitting under the mulberry trees, watercolours in hand, brandy by his side, Vigne spent his days painting. His combination of cheerfulness and obtuseness was remarkably persuasive: most of the Kabul elite, including Dost Mohammad, ended up sitting for him. Even Masson, for the first time in his life, had his portrait painted. But as soon as it was complete, Akbar Khan, Dost Mohammad's son, claimed it for himself. 'The Amir's son is here and swears you must come,' Vigne wrote to Masson. 'He took possession of your portrait directly he saw it.'⁴²

In August, Masson and Vigne rode out to Bagram together.⁴³ Masson's excitement at his discoveries was still irrepressible. When he first saw Bagram, the plain had been a blank canvas to him. 'Oh,' he had reflected, as he rode past some ancient tamarisk trees, 'that they could tell by whom and in what age they were planted.'[44] Then the faintest scribbles had appeared: copper coins, which he could neither read nor understand. The scribbles had turned into figures: kings and dynasties had lined up, one following the other. Colours had begun to appear: gold and lapis lazuli, coral and silver. The blank canvas had become a huge shimmering painting. Then one of the painted people suddenly turned and spoke to Masson, and he began to understand their long-forgotten language. Suddenly, everyone in the frame was talking. And now, when Masson rode over the plain of Bagram, he felt the ghosts crowding around him and telling their stories.

Generations of kings had ruled from Bagram. Two centuries after Menander I, a new empire took power. The Kushan empire was founded by nomadic tribes who swept west from China on horseback. By the time the Kushans reached Afghanistan, many of Alexander's cities had been destroyed or had slipped into decline. The Kushans built their fortresses from the ruins of Alexandrias. But Bagram had not fallen into darkness during the Kushan period.

In the first century AD, Kujula Kadphises, the first Kushan emperor, built his summer capital at Bagram. One of the strangest coins Masson had found was struck in his mints. Like the others, it had an inscription in Greek on the front, and in Kharoshthi on the reverse. But in place of his own portrait on the front of the coin, the Kushan emperor had chosen one of Augustus, the first emperor of Rome. On the reverse of the coin, Kujula Kadphises sat in a Roman curule chair, traditionally reserved for the empire's highest officials. A Buddhist king, ruling from a city built by Alexander the Great, celebrated the founding of his own dynasty with a coin depicting Rome's first emperor, inscribed in Greek and Kharoshthi. It was dizzying: a multicultural world beyond the imagination of most nineteenth-century scholars. But one discovery after another brought it further into focus. Masson found ivory from India,[45] coins from the Tang dynasty,[46] silver from Constantinople and delicate Roman seals carved from red Chinese amber.[47] This was the age of everything. Masson had found the 'crossroads of the ancient world'.[48]

Masson was still not sure that he had found Alexandria beneath the Mountains. But he had discovered something even more important than Alexander's city: Alexander's legacy.

In 1937, a French archaeological team at Bagram stumbled across a hoard of treasures from the Kushan era, walled up in a hidden room, a few feet below the surface of the plain. What they found left them awestruck. There were glass fish inlaid with lapis lazuli. A hunt in Africa was picked out on translucent Roman glassware. A young man stared out from a plaster medallion, his long hair seemingly caught by the wind from the Hindu Kush. The great lighthouse of Alexandria in Egypt, the Pharos, reared up on a glass beaker.[49] One of the seven wonders of the ancient world, its light shone across the Mediterranean for over 1,000 years. 'It can be seen for more than seventy miles,' the traveller Ibn Jubayr wrote in 1183, 'and competes with the skies in height. Description of it falls short, the eyes fail to comprehend it, and words are inadequate, so vast is the spectacle.'[50] Despite its fame, almost no depictions of the Pharos survive: the glass beaker from Bagram is not just the earliest but perhaps the most accurate one which has ever been found.

The more Masson found, the more he wanted. Coins piled up in shimmering heaps: thousands upon thousands, gold, silver and copper, Afghan, Greek, Roman and Chinese. Pottinger tried to rein him in. 'You have already sent enough to satisfy the whole body of numismatologists in Europe,'[51] he protested. But Masson could not stop. Night after night, he crept out of Kabul in disguise, to check on his excavations. 'The same necessity for caution, however, which had caused me to leave the city without informing any one, precipitated my return to it, and I reached it without having been missed.'[52] 'The collection,' he wrote, 'was not – as indeed no collection well could be – too large.'[53]

The story of Alexander has one inexorable moral: the faster you chase a dream, the faster it runs away from you. In the *Shahnameh*, Sikandar finally reaches the place 'beyond which is nothingness: the world's end'.[54] At the very edge of reality, a magical tree grows. And as Sikandar stands under its branches, it begins to speak to him:

Why does Sikandar travel so far?
He has enough and to spare
Of the bright things of the world.
And when seven years and seven years have passed
He too will pass away …

Sikandar,
Is this truly your heart's desire,
To roam the world,
And bring pain to those you meet?
You have not long to live.
Tread lightly.[55]

For years, Masson had kept a scrap of verse close. It was from an old Persian grammar, and it spoke to him, the hunter who could never be satisfied: 'Wherefore art thou come? If thou art come to learn the science of ancient and modern times, thou hast not taken the right path. Doth not the creator of all things know all things? And if thou art come to seek him, know that where thou first was fixed, there he was present.'[56]

As 1836 turned into 1837, Masson's life was tottering. One of Dost Mohammad's commanders 'urged my seizure upon the Amir, striving to delude him with the notion of finding twenty thousand rupees in my house'.[57] Meanwhile, Masson's finances were in so precarious a state that, far from having twenty thousand rupees stashed away, his creditors were threatening to move in with him until he paid his debts, as was the custom.[58] He lost day after day to crippling headaches. 'I am unable to sit down and compose, a fixed pain in the upper part of my head distracting me.'[59]

'If you can hold on, and bide your time, you will have no cause to regret it,' Brownlow advised him.[60] But Masson was finding it harder and harder to believe in better times. 'I have been only once sorry, and that has been ever since I did not persist in resignation of employment,' he wrote, sadly. 'I have become useless to the world and to myself.'[61]

'My dear Masson,' Brownlow wrote, 'allow me to console you that the worst of your troubles are over.'[62]

Masson did not know it, but his troubles were just beginning.

II

The Second Alexander

A celebrity was on his way to Kabul.

Alexander Burnes liked to call himself 'the second Alexander'.[1] He was born on the Scottish coast, in the greystone town of Montrose. It was a hunched, windswept place of whalers and adventurers, caught between the hills and the sea. You knew who you were if you came from Montrose.

Burnes was bright-eyed, generous, charming and ferociously optimistic; he had the energy and the enthusiasm of a puppy. Unfortunately, he also had the discretion and the morals of a puppy. In the autumn of 1836, the East India Company dispatched him to Kabul to 'strengthen their relations as much as possible, and in order to set the commerce of the interior on a good footing'.[2] Burnes had no idea what he was doing.

In 1831, Burnes, along with the Indian scholar Mohan Lal and Dr James Gerard, had set out on one of the most remarkable journeys of the age. Driven, as Burnes put it, by 'a desire that I had always felt to see new countries, and visit the conquests of Alexander',[3] the travellers crossed the Punjab and took the Khyber Pass into Afghanistan, reaching Kabul on 1 May 1832. 'The people know me by the name of Sikandar, which is the Persian for Alexander, and a magnanimous name it is,' Burnes wrote. 'With all my assumed poverty, I have a bag of ducats round my waist, and bills for as much money as I choose to draw. I gird my loins, and tie on my sword on all occasions, though I freely admit I would make more use of silver and gold than of cold steel. When I go into a company, I put my hand on my heart, and I say with all humility to the master of the house, "Peace be unto thee," according to custom.'[4]

In Kabul, the party stayed with Jabar Khan, and Burnes fell in love with Afghanistan, in his own way. 'The people of this country are kind-hearted and hospitable,' he wrote. 'When they ask me if I eat pork, I of course shudder, and say that it is only outcasts who commit such outrages. God forgive me, for I am very fond of bacon, and my mouth waters as I write the word. I wish I had some of it for breakfast, to which I am now about to sit down.'[5]

After eighteen days in Kabul, the travellers took the road north to Bukhara. From there, Gerard and Lal backtracked to India, while Burnes struck out across the deserts of Central Asia to Persia, finally reaching India in January 1833. When he returned to London that autumn, Britain swooned.

'I have been inundated with visits from authors, publishers, societies, and what not,' Burnes wrote. 'I am a perfect wild beast. "There's the traveller," "There's Mr Burnes," "There's the Indus Burnes," and what not, do I hear.'[6] Burnes pretended wry detachment, but loved every minute of it. He signed an enormous deal with the Scottish publisher John Murray and fussed over the portrait at the front of his book. 'I would like, however, if you could make some alteration in my visage,' he wrote to Murray, 'for it is said to be so arch and cunning that I shall be handed down to posterity as a real Tartar!' He begged the publisher to 'touch it up a little',[7] and label it 'The Costume of Bokhara', rather than a likeness of the author. 'It will be well known that it is a portrait, and will save me from the appearance of vanity.'[8]

Burnes insisted on writing his own advertising copy. 'This work,' he proclaimed, 'lays open to our view a wide extent of country which has not been visited by Europeans in modern times, though it is full of interest from early impressions and classical associations.'[9] His *Travels into Bokhara* became a runaway bestseller, and made Burnes a fortune. 'May I ask,' he wrote hopefully to Murray, 'what prospect there is of my book running to a second edition?'[10]

In Afghanistan, Burnes had often imagined himself standing where Alexander the Great once stood, looking out at the same horizons.[11] But following in Alexander's footsteps was not enough for him. Like Harlan, Burnes wanted to *be* Alexander: a new Alexander for a new world. 'We were daily informed that we were the "second Alexander," the "Sikandar sani," for having achieved so dangerous a voyage,' he wrote happily.[12]

Burnes was fascinated by rumours that Alexander's descendants were still living in remote villages in Afghanistan, cut off from the rest of the world: the last remnants of his cities. 'In speaking of the existence of Greek colonies in the remote regions of Asia, and said to be descended from Alexander of Macedon, it is necessary to premise that I am not indulging in speculation, but asserting a lineage of various tribes of people, that is claimed by themselves, and meriting therefore, our attention.'[13] Such stories are still being told today.

The village of Malana lies high in the foothills of the Himalayas, perched in a steep-sided valley, surrounded by pine trees and rhododendrons. Far below, eagles drift on the wind and mist covers the valley floor. The people of Malana are proud of their ancestor, Alexander the Great. The family business is no longer world conquest, but the cultivation of some of the most potent marijuana on earth.

Burnes was not the first 'second Alexander' and he would not be the last. Nader Shah, who led a Persian army to India in the eighteenth century, capturing Delhi and the Koh-i-Noor diamond along the way, also called himself 'the second Alexander'. But it was not a role to take on lightly. Alauddin Khalji, Sultan of Delhi in the fourteenth century, is said to have lamented to one of his advisers, 'What is the use of my wealth, and elephants, and horses, if I remain content with Delhi, and undertake no new conquests? What will then be said of my reign?' 'These are not the days of Alexander,' the adviser warned him. 'And where will there be found a vizier like Aristotle?'[14] Burnes did not realise it yet, but stepping into Alexander's sandals was risky.

Rudyard Kipling wrote a short story called 'The Man Who Would Be King'. It is the tale of two drifters – one looks a lot like Burnes, and the other looks a lot like Harlan – who proclaim themselves the 'sons of Alexander'. They make a pact to travel to Afghanistan and set themselves up as kings. 'India isn't big enough for such as us,' one says. 'We are not little men, and there is nothing that we are afraid of except Drink, and we have signed a Contrack on that. Therefore, we are going away to be Kings.' One of the kings ends his days in an asylum in India. Little is left of the other apart from a 'dried, withered head' in a horsehair bag.[15] Even Kipling knew that only fools called themselves 'sons of Alexander'.

When Burnes returned triumphantly to India, he was sent to Bhuj as Henry Pottinger's assistant. It was hard to imagine a dustier, more anticlimactic posting. 'The second Alexander' reluctantly settled into a life of paperwork and warm gin. Pottinger was wildly jealous of his glamorous subordinate – 'he has some talent with very little judgment, and even that little was perverted,' he muttered[16] – and soon stopped talking to him. 'Not only has all speaking acquaintance between that officer (Captain Burnes) and myself ceased,' he wrote to Masson, 'but that I have reason to believe him to be one of the greatest of the few enemies I have met with in life.'[17] Burnes fretted and sweated the months away, until the opportunity to return to Afghanistan set him on the road again.

Masson and Dost Mohammad were both delighted that Burnes was heading for Kabul. Masson hoped it would keep the knives from his back. 'I feared my position, unless something was settled, was not tenable another six months. From this embarrassment, the appointment of Captain Burnes, which has given general satisfaction, has relieved me,' he wrote. 'I sincerely trust that no obstacles will be thrown in the way of his mission.'[18] Dost Mohammad also hoped it would keep the knives from his back. In the west, Persia was eyeing up the border city of Herat. In the east, Ranjit Singh's armies saw an open road to Kabul. His treasuries were almost empty, and his courtiers were looking hungry.

Very late one night there was a knock at the door of Masson's house. Two of Dost Mohammad's attendants were outside, 'saying the Amir wished to see me. I observed, the hour was unseasonable; however, as I was still up, I would go.'[19] Masson was led through the streets of Kabul, which were lit only by the moon and the men's lanterns. He realised they were not heading for the palace. The lanes twisted and turned. On either side, the walls were blank, apart from the 'square low doors' of the houses, 'now and then a larger door interposing, the entrance to the residence of some great man, with a mulberry-tree occasionally peering over the wall'.[20] Finally, the men stopped and a door creaked open. Akbar Khan, Dost Mohammad's son, grinned at Masson, enjoying his surprise. Then he 'desired me to follow him, and led the way into a dark passage. I called to him to give me his hand, as I was not a cat that could see in the dark, and he laughed, and did so. After groping our way through a variety of passages, we came upon the roof of an apartment.' On the rooftop, Dost Mohammad and Sami Khan were seated around a paper lantern. Masson and Akbar Khan joined them and, for a while, they all sat quietly together, with the stars above them and the rooftops of Kabul below. Then Dost Mohammad got down to business. 'The reasons for sending for me I found were to ascertain, first, whether Captain Burnes was really coming to Kabul, and secondly, what were the objects of his mission.' But Masson 'could not tell him what I did not know myself'.[21] It would be the last peaceful moment the four of them ever spent together.

Burnes himself did not know whether he was going to Kabul to hawk British goods, or to negotiate an alliance. 'As yet,' he wrote to Masson, 'I have no authority beyond that of conducting a commercial mission; but various hints and letters … have served to convince me that a stirring time of political action has arrived, and I shall have to show what my government is made of, as well as myself.'[22]

Meanwhile, reports of Masson's discoveries were spreading out across the world, as his finds began to arrive in London. 'The first batch of coins and relics has got home,' Pottinger told him, 'and been the admiration of all who had seen them. The collection is stated to be "much finer and more extensive than that of Mr Martin Honigberger, about which so much had been said." '[23] Magazines reported on 'the very important discoveries of a Mr Masson, made during a residence in the country of ancient Bactria. The ruins of an extensive city have been traced at the base of the Hindu Kush mountains, supposed to be the site of Alexandria.'[24] Newspapers praised 'the distinguished antiquary and naturalist Mr Charles Masson'.[25] The greatest scholars of the world wrote awestruck letters.

But in Afghanistan, Masson was sick and miserable. Increasingly, Britain's imperial project, and his role in it, nauseated him. 'The servants of the Honourable the East India Company emerged from the narrow limits of their original factories on the sea coast of India, and extended their conquests far into the continent. One state after another was seized upon by them, under various pretences,' he reflected. 'The Indian government, like a wrongful owner of an estate, conscious of the defect of his title deeds or wanting them altogether, was apparently so well aware of the precarious nature of its tenure of authority, that it was prone to take alarm.'[26] He wanted nothing more to do with the East India Company. His life as a spy had 'brought upon me more misery than I can hope to endure much longer'.[27]

When he rode out of Kabul to meet 'the second Alexander', Masson was half delirious with fever and dysentery. Burnes and Masson had been hearing stories about each other for years, though they had never met in person. 'I have often crossed your path,' Burnes wrote to Masson, 'and I have never done so without finding the impressions which I had imbibed regarding your talents, your honour, and your zeal strengthened.'[28] 'At our camp,' wrote Burnes in his journal, 'we were glad to meet Mr Masson, the well-known traveller and illustrator of the coins and antiquities of this country, who has seen more of it and is better acquainted with it than any European. In this gentleman's society I passed the day and heard his views on Kabul.'[29] 'The second Alexander,' Masson noted, seemed to have a great sense of his own importance. 'I had quite made up my mind to let him [Dost Mohammad Khan] know at once that the British government were not likely to permit any coquetting on his part,' Burnes told Masson. 'The honour of having any agent, however humble, deputed to confer with him, is by no means a small one.'[30] Burnes looked up at the magnificent city of Kabul in the distance, and at Dost Mohammad's palace towering over it, and muttered that 'the Afghans were to be treated as children'.[31]

Charles and Alexander were mirror images of each other. They looked at the world through very different eyes. Burnes saw Afghanistan from above, Masson from below; Burnes was full of strategy and ambition, Masson had dirt under his fingernails, and an obsession with staying alive.

Akbar Khan escorted Burnes into Kabul atop an elephant, with all the pomp and circumstance Dost Mohammad's court could muster.[32] The next day, Burnes rode up to the Bala Hissar to deliver his credentials to the Amir. 'I informed him that I brought some rarities of Europe for him, and he immediately replied that we ourselves were the real rarities of Europe.'[33] Burnes had been worried about his 'rarities'. 'We are not however laden with presents,' he had confessed to Masson, 'but doing the thing as becomes "trading ambassadors" – and if perforce we are converted into political ones, the Amir of Kabul will be too well pleased without an investment of Birmingham baubles accompanying us.'[34] All he had to offer Dost Mohammad was 'a pair of pistols' and a telescope, along with a bag of 'pins, needles, scissors, penknives, silk handkerchiefs, toys, watches, musical snuff-boxes' for the women of his court.[35] But Dost Mohammad accepted the wretched presents 'in a very flattering manner, with many expressions of his high sense of the great honour which had been conferred on him'.[36] Burnes backed out with his hands clasped in front of his chest, very pleased with himself.

As soon as Burnes was out of the room, Dost Mohammad threw the presents to the floor, and 'averted his face'. 'Behold,' he seethed, 'I have feasted and honoured this Feringhi to the extent of six thousand rupees, and have now a lot of pins and needles and sundry petty toys to show for my folly!'[37]

Burnes settled obliviously into Kabul. 'I rode through the town, and am certainly an object of some curiosity,' he wrote. 'What a fine active bustling city this is.'[38] As he trotted through the streets, people cried out, 'Take care of Kabul!' 'Do not destroy Kabul!'[39]

'What will be the turn up of the mission I hardly know,' Masson confessed, 'and I am not certain that he [Burnes] would be able to tell on what errand he has come to Kabul, or that the government would be able to tell why he had been sent.'[40] 'A fatalist I am,' Burnes had once written, 'a sceptical blockhead, whose head, filled with its own vanities, imagines itself more capable than it is.'[41]

Kabul politics were tangled at the best of times, and this was not the best of times. Masson and Burnes spent long hours together, tracing the web of feuds, favours and fears which kept Afghanistan together. 'You have laid before me the rocks which endanger every movement,' Burnes thanked Masson, 'and so foul is the path that I much fear, with such a beacon, I shall yet be involved in great embarrassments.'[42] 'I shall,' Burnes reported to Macnaghten, 'owe much to Mr Masson, whose high literary attainments, long residence in this country, and accurate knowledge of people and events, afford me, at every step, the means of coming to a judgment more correct than, in an abrupt transition to Kabul, I could have possibly formed.'[43]

Dost Mohammad was tired of sleeping with one eye open. He wanted to be free from the threat of invasion from Persia and from Ranjit Singh. He also wanted Ranjit Singh to hand over Peshawar, the city which commanded the Khyber Pass and the trade routes from India to Afghanistan. Ranjit Singh had captured it from one of Dost Mohammad's brothers in 1834. 'I had and have a great desire to make friendship with the British government,' Dost Mohammad wrote to Burnes, 'and to drive the Sikhs from Peshawar through the advice of that government.'[44] There was, unfortunately, a considerable snag. As Pottinger had told Masson months earlier, 'whatever Captain Burnes's mission may end in, he is at present strictly prohibited from the slightest interference in political matters'.[45] Burnes had been sent to talk about customs duties, not grand alliances.

Customs duties bored Burnes. 'Supposing it were found that Dost Mohammad Khan possessed all the influence and all the ability for which he universally receives credit,' he wrote to the East India Company, 'much embarrassment is not likely to accrue to us by either promising to that chief or entering into a secret treaty with him that we should throw our influence into his hands.'[46] Without waiting for a reply from India, he began negotiations.

If Burnes had listened to Masson, and played Kabul's games like an Afghan, things might have turned out very differently. But he did not. 'To myself,' Masson wrote, 'he was always very kind and obliging, although we sadly differed in all opinions. These I always freely expressed to him from a mere point of conscience, and the wish that he might be successful. Nor was I angry that he did not listen to them, for I was aware that I might be presumptuous in offering them, and that as he once said when I was praying him to be a little discreet – "I am the responsible person, Masson, and must act on my own opinions." '[47]

Burnes was having the time of his life. Masson soon realised why he had insisted on having a house that was 'not overlooked'.[48] Burnes spent his evenings in a lecherous daze, in the arms of the women of Kabul. 'Their ghost-like figures when they walk abroad make one melancholy; but if all be true of them that is reported,' he leered, 'they make ample amends when within-doors for all such sombre exhibitions in public.'[49] The Afghans could hardly believe their eyes. Was it this easy to negotiate with the British?

Soon, Masson had a visitor. Sami Khan, 'after a few long-winded observations, proposed that I should imitate the example of my illustrious superior, and fill my house with black-eyed damsels. I observed, that my house was hardly large enough.' So Sami Khan offered Masson a larger one. 'I then asked, where the damsels were to come from; and he replied, I might select any I pleased, and he would take care I should have them. I told him, his charity exceeded all praise, but I thought it better to go on quietly in my old way.'[50]

There was one constant in Kabul politics: nothing was what it seemed. 'The Afghans are members of my body,' Dost Mohammad was accustomed to say, 'and how should I not protect them? According to proverbs, when one member of the body is in great pain, the others cannot remain in a state of rest.'[51] But Dost Mohammad did not actually expect Ranjit Singh to hand over

Peshawar to him. After all, he had never controlled Peshawar in the first place: the city had been governed by his brother. 'Jabar Khan strongly pressed upon Captain Burnes the necessity of firmly rejecting the proposal about to be made to him,' Masson wrote. 'I did the same, in the most forcible manner I could.'[52] But Burnes was too charmed by Dost Mohammad to listen. 'I never had so kind a reception,' he told Masson. 'He is everything to us!'[53] 'The Amir sent for me this afternoon in private,' Burnes wrote in his journal, 'and among other things said to me that he was English in his views and interests, and would do as we wished in everything.'[54]

One evening, Masson found Burnes sitting by the fire in his house, without a 'black-eyed damsel' and looking more preoccupied than usual. 'Masson,' Burnes said, nervously, 'I have gone the whole hog.'[55]

Dost Mohammad's ministers 'had proposed, in return for the cession of Peshawar to the Amir, that one of the latter's sons should reside at Lahore with the Maharaja as a hostage for his father's good behaviour'. Burnes had immediately 'told them all would be settled as they wished'.[56] His offer was soon 'known to every pumpkin-seller in the bazaar'.[57] 'I could,' Masson wrote, 'only express my fears that the worst results would follow.'[58]

'Dost Mohammad Khan,' Burnes wrote to a friend, 'has fallen into all our views and in doing so, has either thought for himself or followed my counsel, but for doing the former I give him every credit. Oh! What say you to this, after all that has been urged of Dost Mohammad Khan putting forth extravagant pretensions? Ranjit will accede to the plan, I am certain.' There was only one cloud on the horizon. 'I hardly know,' Burnes confessed, 'what the government of India will think of my measures.'[59]

In December, the sky grew considerably darker. An enormous Persian army laid siege to Herat. And just before Christmas, a man calling himself Ivan Vikevitch swaggered into Kabul, claiming to have brought Dost Mohammad a letter from the Tsar of Russia.

Vikevitch was born Jan Prosper Witkiewicz in Vilnius. As a teenager, he dabbled in the wrong kind of politics. It was nothing dramatic – he put up a few unwise posters and wrote a few ill-judged letters – but it was enough to have him exiled to the steppes of Central Asia, condemned to serve out the rest of his life as a private soldier in the Tsar's army. Like Masson, he spent years dreaming of freedom. He read voraciously and spent every rouble that came his way on books. In this case, the Russian army was more perceptive than the East India Company had been: Vikevitch was pulled out of the ranks and put to work as a spy.[60]

Masson had been planning to spend a few weeks away from Kabul to escape 'being a spectator, for I am no more, of what is going on'.[61] But just as he was about to leave, a panicked note from Burnes arrived. 'I should feel very much obliged if you could come over here, as I wish to speak particularly with you – the Russian has arrived here!!! and the Amir has been with me to know what to do.'[62] 'We are in a mess,' Burnes wrote to a friend. 'Herat is besieged and may fall, and the Emperor of Russia has sent an envoy to Kabul to offer Dost Mohammad Khan money to fight Ranjit Singh!! I could not believe my eyes or ears, but Captain Vikevitch, for that is the agent's name, arrived here with a blazing letter three feet long, and sent immediately to pay his respects to myself. I, of course, received him and asked him to dinner.'[63]

Vikevitch, smiling blandly, turned up for Christmas dinner in full Cossack uniform. It was not the kind of present Burnes had been hoping for.

Masson was suspicious. There was something wrong with this Russian agent. His manner was too glib. His letter from the Tsar was unsigned. Masson and Burnes spent hours scrutinising it. 'I cannot find a flaw in the correspondence, and am bound to treat it as authentic,' Burnes wrote.[64] But Masson thought Vikevitch was no imperial envoy. His letter had to be 'a fabrication'. At this, 'Captain Burnes shrugged his shoulders, elevated his eyebrows, and rolled his tongue round his cheek'.[65] Like Masson, Vikevitch was a compulsive storyteller who rarely used the same alias twice. But this time, in Kabul, he was exactly who he claimed to be. He was an envoy from the Russian government, and his letter was genuine. Masson had made a colossal mistake.

Despite their disagreements, Burnes was unfailingly kind to Masson. He helped him extract his salary from Wade, whom he disliked almost as much as Masson did. 'I owe him nothing,' he wrote to Masson, 'indeed much the reverse. All this I am led to state as some consolation to one whose feelings have been trifled with as yours.'[66] When Wade was slow to pay, Burnes offered to fund Masson's excavations himself. 'If my own purse can avail you,' he wrote, 'and if you want it now or hereafter, the use of it will always be to me a very gratifying proof of your confidence – I know that you have friends to do such service to you, but they are absent and I am present.'[67] Masson promised himself that as soon as his health was better, and the skies were a little clearer, he would take up his pursuit of Alexandria again.

'Do you,' Dost Mohammad asked Harlan one day, 'know the story of the hungry fox?' A half-starved fox had been searching for food when he 'suddenly came face to face with a large ram of the broad-tailed breed'. Now the ram was larger than the fox but, 'looking wistfully after him as he slowly moved away, the fox was astounded to see the large pendulous tail, which appeared like a load of flesh, dangling precariously, and on the point of falling from its attachment. New hopes kindled in his hungry stomach, and he stole softly after the ram', expecting the tail to fall off at any moment. But, of course, it did not, and 'at length reaching his fold he [the ram] walked in, and left the disappointed fox, hungry and hopeless, standing at the door'. 'Now this is just my condition,' said Dost Mohammad to Harlan, 'I shall be looking after this European agent in momentary expectation of something falling from him, and eventually turn away like the miserable fox, to feed on the hard fare which has always been the lot of us mountaineers.'[68]

'Our country is good,' Burnes was told. 'It is like a beautiful widow who voluntarily avows her attachment, and you cannot refuse to accept her as a wife.'[69] One of his Afghan friends 'saw the Feringhis in a vision seated on Babur's tomb receiving the salutations of the Afghans. The morning call to prayer awoke him, and he knows not what followed.'[70] But Burnes's promises to Dost Mohammad still hung in the air: from India, there was no reply, and the Amir was beginning to wonder 'whether the confidence of Captain Burnes as regarded Peshawar would be shared in by his superiors at Calcutta'.[71] Burnes wrote to Lord Auckland again, telling him that 'it was now a neck and neck course between the Russian and us'.[72] He had quite forgotten that he had promised the East India Company 'not to allow Dost Mohammad to play any other power off against us'.[73]

While Burnes and Dost Mohammad waited for an answer to arrive from India, Harlan and Vikevitch happily stirred the pot. 'The Amir has been strengthened in his views against our policy by Mr Harlan, an American in his service who has told him that we are seeking to remove him,' Burnes wrote. 'To Mirza Sami I made objections of Mr Harlan being a bad councillor – of having been in Ranjit Singh's service, once an agent of Shujah, and now a servant of the Amir – but these are after all objections to the man and not the policy.'[74]

One day, Dost Mohammad called on Burnes. 'He was greatly delighted with an inflated paper globe of the earth' which Burnes happened to have. The Amir and 'the second Alexander' spun the globe together, 'asking the names of the different countries – pondering on cutting the isthmuses of Suez and Darien [Panama]'. Dost Mohammad said to Burnes that 'Afghans were by profession and inclination soldiers, and the British might now make anything of them, though there was a time when they might not be so easily secured, and which might again return. I agreed with him.'[75]

'We shall,' Dost Mohammad told Burnes, 'adhere to you until you cast us off.'[76]

The East India Company decided to cast him off. They washed their hands of the promises Burnes had made to Dost Mohammad. 'His Lordship sees nothing in any facts yet reported to him to induce him to run into the dangers of such embarrassment as would attend the course which you have pressed upon him,' Macnaghten wrote to Burnes. 'These promises were entirely unauthorized by any part of your instructions.'[77] Burnes was told to unpick every agreement he had made, in such a way that no room was left for doubt. For someone who believed in telling everyone what they wanted to hear, especially himself, it was a hideous experience. But Burnes had no choice.

'You must,' Burnes told Dost Mohammad in March 1838, 'never receive agents from other powers, or have aught to do with them, without our sanction; you must dismiss Captain Vikevitch with courtesy; you must surrender all claim to Peshawar on your own account, as that chieftainship belongs to Maharaja Ranjit Singh; you must live on friendly terms with that potentate.' 'Are we,' he went on, 'to allow you to sit in Kabul, address Russia and Persia, bring agents from those countries, and publicly avow that you wish to disturb the peace of a friend on our frontiers?'[78]

After Burnes had finished, there was a long 'embarrassing silence'.[79] Dost Mohammad 'stated that he had been viewed by our government as no-one; that his friendship was worth little; that he was told to consider himself fortunate at our preventing the Sikhs coming to Kabul, of which he himself had no fear'.[80] 'It is impossible to write all,' Burnes confessed to Masson later, 'and for me to come to you, or you to me, before dinner might show our funk. I gave it fearfully and left him in a furious rage, but not a word was forgotten of which I prepared for him. He gave the old story – no benefit – no one cares for a falling nation – I offered my wares for sale, and you would not buy.'[81]

Then Burnes 'abandoned himself to despair. He bound his head with wet towels and handkerchiefs, and took to the smelling-bottle'.[82] 'I cannot hold on much longer,' he wrote in his journal. 'They think to make this man their friend without benefiting him.'[83]

Dost Mohammad's ministers were baffled. Sami Khan took Masson aside one day and asked, ' "To what are we to agree?" No question could be more perplexing. My reply was, "By heavens! I know no more than you, but I am certain you will not be required to agree to anything hurtful," and then added, "We must agree to everything without knowing what, and then we shall find out." '[84]

Vikevitch could not believe his luck. As winter gave way to spring, Dost Mohammad 'entered more and more into close intimacy and conversation in public with him and invited him openly to pass evenings and have dinners in the palace with him'.[85] Burnes gloomily reported everything to Macnaghten. No one in Kabul realised how much this single Russian officer was terrifying the East India Company. For many in Calcutta and London, Vikevitch's mission looked like the first move in a vast, sinister conspiracy, one which would end with a Russian army pouring through the Khyber Pass into India. Afghanistan and Russia had to be kept apart, no matter the cost.

Burnes heard rumours that he was about to be 'seized'. Someone in the bazaar 'declared he had been bribed to do it for 200 rupees'.[86] Masson's sleepless nights continued.[87] Men continued to shadow him, and to watch his house. He knew that if Burnes could not patch up the East India Company's relationship with Dost Mohammad, Kabul would no longer be safe for him. Britain and Afghanistan were drifting from friendship to enmity.

'Matters are over in Kabul,' Burnes wrote. 'Our position here is precarious, and the sooner we alter our view or leave Kabul the better.'[88] He sat at home, glumly eating grapes. Every letter he received from India made it clearer that the East India Company was alarmed by Dost Mohammad's refusal to submit. Burnes warned the Amir that he would soon 'repent that he did not listen ... The Amir may reflect well, before he abandons the friendship of the British government.'[89] 'As my hopes on your government are gone,' Dost Mohammad replied, 'I will be forced to have recourse to other governments. It will be for the protection of Afghanistan, to save our honour, and God forbid, not from any ill designs against the British.'[90]

'Some of the people, who had kept aloof since the arrival of the mission, one evening ventured to ask the Amir what he was doing with Sikandar. He replied that he did not know. He had told him to go, but he stayed.'[91] 'If I had become a convert to the Afghan belief in dreams,' Burnes wrote, 'I should have had, during every week of my residence, proofs of our ultimate success and supremacy in the country.'[92] But dreams could only take him so far. 'Reports are rife that Dost Mohammad Khan is done with the British,' he wrote sadly in his journal.[93] It was time to go.

The suddenness of it took Masson by surprise. 'I was wholly unprepared for so abrupt a departure,' he confessed.[94] His friends all told him the same thing: remaining in Kabul was now too dangerous. 'Masson goes with me,' Burnes wrote. 'He cannot stay, he thinks, and I agree with him.'[95] Masson had been close to solving the mystery of Alexandria. But now he had to pack up and leave. Half a decade's work went with him: thousands of coins poured into boxes; artefacts crammed hastily into sacks. He had spent the happiest days of his life in Kabul. When he walked through its gates in 1832, he was a drifter with nothing to his name. Since then, he had discovered a lost city, unravelled a forgotten language, and seen the world through new eyes. He had no idea when he might be able to return, or what the future held for him.

On 25 April 1838, Burnes 'had my leave of the Amir in the evening. It was a trying scene and I cannot now describe it. Everyone was excited, and no wonder – I sat up till midnight.'[96]

It was all over.

There is an old Jewish story about Alexander the Great. Once, he travelled for weeks through a unknown land, until he reached the gates of the Garden of Eden. He knocked three times, until an angel appeared, holding a skull made of the purest gold. Alexander demanded entrance to Eden, but the angel refused:

'Only the righteous who bring peace to mankind may enter Paradise alive,' said the angel, gently.

Alexander hung his head, abashed; then, in a voice broken with emotion, he begged that at least he should be given a memento of his visit. The angel handed him the skull, saying: 'Take this and ponder o'er its meaning.' The angel vanished and the golden door closed.

The skull was so heavy that, with all his great strength, Alexander could scarcely carry it. When he placed it in a balance to ascertain its weight, he found that it was heavier than all his treasures. None of his wise men could explain this mystery and so Alexander sought out a Jew among his soldiers, one who had been a student with the rabbis. Taking a handful of earth the

Jew placed it over the eyes, and the skull was then as light as air. 'The meaning is plain,' said the Jew. 'Not until the human eye is covered with earth – in the grave – is it satisfied. Not until after death can man hope to enter Paradise.'

Alexander was anxious to hasten away from that strange region, but many of his soldiers declared that they would settle down by the banks of the River of Life. Next morning, however, the river had vanished. Where all had been beautiful was now only a desolate plain, bounded by bare rocky mountains, reaching to the clouds. With heavy hearts, Alexander's men began their march back.[97]

If you had told this story to 'the second Alexander' it is likely that he would have understood it. But it is unlikely that he would have appreciated it.

As the sun set on 26 April 1838, Masson rode out of Kabul. He could not bring himself to look back. 'And Bagram, I suppose, became partially neglected, or its antique treasures, as previous to their diversion by me, fell into the hands of coppersmiths and were either melted up by them, or by the mint officers at the city.'[98] His heart was breaking.

12

Last Resort

On the morning of 2 May 1838, the directors of the East India Company assembled in London. Their carriages rattled down the broad, grey expanse of Leadenhall Street, past brothels and churches, coffeehouses and Hebrew bookshops, and pulled up at a long stone building: East India House. From here, India was governed, greedily and uneasily. Clerks toiled and scratched in its rafters. Secrets, scandals and money (above all, money) poured through its doors. East India House was loot made manifest.

The Court Room, where the directors met, was a high, golden space, lined with velvet chairs. Above the chimney, Britannia was 'seated on a globe by the sea-shore, receiving homage from three female figures, intended for Asia, Africa, and India. Asia offers spices with her right hand, and with her left leads a camel; India presents a large box of jewels, which she holds half open ... The whole is supported by two caryatid figures, intended for Brahmins, but really fine old European-looking philosophers.'[1] Here, curiosity and wonder met capitalism and bureaucracy. Curiosity and wonder never stood a chance.

For the last two years, Masson's supporters had been trying to persuade the Company of the brilliance of his finds. They had not been successful. H. H. Wilson, the Company's Librarian, had almost swooned on the spot 'after inspecting the first batch' of Masson's discoveries. He suggested to the directors that he might 'give them a lecture upon them. Each individually said, "Oh, delightful!" – but it appears when they talked it over in Council, some of them thought it would be an inadvisable innovation to receive lessons from their Librarian, and the measure was abandoned.' Wilson sent them a stack of notes instead. He should have known better. 'They have expressed themselves very graciously,' he remarked ruefully, 'but perhaps have not read much.'[2]

That day in 1838, Masson was again on the agenda. The directors – a Dickensianly named bunch, Mr Lushington and Mr Muspratt, Mr Thornhill and Mr Shank – were anxious that they had overpaid him for his labour. 'An exact appreciation of the value of articles like those which are the subject of our observations is utterly impracticable,' they sniffed. 'It depends upon arbitrary and fanciful notions of their rarity and curiosity.' However, once they scrutinised Masson's finds, they were convinced that they had made a handsome profit. 'The collection is worth much more than the sum which it has cost. We are therefore satisfied that the outlay has been fully justified by the value of the articles which it has procured.'[3] At East India House, that was all that ever mattered.

The directors sent a letter to India about Masson which, on the surface, looked remarkably warm and generous. 'It is our wish that the field of his [Masson's] labours should be as wide as is compatible with his official duties, and that it should be investigated as fully as possible.' But a series of pencilled scribbles in the margins showed what the directors were really thinking: 'We had better stop, I think' – 'We are not collectors or antiquarians' – 'Throwing a light on history, but this is out of our way' – 'Better stop.'[4] The East India Company, the hungry god of capitalism, was not about to start chasing lost cities. Masson, the directors instructed, was to be cordially thanked, given a token sum of money and cut off from all future assistance with his excavations. He was a spy, and from now on he would only be paid to spy. If he still hoped to find Alexandria, he would have to do it on his own. Pothos had no place in East India House.

Two days later, Masson and Burnes arrived at Peshawar, city of last resort.

Its dusty mud walls sat across the base of the Khyber Pass. If you wanted to get into or out of Afghanistan, Peshawar was difficult to avoid. Spies and traders, footsore camels and anxious exiles passed through its gates, though few stayed longer than absolutely necessary.

Masson and Burnes were miserable. Their first glimpse of Peshawar did nothing to cheer them up. All around its walls, stretching out as far as the eye could see, the setting sun shone on fields and fields of corpses. Bodies were hung from gibbets, strung from withered palm trees, and lashed to posts. Some were no more than bleached skeletons, turned gold by the last of the light. Others were barely cold. Eager birds were tearing out their eyes and at their flesh. The dead were the 'silent sentries'[5] – and the particular pride – of General Paolo Avitabile, Peshawar's governor.

Avitabile looked like an angry dumpling: huge, heavy lipped, and bulging in all the wrong places, 'just the picture of one of Rubens' satyrs', according to a British officer, Henry Lawrence, but 'one of the world's masterminds'.[6] He was, all things considered, one of the worst people in the world. A washed-up former lieutenant in one of Napoleon's less distinguished armies, he had arrived at Ranjit Singh's court in 1827, with a cargo of pornography.[7] Soon, he was calling himself 'General' Avitabile. In 1834, due to the lack of any other interested candidates, Ranjit Singh put him in charge of Peshawar. The city was then in the grip of full-scale anarchy: no one expected the new governor to live more than a few weeks. Avitabile loved to tell the story of how he had proved them all wrong.

'When I first marched into Peshawar,' he would begin, 'I sent on in advance a number of wooden posts, which my men put up round the walls of the city. The people scoffed aloud at this new madness of the Feringhi, and louder still, when my men came in again, laying coils of rope at the feet of the posts. Guns and swords, it was whispered, are the arms to rule a city, not sticks and tackle. However, when my installation was complete, there was found one fine morning dangling from these crosstrees, fifty of the worst characters in Peshawar; and the exhibition was repeated on every market day with new subjects, till I had made short work of brigands and murderers. Then I had to deal with the liars and talebearers. My method with them was to cut out their tongues. And then a surgeon appeared and professed to be able to restore them to speech. I sent for this surgeon and had his tongue cut out also. After this, there was peace: and in six months – ecco! – crime became unknown in Peshawar.'[8]

Avitabile never moved out of doors without an executioner or two.[9] Most days, he would kill a dozen people before dinner.[10] By the time Masson and Burnes arrived, he was bored, and was experimenting. One day, he might hang someone upside down. Or he might get creative and skin them alive. 'The executioner begins this operation by raising the skin on the soles of the feet, which is then torn in strips upwards, and the wretched creature is left vainly to wish for the relief which death sometimes does not afford within two hours of the infliction.'[11] Every day at sunset, Peshawar's vultures descended on their daily feast, with 'discordant screams of health and prosperity to Governor Avitabile, whilst circling round their hideous repast'.[12]

Avitabile, or Abu Tabela, as the Peshawaris knew him, was literally the bogeyman. Well into the twentieth century, mothers in Peshawar were still telling their children to behave – or Abu Tabela would come for them.

Avitabile did, however, throw quite a party. For most visitors, this was enough to count him on the side of the angels. His eight cooks were 'well versed in all the mysteries of Persian, English, and French gastronomy'.[13] There would be music and fireworks, and the gigantic courtyard of his headquarters would be lit up like fairyland. Avitabile would slouch at the head of the table, working his way through an enormous mound of rice, with two thin Afghan boys shivering behind him. For guests with weaker stomachs, the meat course was not pleasant. 'I confess that the paraphernalia of the surrounding gibbets haunted me so much at the table,' remembered one, 'I could scarcely persuade myself that the boiled kid and trussed-up capons were not some novel delicacies artistically carved from a skinned criminal!'[14]

Afterwards, there would be more wine, and nautch dances, and spectacularly beautiful women[15] – with Avitabile sometimes reading official papers with one hand, and groping a woman with the other: 'a picture of Nero's feast'.[16] (It was not advisable to make remarks about Avitabile's sexual tastes. After one unwise comment, an aide – so the Peshawari legend ran – 'was forthwith ordered to be hurled from the top of a minaret. The wretch was hurled; but half-way down caught hold of a projecting cornice, thence screamed aloud to Avitabile for "Mercy, for the sake of God." Avitabile unmoved replied, "God may have mercy on you if he likes, but I'll have none. Throw him off the ledge!" ')[17]

Needless to say, Avitabile's bluster and bloodlust were designed to hide his abject terror. During his first months as governor he 'never slept twice in the same room, but shifted his bed nightly and had a fleet horse waiting saddled at all hours under the private gate of his palace'.[18] He was 'afraid of his men,' wrote Henry Lawrence, 'and afraid of his government, and of ours, too'.[19] When Joseph Wolff, the occasionally naked missionary, passed through Peshawar, Avitabile pulled him aside, dropped the mask and begged for help: 'For the love of God, help me get away from this country!'[20]

Masson and Burnes were in no mood for feasts or nautches. Both felt like they had lost, and lost badly. Burnes, for the first time in his life, was crushed. 'The game is up,' he wrote to a friend, 'the Russians gave me the coup de grâce, and I could hold no longer at Kabul.' Most of all, he was angry: angry at having the rug pulled out from under him in Afghanistan, angry at being ignored, angry – as only Burnes could be – at being right about everything. 'All I said and wrote received high applause, cordial approbation and so forth – but when the vessel was sinking, and I cried "To the pumps!", they told me not to be too precipitate, but to wait – be it so.' 'I wish the fault were mine and not my country's,' he sighed, insincerely.[21]

Burnes had no idea what was waiting for him: would he be expected to take the blame? Or to fix things? Now that the British had done such a good job of alienating Dost Mohammad, he had a suspicion they might call upon Shah Shujah, the exiled Afghan king who had spent the last few decades plotting and lopping off ears in Ludhiana. If that was the plan, Burnes wanted nothing to do with it. 'I await orders at Peshawar and shall either be ordered to Shimla or … to lead the ex-King against the Barakzais [Dost Mohammad and his family]. This last I will not do. The Barakzais consigned themselves to us, and merely asked for Persia to be warned off, and we would not do it. Fear therefore made them desert us.'[22] 'After all my travail,' he wrote in his journal, 'I hope now to be left alone.'[23]

Masson was in an even worse frame of mind. 'Our retreat from Kabul partook a little of the nature of flight,' he wrote, ruefully. 'It is an awkward business, and one to be regretted.'[24] Now he had time to gather his thoughts after the chaos of the last few weeks, he realised the consequences for his work had been hellish. Many of the treasures he had been trying to catalogue were a jumble again. His plans were adrift: he had no idea whether any of his Afghan collaborators would be able to get back in touch with him, let alone send on what they had found. He might be able to buy a few coins while in Peshawar, but that would bring him no closer to Alexandria. Every day away from Afghanistan felt like torture.

Masson realised that his relationship with the East India Company was reaching breaking point. For years, he had felt weighed down by his obligations, but too scared to walk away from them. In Kabul, he had at least been able to rationalise the relationship: it made him miserable, but it let him pursue – occasionally, anxiously – the things he longed for. But now, thanks to Burnes, he did not even have that. He hoped the East India Company would do right by him, and finally set him free to follow his dreams.

He felt numb: ashamed of himself, and ashamed for the work he had not been able to do. For months, he had put off writing to Pottinger.[25] He had gone years without being able to pick up a pen and write to his friends in Britain. 'I have replied to no letters from Europe since my appointment [as a spy], so much it cut me up – before I used to write expressing my hopes and purposes, but I found that if I continued to do so, I ran the chance of being considered an imposter, or of one willing to deceive. Nothing ever gave me so much mortification.'[26] It felt as if part of him, the part which had sauntered so confidently into Afghanistan, had been frozen for years.

Now, he promised himself, things had to change. That meant, as he knew very well, that he had to change. He had to stop shaping himself around everyone else's wishes. He definitely had to stop spying. But how? Perhaps he might simply fade away: since he was no longer in Kabul, the East India Company might decide he was no longer useful. 'Then, my services being at an end, my request for liberty to decline serving would be easily granted.' He dreaded the thought of being put to work again. 'If it be attempted,' he wrote, trying to find courage in the words, 'I shall resist it.'[27] 'If I submit, I am ruined for life.'[28]

After several weeks of stewing – Peshawar did not improve on closer acquaintance – Masson and Burnes received unctuous letters from Macnaghten. 'Would you oblige me,' he wrote, 'by stating what means of counteraction to the policy of Dost Mohammad Khan you would recommend for adoption, and whether you think that the Sikhs using any (and what) instrument of Afghan agency could establish themselves in Kabul?'[29] As he read, Burnes realised the East India Company had taken his failure for granted. While he was clinging to a raft, soaked to the skin, on the river down from Kabul, Macnaghten had been plotting to topple Dost Mohammad. 'They shall have my sentiments sharp enough,' Burnes wrote to Masson. 'What theirs are I do not know, but you may guess.'[30]

Burnes was soon summoned to meet Macnaghten at Ranjit Singh's great summer palace of Adinagar. Masson was left in Peshawar, with Avitabile and the vultures for company. Before Burnes left, the two talked about their futures. Generous as always, Burnes promised to help Masson get away from Wade and the East India Company. (Both were so paranoid about Wade reading their letters that they devised elaborate schemes to avoid the tentacles of Ludhiana. Burnes told Masson to use unofficial couriers, and to 'send the packet under a Persian cover' so that Wade's men would never suspect it came from him.)[31] On the way to Adinagar, a dust storm howled down from the north onto Burnes. 'Dust engulfed us such we could not see a yard in front,' he wrote. 'The heat was insufferable – I cannot note the temperature, but suppose it must have been 126–130 [52–54°C].'[32] Broiled, blinded and lost, he stumbled onward.

Adinagar was the scene of a diplomatic disaster which made Burnes's fumbling in Kabul look positively masterful: Macnaghten's attempt to outmanoeuvre Ranjit Singh.

Macnaghten – dressed in striped trousers and yellow waistcoat[33] – crept across the carpets towards Ranjit Singh, looking like a tropical beetle about to be squashed. Outside, 'the troops of the Maharaja,' the court writer reported, 'covered from head to foot with silver, jewels, and all manner of beautiful clothes, were drawn up before his doors, and such was their appearance that the jewel-mine, out of envy, drew a stone upon its head, [and] the river sat upon the sand of shame'.[34] The Maharaja met Macnaghten with an unexpected hug. Then, sitting cross-legged in a golden chair, all in white, with the Koh-i-Noor diamond gleaming on his arm, he put the envoy through his paces.[35] 'Do you drink wine?' 'How much?' 'Did you taste the wine which I sent you yesterday?' 'How much of it did you drink?' 'What artillery have you brought with you?' 'Have they got any shells?' 'How many?' 'Do you like riding on horseback?' 'What country's horses do you prefer?' 'Are you in the army?' 'Which do you like best, cavalry or infantry?' 'Does Lord Auckland drink wine?' 'How many glasses?' 'Does he drink it in the morning?' 'What is the strength of the Company's army?' 'Are they well disciplined?'[36] By the end of the meeting, Macnaghten was breathless, dazed and confused.

Within a few days, the British were seriously floundering. Each meeting went along the same lines: an endless barrage of unanswerable questions from Ranjit Singh. 'Did you see my Kashmiri girls?' 'How did you like them?' 'Are they handsomer than the women of Hindustan?' 'Are they as handsome as English women?' 'Which of them did you admire most?' 'I will send them this evening and you had better keep the one you like the best.'[37] 'Is Lord Auckland married?' 'What! Has he no wives at all?' 'Why doesn't he marry?' 'Why don't you marry?' 'Are English wives very expensive?' 'I wanted one myself some time ago and wrote to the government about it, but they did not send me one.'[38] By the end of the negotiation, Macnaghten was checkmated. He had arrived hoping to persuade Ranjit Singh to send an army against Dost Mohammad. 'Should he [Ranjit Singh] make an instrument of Shah Shujah,' Macnaghten's instructions ran, 'you will appraise him that the Governor General attaches too much importance to the person of the ex-King to admit of his going forth otherwise than with the almost certainty of success.'³⁹ Instead, Macnaghten left having made a whole basketful of expensive promises, with very little to show for it in return.

While the negotiations were unravelling, Masson and Burnes each reluctantly responded to Macnaghten's oily letter. Both thought it was perverse. Why try to topple someone who was so eager to be your friend? 'It remains to be reconsidered,' wrote Burnes, vainly, 'why we cannot act with Dost Mohammad. He is a man of undoubted ability, and has at heart high opinions of the British nation, and if half you must do for others were done for him, and offers made which he could see connected to his interests, he would abandon Persia and Russia tomorrow.'⁴⁰ The whole business felt doubly unsavoury, as both Burnes and Masson had assured their friends in Kabul of Britain's good faith. Giving Macnaghten a how-to guide for regime change – which was what he was asking for – did not feel like good faith. It felt like treachery.

'Of Shah Shujah al-Mulk, personally, I have, that is as ex-King of the Afghans, no very high opinion,' wrote Burnes. Then he crossed it out. 'As for Shah Shujah al-Mulk, personally', he tried again – and at this point, you can almost hear the sigh of resignation – 'the British government have only to send him to Peshawar with an agent, and two of its own regiments as an honorary escort, and an avowal to the Afghans that we have taken up his cause, to ensure his being fixed forever on the throne … It is, however, to be remembered always that we must appear directly, for the Afghans … believe Shujah to have no fortune; but our name will invest him with it.'⁴¹ Burnes was beginning to reconsider his vow not to lead Shah Shujah into Afghanistan. 'My belief,' he wrote privately, 'is that we are to set up Shah Shujah, and your humble servant is to be sent to effect it. By my truth, this is a Herculean, though possible task, and made more so by our own blundering.'[42]

Masson's response was even more uncertain. Above all, he hoped to avoid saying anything that might provoke a full-scale war. An invasion of Afghanistan by Ranjit Singh – with Avitabile, perhaps, in charge of pacifying Kabul – could only be disastrous. 'Can the Sikhs by their own power hope to conquer Kabul? I would not venture to assert that they could not,' he wrote. 'Although they might, in my opinion, perhaps with care overrun the plains of Kabul and its vicinity, they would retain possession of them in much the same manner as they are compelled to retain Peshawar.' Masson had no desire to turn Kabul, the city of his hopes and dreams, into another Peshawar, still less to set Avitabile loose upon his friends. The only result of a full-scale invasion, Masson wrote, would be mutual devastation. 'If it were resolved to devote Kabul to destruction, and to give Ranjit Singh a fair chance of destruction also, the best plan that could be devised would be to encourage him to proceed against that place.'[43]

That left Shah Shujah. Like Burnes, Masson imagined that this option would be relatively straightforward: the Shah could approach Afghanistan accompanied by a nod and a wink in the right places, a little money passed from hand to hand, and a British officer or two in his retinue, to indicate that more money was waiting in the wings. 'Had the Shah, as I think he ought to have been, been sent to Peshawar, acknowledged by the British government and attended by two or three British officers, in all probability the Afghans would have themselves carried him in triumph to Kabul, or they would have brought Dost Mohammad bound hand and foot to him.'[44]

It was not a noble plan, but at least it stood a chance of working, and of keeping the fragile peace. Unfortunately, it bore no resemblance to the plan currently being hatched a few hundred miles away, in Shimla.

Imagine a miniature British town, perfect in every detail – church steeples, mock-Tudor houses, roaring fires and china teacups, gossip and whispers – slung across a ridge of the Himalayan foothills, and you have Shimla. Lord Auckland was ensconced there, with a retinue of thousands. It was the perfect place for scheming. That summer, the schemes were about the invasion of Afghanistan and amateur theatre, in roughly equal measure. 'There is a little sort of theatre at Shimla, small and hot and something dirty, but it does very well,' wrote Emily Eden, Lord Auckland's sister. 'But then the actors fell out. One man took a fit of low spirits, and another who acted women's parts well would not cut off his mustachios, and another went off to shoot bears near the Snowy Range. That man has been punished for his shilly-shallying; the snow blinded him, and he was brought back rolled up in a blanket.'[45] When it came to Afghanistan, many of Auckland's advisers, none of whom had ever set foot in the country, were all for launching an invasion, and convinced that the threat from Russia was real. ('Anyone demanding an explanation of the words "Russian influence," or daring to doubt the potency and malignancy of its effects on his country,' wrote an Indian newspaper editor, a few years later, 'must run the risk of having his sanity, sincerity, or patriotism called in question.')[46] But when two Russian letters were intercepted – surely proof of some grand conspiracy – 'unluckily nobody in India can read them. The aides-de-camp have been all day making facsimiles of them, to send to Calcutta, Bombay, etc., in hopes'[47] of finding a translator.

Thousands could be dying on the plains below, but in Shimla the band would always play on. Its illusions were fragile, but they held. True, a marauding troop of monkeys might descend on your perfect English tea party and carry off everything in sight (today in Shimla, billboards still warn about the 'Monkey Menace', and huge grey apes barrel along Mall Road, sending the crowds scattering), but you would never have to look straight at the consequences of empire.

Burnes travelled up from Adinagar to Shimla to present himself to Lord Auckland. 'I told them, you have lost your influence,' he wrote, 'and they reply, "Come and see us, let us hear what is to be done, we are now ready to act." '[48] He was anxious, and still in a foul temper. 'They are now lamentably at fault, and have most assuredly written themselves down as asses.'[49]

Burnes cut a lonely figure as he followed the path up into the Himalayas. It curved around one hill after another, winding slowly upwards, towards the clouds. Thanks to Auckland, an entire empire's worth of paperwork was being hauled, one mule at a time, up and down this unpaved track. For the first time in weeks, the heat started to lift and Burnes felt a cool breeze in his face. Mist spread out above and below him, a light rain fell and the hills reached up to the sky and down to the abyss. Burnes wondered if he had been set up to fail. 'I have had the satisfaction of being told that I was sent to do impossible things at Kabul, so all my labour that did not succeed was not expected to succeed! Politics are a queer science.'[50] The trees were tall now, and the hills looked more like mountains: solid walls of green, slashed with clouds. He was closer by far to Tibet than to his old home in Scotland. The narrow road seemed like a pathway to the world of the gods – albeit one patrolled by fat, sway-bellied monkeys.

In Peshawar, Avitabile was having a fine time. Stories about him were everywhere. One village had to pay its taxes in severed heads.[51] When some Afghans could not come up with the money he demanded, he shut them in a cell and began bricking up the entrance, 'raising a course of bricks daily. They held out on their ration of bread and water, till the last course was wanting, although one of their number died and they had his body with them for days in the hot weather. The poor wretches had stopped up their nostrils with linen rags to keep out the stench.'[52] Avitabile diverted a healthy chunk of the district's revenue straight into his own pocket. Every few months, sacks of silver were loaded onto camels and sent to Ludhiana, where Wade cheerfully laundered Avitabile's looted rupees, extracted from the desperate, the dead and the dying, into fresh East India Company bonds.[53]

Masson still had no idea what the future held for him. 'I wish,' he wrote despairingly, 'to be at perfect liberty – of politics I am sick.'[54] Day after day, he remained in suspense. 'Two, three, four or five days, should bring me an account of some kind.'[55] He was still convinced of an untrue thing: that the East India Company cared; that a thoroughly amoral, capitalist empire could also be kind.

13

No Return

In Shimla, Burnes was starting to feel more like his old self. The air was clear and cool. Everyone seemed pleased to see him. He moved into the Secretaries' Lodge, just down the hill from Lord Auckland's own house. In the evening light, its green lawns, white walls and red-tiled roofs turned shimmering gold. To the east, range after range of hills stretched away to the horizon, shading imperceptibly from green to darkest blue. Inside, the lamps were lit in the long, wood-panelled rooms and the table was laid for dinner. For those who have travelled too far and seen too many horizons, Shimla gives comfort. There is an armchair by the fire, a pile of blankets on an old brass bedstead, and a cup of hot, sweet morning tea. From that armchair, you may even start to believe you understand India. That is Shimla's great solace, and that is why, in 1838, it was one of the most dangerous places in the world.

When Burnes, trying his best to look respectable, went to report to Lord Auckland, two of Auckland's private secretaries 'came running to him and prayed him to say nothing to unsettle His Lordship: that they had all the trouble in the world to get him into the business, and that even now he would be glad of any pretence to retire from it'.[1] 'The business' turned out to be a full-scale invasion of Afghanistan.

Over the course of a few weeks, the small-scale plan suggested by Burnes and Masson – a British officer here, a handful of cash there – had turned into a gigantic military expedition. Burnes's first reaction was shock. His second reaction was that he wanted to be in charge. 'We are now planning a grand campaign to restore the Shah to the throne of Kabul,' he wrote. 'What exact part I am to play I know not, but if full confidence and hourly consultation be any pledge, I am to be chief. I can plainly tell them that it is "aut Caesar aut nullus" [either Caesar or nothing], and if I get not what I have a right to, you will soon see me en route to England.'[2] Despite Burnes's confidence, one of Auckland's secretaries, John Colvin, had already sent a 'private letter to Macnaghten on his assuming the diplomatic direction of the Shah's expedition'.[3] (When Masson eventually found out, he thought 'the unfortunate secretary was the last man in India who should have put himself forward.')[4]

Auckland's vast troop of secretaries was in a bloodthirsty mood. 'Military croakers have always called our army inadequate,' Colvin sniffed, 'yet it has never been founded.'[5] A few weeks earlier, Burnes had sworn off any involvement in re-establishing Shah Shujah in Kabul. 'This last I will not do,'[6] he vowed. But now that he had seen the chessboard, he made a different move, and began to insist that 'the British have no resource but in instantaneous movement, and the most cordial support of Shah Shujah'.[7] 'You must,' Burnes took to saying, 'set up Shah Shujah as a puppet, and establish a supremacy in Afghanistan, or you will lose India.'[8] Auckland himself was not the most decisive of men. He spent the summer wobbling. 'If we can only get him to seize the gun he has loaded,' Burnes complained, 'but His Lordship hesitates.'[9]

The rains came down day after day, and the roof of the Secretaries' Lodge leaked relentlessly. Burnes had dinner under an umbrella, with a servant to hold it over him.[10]

In Peshawar, Masson was trying to stay positive. 'I hope and almost believe,' he wrote, 'that I have a chance of some change in my situation, whatever it may be. I trust in God, I shall recover my liberty.'[11] He still had not heard anything definitive from Burnes, and Avitabile's city was no place for scholars. ('Ah, my friend!' Avitabile was known to exclaim, 'Don't read! It's very bad for you!')[12] Rumours of the coming invasion of Afghanistan were everywhere. 'The business' made Masson feel physically sick. He confessed to an old Afghan friend that 'I feared I should be unable to take any part in the measures determined upon, and he replied: "Your people will be coming here – they know nothing of our ways, nor we of theirs – you are acquainted with both us and them – you will be of service to us – do not think of leaving us." '13

Masson wanted to slip away and go back to work in Afghanistan. But he was afraid: was his pardon really unconditional? Try as he might, he could not find the courage to burn his bridges with the East India Company, when the consequences could be so catastrophic.

Finally, in early August, a letter arrived from Shimla.

On the morning of 27 July, Burnes had sat down with Lord Auckland to plead Masson's case. In a quiet, overstuffed room, he tried to translate Masson's misery into words the East India Company might understand. He 'plainly told the Governor General that I was not of the opinion that your merits had been properly rewarded, that I was forced to coincide with opinions I knew you to entertain, that government employ had stood between you and your fair fame in the literary world'. Auckland, used to men desperate for his favour, was bemused. 'Surely Mr Masson cannot know,' he said to Burnes, 'how we all think of him.' Good wishes, Burnes was obliged to point out, hardly made up for years of dealing with Wade. 'To this, he [Auckland] said, "Point out how I can serve Mr Masson." I replied that you wanted liberty, that though you made no complaint your pay was totally inadequate, that you should be freed from all constraint, allowed to go where you pleased from the ocean to China – be tied by no instructions, and in return for this, as you yourself saw fit, you would give the government of India the benefit of your observations, all other matter being your own.'14

Very few people had the nerve to talk to the Governor General like that. But 'Lord Auckland said he would agree most readily to this, and only wished me [Burnes] to say if I had full authority from you. I said I had not, but from a long experience of your modes of thinking, I thought I could answer for your agreement.' That was when things began to go wrong. 'Well, but,' said Auckland, 'Mr

Masson cannot prosecute his vocations in Kabul when we are to go to war, and it is clear therefore he cannot follow the bent of his own inclinations now. Besides he is a gentleman' – this may be one of the few instances of a penniless deserter being called a gentleman – 'of such knowledge that he could not be spared, and would not seek to leave us at present, particularly if we free him in the manner you propose after the Shah is put on the throne.'[15]

It was the same empty promise Masson had been forced to swallow for years: tomorrow, perhaps, may be yours – but today, you are ours. To Burnes, dreaming of his own glory, Auckland's proposal sounded wonderful. 'I at once answered for you on this point,' he wrote breezily to Masson, 'and said that during seven months, I had never applied to you in vain, and I was sure the same zeal would now animate you in this crisis, it being distinctly understood you were to have your own way in some such manner as I had proposed afterwards. "That, then, is settled," said His Lordship.'[16]

In Peshawar, Masson came to the end of the letter and felt despair reaching out for him. Burnes had, he reflected ruefully, 'explained my wishes and feelings not only inaccurately but even ridiculously'.[17] In truth, Burnes had done exactly what he always did. With the best of intentions, he could never see the world through another person's eyes. When asked to speak for someone else, he always ended up speaking for himself instead. It was, all things considered, an unfortunate trait in a diplomat.

Auckland's secretaries followed up, to ensure Masson knew his place. 'Write to Mr Masson to say that Lord Auckland is really sensible to his merits,' Colvin instructed Burnes. 'While the present crisis lasts, his services are too valuable to his country to admit of his being detached to a distance.'[18] 'His Excellency,' Burnes wrote, 'would place the intelligence department under yourself from your great local knowledge and acknowledged fitness.'[19] Masson was to be a spy, for as long as the East India Company needed a spy. Why not, then, walk away?

What if you walked off into a bright future, and fell, and kept falling? Masson did not have to look very far, in Peshawar, to see what that looked like. The last few years had stripped much of his hope away. What if life was not about chasing dreams, but making peace with unhappiness? 'I had much rather have taken my chance, and have obtained my liberty at once,' he wrote, 'but under all circumstances, I judged it best not further to press upon the good disposition of Lord Auckland at this time.'[20] Even holding onto a fragment of his dreams was better than nothing.

No one else in Britain or Europe knew Afghanistan as well as Masson. Pottinger, assailed by gallstones, urged him to snatch his chance for celebrity and rush a book out. He had seen enough of Masson's notes to be sure that his friend had 'material for a most valuable and interesting work, and I only wish it were possible to get it out within any moderate time as the thirst for information upon Kabul ... will be unquenchable with John Bull [the British public], to whom something must be "the rage," and the pending war will no doubt be much talked of not only in England, but all over Europe. I am not sure but it would be a good plan for you to authorize your journals and papers to be sent to England, where I have little doubt but some efficient person would be found to arrange them, and some publisher glad to bring them out on liberal terms.'[21] Never mind the rights and wrongs of the coming war, he urged Masson – just think of the royalties.

Masson's work was suffering badly. A few finds still trickled in from his collaborators in Afghanistan – '15 gold coins, 104 silver coins and 1 engraved gem' arrived from Kabul at the end of July[22] – but his discoveries were at a standstill. 'I am pleased to observe that the manuscripts exceeded your anticipation, but I much regret I have not been able to arrange them,' he wrote sadly back to Pottinger. 'In fact so completely baffled have I been, that I have not, to tell the truth, effected one purpose which I had proposed when I set out from Tabriz in 1830.'[23] More and more, he was starting to wonder if he was a failure.

Fortunately, the East India Company had some ideas about how he could fill his time. 'Mr Macnaghten wants to get one hundred good mules,' Burnes wrote to Masson, 'sent forthwith to Ludhiana from Peshawar, and I have had no hesitation in saying you will do the needful.'[24] Masson did not know whether to laugh or cry. Some weeks later, an anonymous letter written in a distinctive, jagged hand would arrive at the offices of an Indian newspaper. 'I observe that jackasses are employed in place of camels for the transport service of the troops employed in Afghanistan,' wrote Masson. 'Seeing that jackasses have been for a long time employed in the Political Department, is it the commencement of a system to introduce them in to the military one, with a view of establishing uniformity in the services? Does the respectable envoy [Macnaghten] feel a certain sympathy for the long eared gentry, or consider them in the light of relatives whom he is bound to advance to place and employment?'[25] Slowly but surely, Masson's long-suppressed anger was coming to the boil.

In Shimla, George Jephson, an old friend of Masson's from his Bengal Artillery days, was working at top speed. Jephson had climbed the bureaucratic ladder to become one of the East India Company's chief clerks.[26] He was a shameless gossip: unsurprisingly, he and Masson got on tremendously. They had been exchanging letters for the last few years, rolling their eyes at the amoral fools who called themselves the masters of India. But Jephson had heard some things about Masson which puzzled him. He had assumed Masson's 'situation was that of "British officer in Kabul" ... accredited and respectable'. But Burnes had suggested otherwise. So Jephson started pulling out old volumes of government reports, where all appointments were listed, going back years and years. He flipped pages, increasingly anxiously, as his clerks worked around him, and the smell of ink hung in the air. Masson's name was nowhere to be found. 'Your appointment never appeared in print,' he wrote to his friend, 'it would not have escaped my eye, although at the time I should not have known who Charles Masson was.'[27] In Shimla, the penny finally dropped. 'I wish I could express to you, my dear Masson,' Jephson wrote, 'how sorry I am.'[28]

Masson could not quite believe it. 'The appointment of Agent at Kabul had been announced to me by Captain Wade "as conferred by G.O.G.G. 7 January 1835." The initials meaning, I presume, General Orders by the Governor General, and to my surprise,

I afterwards discovered no such orders had been issued.'[29] In fact, Macnaghten had only suggested that Wade 'encourage Mr Masson to furnish you, by every opportunity, with his notions of the prevailing state of politics and of the feelings of the people in the different countries which he may visit'.[30] Wade had dressed up that informal suggestion as an official posting: 'Government,' he told Masson, 'has at my recommendation been pleased to appoint you our Agent in Kabul.'[31] 'The case was one of artifice and deception,' Masson wrote. 'Why practiced? Because it was known that had such employment been proposed to me, I should have rejected it. I was therefore led to believe I had no option.'[32]

Jephson thought it was time Masson stood up for himself. 'If not,' he warned, 'you will be made a cat's paw of until you sink into an early grave.'[33] 'A man having no other views or hopes, and knowing less of the country and people, might have allowed the government to take an ungenerous advantage of the error he had committed in quitting the service as you did',[34] but Masson was far from helpless. Masson's Afghan friends agreed. 'Now you have no alternative but to retire,' one told him. 'They have disgraced you, and care nothing about you.'[35]

In Shimla, Burnes had been knighted, and promoted, and showered with praise. Along the way, history had been rewritten. 'All things went well at Kabul,' Sir Alexander Burnes now told everyone.[36] Rather than being given 'the coup de grâce',[37] the 'mercy blow' delivered to put a helpless victim out of its misery, he had done his country proud. 'I met the Russian agent publicly, and I demanded my dismissal, and I got it.'[38] He had been the hero all along. Now, even greater fame and fortune were waiting for him.

'I bask,' Burnes smiled, 'in the sunshine of my Lord.'[39]

'I may yet,' Masson wrote, 'be able to show my Lord Auckland my grey hairs, and ask him if they have been caused by fair play.'[40]

Masson took a long look at himself. 'I am in so terrible a state of mind and health, the latter I believe caused by the former.' For years, he had compromised. Day by day, he had bent a little more, and a little more. 'I was unwilling to offend, and this unwillingness has,' he wrote, 'induced me to delay the final step in hopes that the government themselves would permit me to follow my own plans, until, I verily believe, I am brought on the verge of insanity.'[41]

Masson realised that the East India Company was never going to give his story a happy ending. Instead, 'I was to be thankful for anything':[42] whatever crumbs might happen to fall his way. He remembered, long ago, a person called James Lewis, who dared to live life on his own terms, no matter the consequences. He listened to the vultures over Peshawar, circling round their latest meal. And – still unsure whether he was signing his own death sentence – he found the words he had been looking for:

> I have the honour to request that you will signify to the Right Honourable the Governor General of India in Council my resignation of the service of the Government of India.
>
> I have not one reason for taking this step, but many reasons, the only one I need mention is that I am willing to ascertain whether or not I am a free agent.[43]

14

Worlds to Conquer

Today, woodsmoke still curls up from the chimneys of the former Secretaries' Lodge in Shimla. In the early evenings, the lamps are lit and the dining table is set for poulet au citron and ginger pudding. Gin waits on silver trays, and a yellow light hangs in the long rooms. 'Would you press the bell over there?' Reggie Singh asked. An elderly attendant brought tea and biscuits, bowed, and passed china cups. Reggie's grandfather, Raja Charanjit Singh, bought the house decades earlier. A picture of it as it was in Masson's time hangs in the conservatory. Here, one of the most disastrous decisions of the nineteenth century was made, just after an excellent breakfast, on 1 October 1838. 'This house was where it all began,' said Reggie quietly.

***

The autumn of 1838 brought heavy morning mists to Shimla. The hills were deepest evergreen, and the air was crisp and cold. Log fires were lit and tea was ordered. Emily Eden had promised to paint a portrait of the newly crowned Queen Victoria for Ranjit Singh. Unfortunately, she had no idea what Victoria looked like. 'It has cost me much trouble,' she wrote, 'to invent a whole Queen, robes and all.'[1] Macnaghten had made a terrible mess of his 'eating stall', at one of the last fairs of the summer.[2] He was ready to get his hands on Afghanistan.

On 1 October, the East India Company declared war on Afghanistan. 'The Governor General,' ran Macnaghten's declaration, issued from the Secretaries' Lodge, 'was satisfied that a passing necessity as well as every consideration of policy and justice warranted us in espousing the cause of Shah Shujah al-Mulk, whose popularity throughout Afghanistan has been proved to His Lordship by the strong and unanimous testimony of the best authorities . . . The Governor General,' it continued, 'rejoices that in the discharge of his duty, he will be enabled to assist in restoring the union and prosperity of the Afghan people.'[3]

In the third century BC, seventy years after Alexander died in Babylon, much of India was ruled by the emperor Ashoka. Late in his reign, Ashoka issued a proclamation to his people which was very different from the East India Company's declaration of 1838:

> When the king, God's Beloved, had ruled for eight years, he conquered the land of the Kalingas. A hundred and fifty thousand men fled, a hundred thousand were slain, and many times that number died.
>
> But afterwards, having taken the land of the Kalingas, the king, God's Beloved, devoted himself to the study of right and wrong, and to instructing his people in morality. For the king, God's Beloved, repented of his conquest of the land of the Kalingas. He considered it an abomination ...
>
> My sons and my great-grandsons must remember this: never again should they set out to conquer a country ... They must remember that the only true conquest takes place in the mind and the heart: the victory of right over wrong.[4]

Ashoka turned his back on his former life: he recalled his armies, gave away much of his wealth and ordered gigantic inscriptions to be set up in every corner of his kingdom proclaiming tolerance and respect for all. Each was written in the local language: Brahmi and Kharoshthi, Aramaic and Greek. One of the best preserved of Ashoka's inscriptions lies sixty miles from Peshawar, in the village of Shahbazgarhi. While the East India Company was preparing for war, Masson was carefully scraping centuries of moss from its surface.

He had heard rumours about the inscription and, after sending in his resignation, had ridden out to see it for himself. His old travelling habits were coming back: on the way, he slept in a village mosque, shaded by plane trees. The road from Peshawar was a dangerous one: 'many were the efforts of our village friends to dissuade us from crossing the plain with so small a party; and abundant were the conjectures as to our probable fate.'[5] Masson rode through tall, thick grass, which 'attained the height of six or seven feet', towards the 'low range of hills on which the inscribed rock is found'.[6]

When he reached Shahbazgarhi, Masson was hopeful and gleeful, in ways he had not been for years. 'A glance at the surface of the rock convinced me that my journey would be recompensed.'[7] It was covered in dense lines of characters. Looking closely, he realised that this was the same Kharoshthi script he had found on the coins at Bagram. Carefully, over several days, he traced the inscription onto yards of fine calico. The occasional 'reports of cannons and small arms' in the distance speeded up work considerably.[8]

Masson did not know it, but the Shahbazgarhi inscription was the last piece of a puzzle he had started to assemble years earlier in Kabul, when he began to decode the unknown script on the coins. Because Ashoka's edicts had been issued in so many different languages, each line of Masson's Kharoshthi inscription could be compared to the same line from the same edict in ancient Greek. The lost language was about to become an open book.

When Masson returned happily to Peshawar, news of the East India Company's declaration of war had just reached the city. As he read through it, his heart sinking, Masson realised that 'the authority of Mr Masson' and 'the reports of Mr Masson'[9] lay behind almost every line. Every good thing he had ever written about Shah Shujah, and every bad thing he had ever written about Dost Mohammad, had been plucked out of his letters and lined up behind the war.[10] He, above all others, had shaped the government's knowledge of Afghanistan. His advice had been highly thought of. And now his words had been twisted in ways, Masson wrote desolately, that 'I never dreamed'.[11]

Years earlier, in one of his first reports to Wade, Masson had urged the East India Company to accept Dost Mohammad's friendship. 'Disappointed of his hoped for British mediation,' Masson wrote, 'the detested Persian alliance will probably be sought – a Russian is even agitated.' Dost Mohammad, Masson pointed out, was 'offering to the British government the paramount ascendancy in the country seated west of it, an ascendancy not to be acquired by conquest and the destruction of life but to be assumed at the invitation of their rulers themselves … An important object which might be esteemed cheap if purchased by a large expenditure of life and treasure may be accomplished by a few strokes of the pen, and the British influence will be introduced into Central Asia in a mode honourable to the British character and acceptable to all parties … There can be little doubt but that the British government will hereafter have ample reason to congratulate itself.'[12]

At the time, Wade, scornful of any strategy which did not rely on force or fear, had scribbled dismissively on Masson's dispatch that 'I cannot concur in his opinion that if disappointed in his hope of British mediation, Dost Mohammad Khan . . . would throw himself into the arms of Persia or Russia. The Barakzai chiefs [Dost Mohammad's family] are too well aware of the means which we possess both to injure and benefit them rashly to change their present position in respect to us, by seeking an alliance with a rival power. Neither the Persians nor the Russians can exercise so fatal an influence for the destruction or consolidation of their rule in Afghanistan as the British government.'[13] Masson's advice was ignored, and soon forgotten.

Masson finally understood his place in history. He knew that once a British army marched into Afghanistan, the relationship between it and Britain would never be the same again. A door was closing for ever.[14]

Dr Percival Lord – fussy, ill-informed and thrilled by the coming war – had arrived in Peshawar to take Masson's place. 'I have never met a sentiment,' Lord wrote, 'which might more properly be termed national and universal than the desire of the Afghans for the return of Shah Shujah. They can seldom converse with [the] English for five minutes without alluding to it.'[15] Lord had a long list of people to convert to the British cause, which he waved triumphantly at Masson. 'There was not a man of them could be of any use to him,' Masson realised at a glance, 'while some were even dead.'[16] Undaunted, Lord spent his days 'talking, persuading, threatening, bullying, and bribing'.[17] When Masson left Peshawar, Lord followed him out of the city, 'shed tears when we parted, and afterwards confidentially reported to government that I was insane'.[18]

December found Masson in the little town of Firozpur, on Ranjit Singh's borders. He was not alone: a vast British army was gathering there, along with Burnes, Macnaghten, Lord Auckland and seemingly every important and self-important official in the East India Company. Emily Eden brought her portrait of Victoria. Ranjit Singh brought just enough troops to make the British uncomfortable: 'they were quite as well disciplined [as the British],' remarked Eden, 'rather better dressed, repeated the same military movements and several others much more complicated, and, in short, nobody knows what to say about it, so they say nothing, except that they are sure the Sikhs would run away in a real fight. It is a sad blow to our vanities!'[19] At his meeting with the British, the Maharaja took off one of his stockings, 'that he might sit with one foot in his hand, comfortably', and 'said he understood that there were books which contained objections to drunkenness, and he thought it better that there should be no books at all, than that they should contain such foolish notions'.[20] Macnaghten 'was much occupied in contriving to edge one foot of his chair on to the carpet, in which he at last succeeded'.[21]

Masson had become a minor celebrity. Colonel Lewis Stacy, whose mania for ancient coins almost equalled Masson's, considered marching his regiment all night through the winter mud, to improve his chances of meeting him. 'Pray send me a line saying when you propose leaving camp, because for the pleasure of meeting you I would make a forced march into Firozpur,' he wrote.

'My hands are too cold to write for the present – I hope so much for the pleasure of meeting you.'²² Stacy sealed his letter with an ancient goddess of victory, which he had snapped up in the bazaar in Ludhiana. He was an obsessive collector, and 'would be seen putting up with every inconvenience, under trees or in common serais [caravanserais] in Central India; digging in deserted ruins, or poring over the old stores of village money-changers.'²³ 'May I ask,' he wrote to Masson, 'have you any intention of publishing?'²⁴

Masson had been planning to write a book for years. But the more he thought about it, the more it daunted him. His notes seemed like a hopeless jumble. Reading back through the yellowing scraps and sketches, even he could barely understand them. 'I am conscious there is much, indeed the greater portion, intelligible to no one but myself, and I am also conscious that everything is sadly incomplete.'²⁵

Instead, he wandered aimlessly through the army camp at Firozpur. Of all the thousands of people, the soldiers and camp followers, officers and spies, he was the only one who had no place to be, and no role to play. Nothing about the expedition made sense to him. 'No new circumstances of alarm had arisen – neither so far as I am aware had any new ideal armies of Russians been called into existence by the prolific brain of Sir Alexander Burnes.' (Masson crossed out 'Sir Alexander Burnes', and wrote 'the Russophobes of Shimla'.) 'Yet how happened it that with a diminished pretence for anxiety, an expedition so formidable was set on foot? One so wonderfully in contrast with the original intentions?'²⁶ Justified or not, here the army was, and there was nothing he could do to stop it. 'Volumes would not suffice to express the frivolity of the grounds on which the powerful armies employed were put into motion – the errors and misconduct of those directing the operations, nor the evils attending and to be apprehended from the line of policy adopted.'²⁷ It seemed, to him, to be 'the very child of madness'.²⁸

After a decade of conquest, having travelled further than any Greeks before them, Alexander and his army reached the end of the world, and the shores of the last sea. The soldiers jumped for joy, feeling the salt breeze on their faces for the first time in years.

Alexander stared out at the horizon, looking in vain for land, and seeing nothing but limitless ocean. 'King of everywhere and everything'²⁹ at last, 'Alexander, thinking that the boundaries of the earth had been reached, and a limit set to his ambition, wept because there were no more worlds to conquer.'³⁰

This story – of how Alexander conquered the world, then shed manly tears by the shores of an unknown sea – is not an ancient Greek one. It is a nineteenth-century one.

There is also an ancient story of Alexander's tears, but it is very different. 'There was a time,' wrote Plutarch, 'when Alexander learned the true nature of the universe. He was told how it contained infinite worlds. When he heard this, he wept. His friends asked him why, and he said: "How can I not weep? There are more worlds in the sky than anyone could count – and I have not yet conquered one of them." '³¹ Plutarch's Alexander learns that the universe is too vast for anyone to understand, let alone conquer, and that he must accept his place in it. He realises his own insignificance and is inconsolable. But in the nineteenth-century story, all Alexander needed to dry his tears was some more people to kill.

The night before the army was due to leave, neither Masson nor Burnes could sleep. They sat and talked together, far into the night, each trying to understand the story they were part of. Ultimately, Masson knew, he and 'the second Alexander' were on different paths. 'Our interests clash in some respects, as do our habits,' he reflected. 'To act with him or under him is so painful as to be nearly impossible ... We differ too much to be companions, and I scorn to be an accomplice.'³²

That night, Burnes was like a man balanced on a high ledge, terrified of what he might see if he looked down. His optimism, which grated on Masson at the best of times, had a new, desperate quality to it. 'A long conversation,' Masson remembered, 'terminated by a singular confession on his part, that he had been fourteen years labouring to bring about the present moment, and had at length succeeded.'³³ All was for the best: the invasion, which Burnes had argued so passionately against, had been his idea all along. 'It is indeed transcendentally great,' he wrote to a friend. 'My views are adopted.'[34] 'Sometimes sanguine; sometimes desponding – sometimes confident; sometimes credulous – he gave to fleeting impressions all the importance and seeming permanency of settled convictions, and imbued surrounding objects with the colours of his own varying mind,' argued the historian John Kaye. 'If he deceived others, he first of all deceived himself. If he gave utterance to conflicting opinions, they were all *his* opinions at the time of their birth.'[35]

The night was very cold. (Emily Eden had been horrified by the weather. 'Nobody has been without a cold since we were at Firozpur, but the sneezing and coughing never ceases now. Everybody is paddling about in overshoes, and we are carried to dinner in palanquins, and have trenches dug round our bedrooms.')[36] Masson tried to sleep, listening to the sounds of the camp around him. The last time he had been among British soldiers, he had been Private James Lewis. Now, after so many nights alone, he was no longer sure who he was.

In the morning, dizzy with exhaustion, Masson watched the army forming up: thousands of men in red coats, horses stamping and steaming, long lines of servants. 'The officers regarded the expedition as little else than an extensive pleasure promenade – an enormous picnic.'[37] Camels were loaded with 'jams, pickles, cheroots, potted fish, hermetically-sealed meats, plate, glass, crockery, wax-candles, table-linen'.[38] Even the most junior officers had 'their dressing-cases, their perfumes, Windsor soap, and eau-de-Cologne'.[39] Burnes had brought several spectacularly beautiful women from Kashmir.[40] It was a long way from how Masson had travelled to Kabul all those years ago, with 'no stockings nor shoes, a green cap on his head, and a fakir or dervish drinking cup over his shoulder'.[41]

Amidst the chaos, 'an officer, a friend of Sir Alexander Burnes', drew Masson aside, and 'made a final proposal for me to accompany him: "Now, Masson, pray do go with him. Before he did not, but in future he will do everything as you advise him. I have seen on many occasions that you have a clear head and he has not. Horses and servants are all at your command, and he will remedy as far as he can the neglect of the government." '[42]

With a British army behind him, Masson knew that Alexandria would be his. But he loved Afghanistan deeply. For almost a decade he had called it home. His greatest friends were there, people who had saved his life, and taken care of him when no one else would. Could he bear to betray them? The East India Company had hunted him, blackmailed him and lied to him. He had to choose between his loyalties and his deepest desire. Masson hesitated. After a long moment, he simply said: 'It is too late.'[43]

The army left without him. Soon afterwards, Masson disappeared.

Across the border, in Afghanistan, a sallow, heavily bearded American was watching the advancing British army warily. Josiah Harlan had been busy. After Masson and Burnes left Kabul, he had attached himself to a small force, commanded by one of Dost Mohammad's sons. Harlan was, as ever, the hero of his own melodrama, in search of new worlds to conquer. 'We ascended passes through regions where glaciers and silent dells, and frowning rocks, blackened by ages of weatherbeaten fame, preserved the quiet domain of remotest time, shrouded in perennial snow. We struggled on amidst the heights of those Alpine ranges – until now, supposed inaccessible to the labour of man – infantry and cavalry, artillery, camp followers, and beasts of burden – surmounting difficulties by obdurate endurance, defying the pitiless pelting of the snow or rain ... toiling amidst the clouds like restless spirits of another sphere.'[44] When the force halted at the top of a mountain pass, Harlan seized the moment and unfurled his battered American flag. 'I surmounted the Indian Caucasus, and there, upon the mountain heights, unfurled my country's banner to the breeze, under a salute of twenty-six guns. On the highest pass of the frosty Caucasus ... the star-spangled banner gracefully waved amidst the icy peaks.'[45]

Harlan returned to Kabul calling himself prince of Ghor. He told anyone who would listen that 'the chief of Ghor', Mohammad Rafi Beg, 'transferred his principality to me in feudal service, binding himself and his tribe to pay tribute for ever. The absolute and complete possession of his government was legally conveyed according to official form, by a treaty which I have still preserved.'[46] Mohammad Rafi Beg was not exactly a prince, nor had he bestowed that title on Harlan. He did, however, give Harlan a very impressive-looking piece of paper, written in courtly Persian. (It was translated in 2008 by Eckart Schiewek, who was at the time an adviser to the UN mission in Kabul. 'The documents,' he remembered, 'reached me in the middle of the battle over Kandahar.')[47] It was what the American had been dreaming of since he first met Masson:

> Because in these days I did develop towards Harlan, this noble abode of welfare, this tool of glory and pride, the ideal of the splendid Khans, the trustee of the state, such a friendship ... whenever the affectionate and kind friend Harlan comes to the lands of the Red River, the order of the aforementioned Harlan will not be disobeyed by the breadth of a hair by me. Whatever would be required as service, and sacrifice of life, will not be evaded by me in any aspect. On the contrary, from morning to evening, at all times, will I be at service of the kind Harlan. Over countless years and centuries will I, and alongside me my sons and brothers, not evade his orders.[48]

'The sovereignty of his possessions was,' Harlan claimed with satisfaction, 'secured to the writer and his heirs for ever.'[49] American audiences swooned at the news of Harlan's campaign. The *United States Gazette* – in an article which Harlan reprinted, modestly, at the start of his *Memoir* – anointed him another Alexander the Great. 'Retracing the steps of Alexander', Harlan's little raid was 'an incident altogether unique since the period of Alexander's conquests'.[50] (The current heir to the throne of Ghor, Harlan's descendant, lives in Los Angeles, and is known for his zombie films. He has no plans to reclaim his kingdom.)

It was a shock for Harlan to learn that his rule would be short-lived. The British army currently bearing down on the city had no need for American princes. Accounts differ as to what happened next. According to Harlan – when he told the story later in life, back home in Pennsylvania – he organised the defence of Kabul almost single-handedly. Dost Mohammad 'constituted General Harlan generalissimo of his forces, and himself assumed a subordinate station in the contemplated arrangements for meeting, and opposing, Shujah al-Mulk and the English'.[51] Harlan (according to Harlan) was a true American hero, who led the people of Afghanistan against the British. And though he was an Afghan prince, 'the General looks upon kingdoms and principalities as of frivolous import, when set in opposition to the more honourable and estimable title of American citizen'.[52]

The truth was more complicated. Long before the British army reached Kabul (before, indeed, it set out for Kabul) Harlan had jumped into bed with the East India Company. In December 1838, Colonel Stacy was writing warmly to 'my dear Harlan' in Kabul and gossiping about the British force – hardly the kind of information one would share with the opposition's 'generalissimo'. 'I am very anxious to know your intentions as to the future,' Stacy wrote, 'whether you will remain in India or return to your country. Pray write me as soon as possible if there is any way in which I can be of service to you.'[53] When the British reached Kabul with Shah Shujah, and settled into their occupation of Afghanistan, Stacy wrote to 'my dear Harlan' again, making plans to spend several days together, but 'happy to see you at any time you please'.[54]

Once Kabul fell, Harlan found that the 'bland intimidation' of the new regime was not to his taste. 'Everyone,' ran one of Shujah's proclamations, 'is commanded not to ascend the heights in the vicinity of the Royal Harem under pain of being embowelled alive. May the King live forever!'[55] What tipped Harlan over the edge, however, was not the threat of being disembowelled. Rather, it was the appropriation of his house and horse by the British upon their arrival in Kabul. One day, Harlan saw the horse again, grabbed it from its current owner and rode off. A series of angry letters between himself and the British Superintendent of Police followed. 'Having been deprived of my property by an act of spoliation,' Harlan seethed, 'I am entitled by that law to reclaim and seize upon the effect as my bona fide property.' Even frothing with rage, he was careful to note how 'friendly' he had always been towards the British. 'Had the horse been the property of Dost Mohammad, or of any individual found in arms against the King and his allies, it would have become prize. But as it belonged to an alien and temporary resident ... on friendly terms with the captors, I therefore confess myself unable to recognize the right of the prize agents of the British army to the property of an American citizen.'[56]

Meanwhile, Masson's friends all had the same message for him: finish your book and do it soon. Everything pointed towards it being a triumph. A snippet of his notes had been read at the Bombay Geographical Society, and 'it was pronounced at a meeting', reported Pottinger, 'the best paper the Society has ever received'.[57] Pottinger had seen his friend's plans for the whole volume and was utterly 'delighted with them. They are just what was required, and will place you at the top of all the antiquarians of Europe. I do think you should not allow anything to interfere with the completion of your book.'[58] Charles Masson – deserter, traveller, pilgrim, doctor, archaeologist and spy – had been many things, but never famous. Now everyone in his life, even Burnes, thought he should prepare for immortality. 'No one,' Burnes wrote, 'will rejoice more in your increase of fame than myself.'[59]

All Masson had to do was write.

Months later, in the winter of 1839, Henry Rawlinson rode into the ancient port of Karachi in search of Masson. Rawlinson, like Stacy, was a soldier who was more comfortable digging up the past than blowing up the present. He had been following Masson's work for years. The chance to meet the man 'of whom I have heard and read so much' made Rawlinson positively giddy.[60] He picked his way through the old city in the morning light. Dust and smoke hung in the air. The houses were tumbledown 'shells framed of wattles and mud plaster, and are but a poor defence against rain'.[61] Uncertainly, Rawlinson knocked at the door of 'a wretched hovel'. Inside, 'nearly naked and half drunk', was Masson.[62]

After so many years as a master storyteller, able to wrap his tales around the world and transform it, Masson's unfinished book had driven him to despair. He had no 'means of access to any library'.[63] He did not even have enough paper, and had to beg friends for 'a small supply'.[64] Racked with fever and pounding headaches,[65] he could barely sleep or think straight.[66] He started drinking. Then he found it hard to stop. Believing in himself was a daily battle:[67] fewer and fewer things were able to make 'a man think better, even of himself'.[68] 'I remember,' he confessed to Pottinger, 'that you told me book-making was not so easy as I supposed it, and I have found that your experience was correct.'[69]

'I remained with him [Masson] several hours,' remembered Rawlinson, 'and was extremely pained with all I witnessed. His language was at first so insolent that I thought he had become quite foolish, but at last he told me that having sat up writing near morning, he had dined of a bottle of wine and had risen at daylight and written with the fumes still in his head. I almost think, however, that his mind is really giving way.'[70]

For years, Masson had kept his temper under control, said 'no' as little as possible, and been almost unnervingly eager to please. Now, whether or not it was 'advisable, or prudent, or anything else',[71] he was letting loose. Rawlinson was shocked at how 'bitter' he was: sloppily angry at Wade, Burnes and the East India Company.[72] Periodically, Masson would snatch up a page, and scribble furious verses all over it.[73] 'If any of the remarks in the latter part of my narrative should be deemed too personal, I pray it be remembered, that the insults and injuries offered to me were also personal,' he wrote.[74] Burnes, characteristically, laughed it off to a friend: 'I have been much amused with your report of your interview with little Masson. I was aware of his wrath, but I did not think I was to come in for a share of it … I suppose he is ashamed of himself.'[75]

Masson was ashamed. 'I had kept from writing to you, even at the risk of being unfavourably thought of,' he confessed sadly to a friend. 'I had nothing but crisis and ill fortune to write about and I would not trouble you with that.'[76] Almost every night, guilt at his part in the war left him lying awake.[77]

Yet day after day, sometimes weeping, sometimes shivering, sometimes clenching his fists with fury, he kept writing. And in February 1840, his book was finally finished. His hopes rested in its pages. 'So much depends upon them and the fate they meet with,' he wrote to Pottinger. 'I dare not be so sanguine as to hope what your goodness suggests, that I shall find myself at the top of the antiquarians of Europe.'[78] Pottinger promised to find Masson a publisher in Britain. He was heading back to London to become Queen Victoria's envoy to China (otherwise known as the East India Company's chief opium pusher). The manuscript would go with him.

Masson had no idea how much money his work would make. 'I am rather at a loss in these matters,' he admitted. But once the book was sold, he would have an income of his own. After so many years of having to rely on others, 'independence, without which life, to me at least, has no pleasure', was within his grasp.[79]

But there was a problem. Everyone who read Masson's manuscript had the same reaction: this was unprintable. When Rawlinson met Masson, his hero's drunken slobbering had been painful, but the pages which Masson thrust at him had been heartbreaking. 'He gave me several papers to read,' Rawlinson remembered, 'which were written in the same vague and dreary style as he spoke in, and all of his information appeared to me to be lost by his method of putting it together … I tried to persuade him to go down to Bombay to consult authorities, before just writing. But he was evidently averse to it. He has already written two volumes relating to his travels and work in Afghanistan and was busy with his third – many parts of which he showed me, and are very curious, but they will not stand publication … If Pottinger allows the manuscripts to be printed as they are now, Masson will pass for a presumptuous ignoramus instead of the conscientious, hard-working fellow he really is.'[80]

Masson's friends had been expecting a book about his adventures in Alexander's footsteps: a tale of lost cities and golden coins and hair-raising escapes. Masson had wanted to write that book. Instead, he had written a passionate condemnation of British imperialism, the East India Company and the invasion of Afghanistan. He named names. He spilled secrets. He quoted embarrassing letters. He showed the world 'the second Alexander' with his trousers down. To the dutiful Company men who read his pages, this was heresy. 'I trust,' Rawlinson wrote sadly in his diary, 'something will be done to get him to Bombay.'[81]

Masson knew that he had burned his bridges. 'I do not know,' he wrote, 'that I have a friend in India, or any one person that I know enough to ask a favour of him.'[82] But he was not about to give up and retire meekly to Bombay.

He was heading for Kabul.

15

The Chamber of Blood

By the spring of 1840, Bagram had become a bizarre tourist attraction, inundated with bored British officers, 'breaking the wearisome monotony of military life in cantonments'. 'The immense number of coins found at Bagram, near Kabul, conjectured to be the site of Alexandria,' one wrote, 'was another attraction to many with classical recollections, anxious to traverse and explore the land which had been trod by the Macedonian hero.'[1] Naturally, all those visitors wanted souvenirs. The villagers of Bagram obliged them with heaps of brand-new ancient coins and artefacts. The most gullible were pointed to a low-lying mound, and informed that it was the 'tomb supposed to have been raised over Alexander the Great's mighty steed Bucephalus'.[2]

Every story about following in Alexander's footsteps has one thing in common: the narrator gets conned. 'The amateur archaeologist,' wrote the *Illustrated London News*, years later, 'is well known to the "innocent" peasant of most countries, and many are the "genuine antiques" made for his benefit. The chief difficulty is to give the "finds" the appearance of age. Some "antiques" are buried for two or three years that the earth may give them many years … The patina on coins "of the period of Alexander the Great" may have come into being while the coins were being partially digested by geese. Before this method came into use, coins were made old by being worn for some months tied to the soles of boots.'[3]

British day-trippers called Bagram 'an unpleasurable waste of country',⁴ but in Masson's memories, in Karachi, it became a lost paradise: 'a landscape,' he wrote, 'whose beauty can scarcely be conceived but by those who have witnessed it.'⁵

Every day, Masson thought about Afghanistan. He could not wait to feel the wind from the mountains on his face, and walk through Kabul's gates again. His friends there were 'continually enquiring after you', Burnes wrote to him, and knew 'you could never live without coming to Kabul once more. If you do, I for one shall be most happy to see you.'⁶ Masson's years in Afghanistan had ended with his hopes slipping through his fingers, and his excavations abandoned. Now, he saw a chance to change that. 'My journey,' he wrote, 'I hope will put me to rights.'⁷ This time, he was not going to let the East India Company get between him and Alexander.⁸

First, though, Masson had to get to Afghanistan in one piece. The deserts and mountain passes were unforgiving. And, Masson reflected, 'a new order of things prevailed, and it was very possible that recent political changes and accidents might have induced feelings amongst the people I should meet, to which they were strangers ten years previously'.⁹ Wherever the East India Company's army had passed on the way to Afghanistan, it had left hatred and loss in its wake. 'One or two little bits of smashery took place,' laughed one officer. 'It is perfectly annoying to see a lot of those fellows coming screaming after you that they have been looted. This generally happens during the first or second day you enter a place.' Towns were occupied with brutish contempt. 'Two or three mosques we converted into good Christian dwellings, and rot all Muslim prejudices … The doctor laid hold of a mosque and made it the hospital: the best use it has ever been put to since it was built. The devout may pray outside if they please.'¹⁰ Afghans still tell the story of that invasion: this is how the British will repay your trust.

Hoping to stay safe, Masson attached himself to a caravan of merchants led by an old friend, bound for Afghanistan. Every morning, the slow, plodding camels were swarmed by crows and mynah birds, which 'were so voracious that they perched on the humps of the camels, and actually pecked holes in them'.[11] Masson rode on ahead impatiently, leaving his baggage and papers with the merchants. He planned to wait for them at the desert town of Kalat, one of the last stops on the road before the mountain passes into Afghanistan.

Kalat sat above the desert like a dust-coloured cloud: 800 tumbledown houses, overlooked by a crumbling citadel and palace. When it rained, the lower town flooded, and the poor waded through the shit of the rich. In summer, everyone boiled in the heat. It was an upside-down sort of place: 'what in some countries would have been deemed a proof of insanity, was here judged undeniable evidence of sanctity and wisdom.' A naked man who wandered the streets in search of gold was generally agreed to be the wisest person in town.[12] In Masson's memories, its lanes were full of camel trains and wide-eyed wanderers, hungry spies and an exiled prince selling mules.[13] Years ago, he had spent many happy days there as an alchemist's apprentice, trying (and failing) to make gold from lime juice, 'seven-years-old vinegar' and 'the acrid murky juices of plants in the neighbourhood'.[14]

But the world had not been kind to Kalat, in the years since Masson had been away. The East India Company had been convinced that Kalat's ruler, Mehrab Khan, was responsible for ambushing their army on the road to Afghanistan. There was never any proof of this, apart from some whispers and dubious-looking letters. But that did not stop the British attacking the town, killing Mehrab Khan and looting everything of value inside the walls. Mehrab Khan's young son and heir, Nasir Khan, was now an exile, hunted by the East India Company and protected by a handful of his father's old servants. A more compliant relative, Nawaz Khan, had been placed on the throne, with a British Political Officer, Lieutenant William Loveday, to pull the strings behind the scenes. In the hills and the marketplaces, the songs of rage were already being sung:

The countless army of the Company advanced upon us.
Who can withstand their force?

Men without number were assembled,
Thousands added to thousands.
The far-shooting musketeers could not be counted,
Nor the helmets on their heads,
Nor the shoes on their feet,
Nor their horses dressed for battle.

They set up their engines of war,
Their cannon and tents.
They drank wine and fierce liquors.
The cowards spat at the skies.
The unbelievers made a thousand boasts:
'We shall capture your chief, and make him our slave.'

They crossed the river to us.
Our world was deceived,
It was taken and shared out as spoil.

Praise upon praise,
A thousand praises,
To that son of wrath, generous Mehrab, the sword-wielder.
He gathered men to resist,
He stood beside them in battle.
He did not deliver his city into the hands of the white men.
He gave his life in defence of his family.

Nasir Khan, you are like a rose
In a rich garden.
Your name and fame have crossed the world,
To far-off Delhi and the green fields of Kandahar.
May you find a home in your country,
And your ancestral lands.
May Kalat be yours for ever.[15]

When Masson arrived at Kalat, ahead of the merchants, he was
too busy catching up with his old friends to give much thought

to Loveday. 'Before night, however, I was told that Lt. Loveday had been informed of my arrival, and that he remarked, he knew nothing of me, but I must be a low fellow, for if I had been a gentleman, I should have come to him.'[16] The next morning, more amused than offended, Masson wandered over to introduce himself.

Loveday had a mansion in the old city, but he was busy building his dream home outside the city walls. It was a monstrosity: an elephantine Gothic Revival villa of his own design. He spent most of his days sitting in a tent next to the building site, watching it take shape. 'I wish,' he wrote to his family, 'you could only see some of my pretty designs of couches and tables.'[17] Looking around, Masson realised that many of the workers were slaves.[18] And they were terrified.

Before he could take it all in, a young man bustled up to him, with two bulldogs in tow. 'As I drew near him, he said "Mr Masson, I believe?" I replied, "Yes," when he continued, "We may as well walk into the tent." He led the way, and I followed him. There was, in truth, but one chair in the tent, and he remarked to me: "Sit down on the ground – you are used to do so, I presume?" I smiled, said that I was, and sat down on the ground. He changed his clothes, and while doing so, threw three or four newspapers down before me.'[19] Over breakfast, Loveday told Masson about the men he had killed: he was proud of 'blowing from a gun' one local chief, 'and said he wished he could get hold' of others, to treat them 'in the same manner'.[20] Loveday was particularly looking forward to killing Mehrab Khan's old Darogha, or chief minister, Gul Mohammad. He was also 'to have been blown from a gun. I asked in what the Darogha had so grievously offended, and suggested that if his only crime was attachment to his late master, and now to his son, whether it would not be as well to conciliate as to punish him.' Loveday said that he had 'proof of a diabolical conspiracy – and on that account he was not to be forgiven'.[21] Besides, he remarked, brightly, 'Might is right.'[22] Sitting on the floor, nibbling his breakfast, Masson felt his stomach turn. Something was very wrong here.

The East India Company's armies had left a patchwork of newly captured towns and territories in their wake as they advanced towards Afghanistan. Young men like Loveday, possessed of a little Persian and less common sense, had been left in charge: appointed Political Officers, and given the power of life and death over entire kingdoms. If the young Political Officer was very kind, very clever and very lucky, his rule might not be disastrous. Few were even one of those things. 'If a man is too stupid or too lazy to drill his company,' complained Major General William Nott, 'he often turns sycophant, cringes to the heads of departments, and is often made a Political, and of course puts the government to an enormous expense, and disgraces the character of his country.'[23] Nott recalled, incredulously, when 'a foolish Political destroyed a small village containing twenty-three inhabitants. And why, think you? Because he thought – thought, mind you – he thought that they looked insultingly at him as he passed with his 200 cavalry as an escort! Had I been on the spot, he should have had eight troopers for his protection; he would have then been civil to the inhabitants, or perhaps not cruel.'[24] Even Burnes – not normally one to turn his nose up at ambition – loathed the 'fry and frog-spawn' of the new Politicals.[25]

Loveday had slid up the greasy pole like a man born to the art. 'Once I am brought to Mr Macnaghten's notice,' he wrote before the war, 'it shall be my fault if I do not deserve his good opinion.'[26] At a carefully engineered encounter, he had ingratiated himself with Macnaghten – or, as the saying went, 'eaten toads' – so effectively that he had been plucked out of an undistinguished career in the army and put in charge of Kalat. 'At last,' he gloated, 'I have arrived on the first step of the ladder which leads to renown, and even to wealth.'[27] When Kalat was captured, Loveday proved to be a world-class looter, discovering 'where the Khan had buried his jewels' ahead of the British attack: underneath a light dusting of earth, in an anonymous corner of the city, he dug up 'four boxes filled with diamonds, emeralds, rubies, and pearls as big as peas'. His share, he boasted to his family, 'will be very handsome'.[28]

Masson had been hearing strange, disturbing stories about Loveday ever since he left Karachi. That afternoon, he wandered the town in an uneasy daze. The peaceful and prosperous Kalat of his memories had turned desolate. 'The greater part of the town was uninhabited, and the little bazaar, once busy and well supplied, was nearly deserted. The inhabitants themselves were oppressed with gloom and despondency, as they were clad in the coarse and abject garb of poverty. All of my old acquaintances had suffered most cruelly in the spoil [looting] of their property, and I was hurt to see those who had so recently been affluent and comfortable, present themselves before me necessitous and destitute. The sky, indeed, was as serene as ever, the orchards displayed their verdure, and the valley, as before, was adorned with cultivation, yet there was a loneliness, real or imaginary, on my part, cast over the scene, that was infectious, and with every disposition to be cheerful, I was, in despite of myself, dejected and sorrowful.'[29]

That evening, Masson saw where his old friends' money had gone. Loveday's mansion in the old city was a looter's paradise. 'I found Lt. Loveday in a spacious apartment, hung round with suits of armour, and the corners filled with pikes, halberds, battle-axes, and warlike weapons, the spoil of the late Khan's armoury. He was stretched on his couch, and told me that he had long since dined, but that something had been set by for me.'[30] It was a hideous evening. Masson picked at his plate of leftovers. Loveday 'was extremely restless, sometimes rising suddenly from his couch and taking a chair, and then as suddenly leaving it for his couch. He showed me the plan of the house he was building, and of the Gothic windows he had designed for it.'[31] Before Masson arrived, Loveday had told his servants that he 'was an enemy of his, and illustrating his argument by crossing his little fingers, that he and I stood in such a position, that is in direct enmity'.[32] His twitchy anxiety had a very simple cause: he was afraid that Masson was working for the East India Company, and had been instructed to get to the bottom of what was going on in Kalat. Loveday bid Masson goodnight with a strained smile and invited him to breakfast the next day. Apropos of nothing, he asked if he was going to write a book. 'I have,' Masson took great pleasure in telling him, 'already written one.'[33]

The moment his guest left, Loveday boiled over. Masson was a spy, and a scrounger, and a lot of other things besides. 'I was going to Kabul to get a tikka naan, or a bit of bread, as Burnes was there. Again he observed that I had been an old offender, but had written a book, and Colonel Pottinger had stood my friend, but now the Colonel had gone to Europe and I was friendless.'[34] Masson might have been out of the spy business, but he still had the region's best intelligence network at his fingertips. He had a verbatim report of Loveday's thoughts and feelings within a few hours. The next morning, Masson briefly wondered whether he should keep his breakfast appointment with Loveday, but said to himself, 'What have I to do with him? And what occasion have I to trouble him with my company, or to be annoyed with his?'[35] He decided to keep to himself for the rest of his time in Kalat.

Masson's instincts were right: something was very wrong in Kalat. Alone in the desert, seeing plots all around him, Loveday ruled by fear and 'horror'.[36] A few days later, apparently thinking that Masson had left town, Loveday showed his true colours. He had enslaved a man called Yahya, a local farmer, to build his new house. Yahya somehow 'incurred the displeasure of Lt. Loveday', who flew into a rage and gave 'the necessary signal' to his bulldogs. The dogs leaped onto Yahya, bringing him to the ground in a mess of teeth and spittle. Loveday watched the dogs tear at him – the screams, the growling, the horrified expressions of everyone within sight – and only called them off once they had 'inflicted several wounds on the wretched individual. He was carried home in a grievous state, and in a few days died.'[37] The fear he saw on the faces of everyone around him made Loveday very happy. 'Ere long,' he wrote to his family, 'they will be converted into good subjects.'[38]

Masson was anxious and preoccupied. He knew he could not expect any news about his book for months, but he still thought about those hastily scribbled pages all the time: imagining them being turned over in the office of this or that publisher, and wondering if they would be read with delight, or boredom, or wonder – or even read at all. 'So much depends upon them and the fate they meet with,' he reflected.[39] He was impatient to put Kalat behind him: every day seemed to bring a new idea to pursue. But his baggage remained stubbornly stuck on the road. The merchants had run into difficulties. Camels were dying, and the journey was proving more difficult than anyone had expected. When the caravan finally made it into Kalat, it was in a sorry state. Then, disaster struck.

Loveday found a way to make himself even more unpopular: he started collecting taxes. The people of Kalat were not accustomed to paying taxes. They made their feelings known in an outlying village, by surrounding Loveday's secretary and the soldiers with him, and killing every last one of them. What followed was less a rebellion, more a sigh of relief, as the country's long-suppressed fury boiled over at last:

Our enemies divided the spoil:
A shopkeeper took your helmet,
Men passed out your weapons.
Children I see orphaned,
They sleep in the sun's heat.
The women weep tears of blood.
My soul burns with grief,
My heart answers me thus:
Now, the tiger is growling.[40]

Within days, more than a thousand men were bearing down on Kalat, with Nasir Khan at their head.

Events then sped up considerably. Masson went to bed as usual, in the garden where he was staying, only to be woken by one of his friends, Faiz Ahmed. 'Panting for breath and in the utmost trepidation, he entreated me for God's sake to leave the garden, or I should be murdered.' Gunfire was breaking out in almost every direction. Two of Mehrab Khan's old servants 'had buckled on their arms intending to have assassinated me that night'. Faiz Ahmed 'urged me there and then to leave Kalat. I was still obstinate, being disposed to look upon the matter lightly.'[41] Faiz Ahmed thought that Masson was being an insufferable idiot, and said so. Masson's horse was saddled, a guide for the road was arranged and he prepared to leave.[42] Then, at the last minute, Masson made one of the greatest mistakes of his life. He decided that, whatever was happening, it was not worth leaving town over.

Almost immediately, a message arrived from Loveday, who had retreated to his house inside the city walls, inviting Masson to visit him. 'His reception was very different from what it had been before. He started from his seat, came to meet me with extended hands, and exclaimed mildly, "Mr Masson! Mr Masson!" I immediately gave him my hand, and we sat down; for now I found there were chairs in the house.'[43] The reason for Loveday's sudden transformation soon became clear: now that the town was about to be attacked, he wanted Masson with him. I 'should have been much more gratified if it had been my fortune to have been associated with a person in better estimation than Lt. Loveday',[44] Masson reflected. But his inability to say no resurfaced, fatally, one more time – and, before he quite knew what he was doing, he had agreed.

Kalat, Masson quickly realised, was far from ready to withstand a siege. There were yawning gaps in the walls, large enough for people to step through. Giant blocks of lead were stacked up in the armoury, but no one had thought to turn them into bullets. Several fearsome-looking cannon were sited at the top of the citadel, but they were 'useless; the largest, indeed, might be considered a curiosity, for it was cast at Modena in Italy, and above three centuries old'.[45] Loveday was hoping help would arrive from the city of Quetta, around 100 miles away, where the sour and heavy-eyed Captain J. D. D. Bean presided over a much larger force than his own. But the 'sickly and inefficient state' of Bean's soldiers was the talk of the East India Company[46] – and Bean himself was in no hurry to venture out from behind his walls. Loveday read Masson his letters to Bean, and told him that he was 'bound to represent my exertions and the assistance I had given him to government'.[47] Still, Masson noticed, the only thing Loveday said in his letters was 'Mr Masson is with me'.[48] (That was not actually all that Loveday said, but it was all he read aloud. 'It appears,' the letter went on, 'that he [Masson] was still loitering in Kalat, and when the rebellion broke out he hid himself somewhere – when I heard of it I sent for him to my quarters.')[49] Shut up with a simpering, homicidal, 'obsequiously civil'[50] man-child and his bulldogs, Masson distracted himself as best he could with the town's defences. It had been a long time since he was a soldier, but even he knew that walls with giant holes in them were unlikely to hold off anyone for long. He did his best to help with repairs, and, along with Nawaz Khan, set some reluctant men to work making bullets. Loveday, at least, was on his best behaviour. Masson could not drink a sip of water or wine, without him exclaiming 'God bless you!'[51]

Nasir Khan's army arrived in a rush and tumble – a crowd of perhaps 1,500 men, only half of them armed, 'and many more only armed with sword and shield'.[52] They seemed surprised to find the gates shut and the town defended, and milled around uncertainly for a while before settling down for a siege.[53] That evening, Loveday glumly watched from the walls as the army pulled down his half-built dream home. All that fresh-cut timber was exactly what they needed.[54] Masson – not mentioning his days as Private James Lewis of the Bengal Artillery – did his best with the cannon atop the citadel. He was more of a danger to himself than to anyone outside the walls. None of the guns had been fired for years. They were tied to their carriages with coils of rope, 'intercepting the sight, and rendering it impossible to point them with any tolerable precision. In place of vents were apertures as large as the palm of a hand, and the chambers were so honeycombed, that it startled me to think how they could stand being fired.'[55] Masson tried a few rounds, but when he realised he was more likely to hit the defenders on the walls than any of Nasir Khan's army, he sensibly decided to leave the Kalat artillerymen to it.

The third night of the siege was clear and cool. Torches were lit all along the walls, casting huge shadows over the town, their 'lights tracing the outline of the ramparts, and encircling the turrets'.[56] Masson could not sleep, and paced back and forth on the terrace of Loveday's house.[57] 'Hours passed; no alarm was given and no foe appeared, when, between two and three o'clock in the morning, the torches burning very dimly, the fire of the garrison having for some time relaxed, the shouts of the sentinels being seldom heard, and the appearance of the town being that of repose after some great exertion, a sudden and violent renewal of firing announced that an attack' was underway.[58] On the western side of town, men were clambering up ladders made from the remains of Loveday's Gothic Revival villa, and hauling themselves over the walls. By the time Loveday's soldiers got there and drove the attackers back, almost fifty men had disappeared into the town.

Just as suddenly as it began, the attack was over, and all was quiet again. In the grey dawn light, Loveday cautiously emerged from his house, surrounded by his soldiers, 'to visit the scene of the achievement'. They hurried through the streets of the town, with Masson following behind, and 'ascended the walls, and cast a glance on the corpses strewed about, and on the broken ladders, some resting still against the walls, and some fallen on the ground'.[59] While Loveday and his men examined the bodies to see if there was anything worth taking, Masson took a long look at the ladders. There was something wrong with them, he realised: not a single one was tall enough to reach the top of the walls, yet dozens of men had somehow managed to climb up into the town.

It did not take him long to get the real story of what had happened. 'The attack had been made in understanding with part of the garrison.'[60] At the appointed time, the attackers had scrambled up the ladders, and, when they reached the top, the men on the walls had untied their lungis and lowered them down like ropes, so that they could climb the rest of the way up. Both sides had been firing blanks: their guns had been loaded with gunpowder, but no bullets. The besiegers had not even been able to scrape together enough gunpowder for a fake battle, so some was discreetly passed down to them beforehand.[61] Masson soon had a good idea why the cannon in the citadel never seemed to do any damage to the besiegers: they were not loaded either, and had been firing blanks for days.[62] This was the most absurd game of soldiers he had ever heard of.

Blissfully unaware that he was in the middle of a piece of amateur theatre, not a war, Loveday wrote with great satisfaction of how he had 'saved the town'.[63] Meanwhile, Masson wondered whether he should prepare for the inevitable. Despite the besiegers having 'neither ammunition nor provisions',[64] and the defences being as secure as ever, he realised that the siege was only going to have one ending. One after another, Nawaz Khan's commanders informed Loveday 'that it was dangerous to continue the defence, and that it was necessary to negotiate. This was strange news. The very notion of further resistance seemed as if, by common consent, to be abandoned; the workmen at the citadel ceased their labour, and all preparations were suspended.'[65] Loveday secretly opened negotiations with Nasir Khan and Gul Mohammad. Unfortunately, his secret negotiations were not very secret, and the whole town soon knew about them. His soldiers muttered about 'treachery'.[66]

The luckless Nawaz Khan tried to persuade Loveday to keep up the fight, or at least to make a run for it with him, while they both could. Loveday 'put his arm around him, in the affectionate familiarity of friendship, affecting to concur in his plans, while at the very time his agents were negotiating with the enemy the subversion of the Khan's authority'.[67] The besiegers, naturally, told Loveday what he wanted to hear: if the town was surrendered, he 'was to do exactly as he pleased; he might go to Quetta or remain at Kalat'. In any event, he was guaranteed 'kind treatment and protection'. And, knowing their audience, they threw in one final promise: 'if he remained, a splendid residence was to be built for him, in place of the one which had been demolished.'[68]

That night, Masson and Loveday argued back and forth until it was almost dawn. Masson tried everything to convince Loveday not to surrender the town: shame, fear, self-respect, and the sheer stupidity of 'submitting to a vanquished foe', but Loveday was unmoved, and 'all arguments I could employ were set aside'.[69] 'He was very angry with me for cautioning him, or presuming to suggest that he was deceived.'[70] Once, in the middle of the night, Loveday 'made a theatrical jump, and exclaimed "I will die!" The resolution vanished as soon the words expressing it had passed his lips.'[71] Masson had no intention of dying, but he was starting to be seriously concerned, 'and wearied myself in conjectures as to what would be the end of the drama'.[72] He felt the long, low rooms of Loveday's house starting to close in around him.

Loveday, meanwhile, made plans to open the gates, and burned his papers.[73] Servants began carrying the Political Officer's pots and pans out of the house as discreetly as possible, 'perhaps, on account of their being, in common with much of his property, the spoil of Mehrab Khan, and bearing his marks on them'.[74] Loveday only laughed when Nawaz Khan warned him, in a final, desperate meeting, that the insurgents 'would plunder me, and probably assassinate me'.[75] 'It was expressly stipulated that I should have free permission to remain here,' he wrote blithely. 'I anticipate no danger to myself or men.'[76] At this, one of Loveday's servants murmured a few lines in Persian:

The wicked man has fallen into his own snare,
And he who devoured men with dogs, will in turn be devoured by dogs.[77]

Loveday overheard him and shot Masson an appalled look. But by then, it was too late.

The gates were opened. Every wall and rooftop surrounding Loveday's mansion was soon 'covered with the insurgents',[78] and 'showers of stones were hurled into it'.[79] Anyone showing their face was likely to get shot at, albeit inaccurately. At this point, there was still a chance to conciliate Nasir Khan and his court. But Loveday's approach involved telling 'the young Khan that he should order one of the men who threw stones into the premises to be blown from a gun, with a view of putting a stop to the practice'.[80] He then sent Nasir Khan a breathtakingly beautiful 'sword-blade, the hilt studded with emeralds and pearls'. Unfortunately, the boy immediately recognised it as his own sword, 'which had been presented to him by his late father on the day of his circumcision'[81] and which Loveday had looted when the British took Kalat. When he realised his mistake, Loveday sat frozen, staring into space. Masson asked him 'whether the soldiers had not better stand to their arms. He said nothing; and I spoke again and again to him to no purpose, when I inquired if I should pass the order, and receiving still no reply, I turned to the havildar [sergeant], who was waiting, and told him to call out the men, and to close the doors.'[82]

At night, Loveday's soldiers started vanishing over the walls, 'and in the morning many others, finding the affair drew near a close, followed the example, first throwing over their effects, and then following them'.[83] Masson awoke to find that the 'servants, horse and camel-keepers had disappeared, and the guards at the gate had gone, taking their effects with them'.[84] He should have slipped away in disguise, as he had a dozen times before. But before he could gather his thoughts, the house was 'filled on every side' with people who 'fell to plunder, and were so intent upon it that they hardly seemed to notice us', breaking open Loveday's strong-boxes, swigging from his bottles, stripping the beds and couches, and 'in the highest glee chasing the fowls, now let loose'.[85] Loveday had emptied the wealth of Kalat into his house. Now it was being emptied out again. Masson made a grab for his papers, but it was too late: in an instant, ten years of his notes and sketches vanished into the hands of the crowd. Everything he owned – books, plates, clothes, coins – was seized and scattered.

Dazed and numb, expecting death at any moment, Masson was marched, with Loveday, through the streets and up into the citadel. They were greeted with drawn swords. All the hate Loveday had built up was now coming down on both of them. Expecting the blow to fall at any moment, Masson was stripped and searched, then shoved up a twisting flight of stairs into a room at the top of the palace. Loveday stumbled in after him. It was a bare, tall space,[86] 'where state-offenders were usually put to death'. It was called the Chamber of Blood.[87]

Masson listened to songs and music drifting up from the town below and realised he had lost everything.

Take my song to the wind-blown Balochi!
You said yourself, in former days,
You said yourself, 'I will kill these folk!'
Now, see the battle spread out around us,
See how the world has become wondrous and sweet!

Now come, we will take India by force.
Perhaps we may be masters of the forts,
Perhaps we may receive the salaams of the bald men.

That day, I smote them as a watermelon from its vine,
I smote their perfumed heads.
Our men smashed their skulls into dust.
That morning I laid them out like corn on the threshing floor.
Some the swift-flowing river took away,
Some the jackals ate in the sand dunes,
Some like lost lambs perished,
Some with their shame went home.[88]

16

The Prisoner

Looking down from the window of the Chamber of Blood, Masson had a bird's-eye view of the crowds emptying out Loveday's house. Fights broke out on the roof over particularly prized objects. 'The floors were all dug up, excavations were made in the cellars, and the walls were minutely searched.'[1] Once the excitement died down, people could be seen making their way up the winding streets of Kalat towards the citadel, carrying their prizes, so that they could quiz Masson and Loveday on 'the use of them'.[2] Unfortunately, Loveday's extensive alcohol collection was now playing a role in proceedings. Two men unwisely cracked open bottles of sulphuric acid and swigged away. Once the rest of the crowd got a good look at the effects, all of Loveday's remaining bottles were sent up to the Chamber of Blood. The prisoners would have plenty to drink, if nothing else. 'We were,' Masson wrote wryly, 'reserved for further scenes and perils.'[3]

Life in the Chamber of Blood was not pleasant. Masson and Loveday were considered the best show in town. The rich and poor of Kalat came to gawp at them, 'to gratify their curiosity and to indulge in the expression of their triumph and resentment'.[4] After a few days, Masson was brought down to see Darogha Gul Mohammad, Nasir Khan's adviser. The Darogha – 'a tall, spare, aged, and harsh-featured man, blind of one eye'[5] – knew exactly what Loveday would have done with him if their positions were reversed. 'The old man prefaced his discourse by the declaration that he never

saw a Feringhi, or even thought of one, that blood was not ready
to gush from his eyes, by reason of the wrongs and injuries he had
endured.' He told Masson 'how Sikander (Sir Alexander Burnes),
in that very room had sworn by Hazrat Isa, or holy Jesus, that no
designs were entertained upon the country'. How that promise had
been kept, they both knew – but for emphasis, Gul Mohammad
'expressed his horror that the corpse of his late master had been
exposed in a mosque, unhonoured and unburied: in like manner,
he pointed to a hole in the apartment, made by a cannon-ball at the
time of the assault'.[6] He was still too angry to see the unfortunate
Political Officer – 'a man, as he said, who had devoured men by his
dogs'.[7] As a parting shot he mentioned what Masson had already
suspected: that one of Loveday's closest advisers had been in his pay
all along.

Everyone in Kalat was wondering when a British army might
appear on the horizon. Gul Mohammad had no desire to end his
days as a fugitive. He told Masson and Loveday to write to Captain
Bean in Quetta, in support of making peace. Loveday spent most
of a day drafting and redrafting his letter. As he wrote, he remarked
to Masson 'that it was now necessary to write the truth; to which
I replied, "You should have always done so." '[8] Loveday still refused
to believe that he was in any danger. 'Whilst the fact can no longer
be disguised that we all are prisoners,' he wrote, 'the reason assigned
for placing us under restraint is to protect us.'[9] Masson left his
letter to the last moment, then, with the messengers waiting, 'took
up a fragment' of paper, and 'wrote in support of Lt. Loveday's
wishes for peace'.[10]

No one knew what to do with Masson. 'That I had innocently
become involved in calamity was almost universally allowed, and
from the first of my confinement, not an hour passed, that I did
not hear remarks made by many to that effect. Even the keepers,
when explaining to newcomers who we were, would always
point me out as free from crime, that is the crimes imputed to
Lt. Loveday, my unfortunate companion, in whose favour no one
raised his voice.' His jailers were a little embarrassed about keeping
him locked up, but showed no signs of letting him go. 'I could

not but be conscious,' Masson wrote, 'that I really had very little chance of being allowed to depart, and had reconciled myself to meet whatever happened as an unavoidable end.'[11]

That end began to seem very close. Masson and Loveday were taken from the Chamber of Blood and marched through the streets of Kalat. Punches, kicks, stones and clods of earth rained down on them from all sides. Men and women, on the rooftops of the houses, shouted and laughed as they were dragged by, 'women spitting upon us and crying "Shame! Shame!" and reviling us for having had the presumption to sit on Nasir Khan's throne'.[12] They were taken, surrounded by guards, to the outlying town of Mastung. That night, a man 'came with a pair of fetters, with which he secured Lt. Loveday's feet to the tent-pole.' 'Neither Lt. Loveday nor myself slept,' Masson wrote. 'He did not speak, nor had I the heart to speak to him.'[13] Loveday, 'who never seemed before to understand his situation, only now understood it'.[14] All night, both of them stared into space, lost in despair. Masson watched the sun come up, expecting that it would be the last dawn he would ever see.

Negotiations with Captain Bean had been disastrous. 'If you are desirous of making peace,' Gul Mohammad had written to him, soon after the capture of Kalat, 'we will gladly accept it, but if not, my respected master will leave this [place] on Friday to come to you, and then we will see to whom God gives the victory.'[15] For reasons best known to himself, Bean thought that the appropriate response was to fling insults. 'The style and idiom of your letter was so bad, and the answers not adapted to the questions put, that I can with difficulty reply to it,' he wrote. 'If you are bringing an army to plunder the suburbs you had better come on Thursday. It is clear as noonday that fortune is on our side.'[16] At this point, Gul Mohammad had begun to wonder if he was dealing with an idiot. 'When we inhabitants of the mountain are unable to comprehend a thing,' he had written, with exasperation, 'it is not to be wondered at, but it is a pity that you, who consider yourself the wisest of the wise, should be so ignorant.'[17] In response, Bean wrote directly 'to the young Khan in the manner in which a master addresses a slave.'[18] 'No-one has gained aught from our government except by submission,' his letter ran. 'If you have your own welfare and the welfare of your people at heart you should agree to the terms proposed.'[19] 'You say in God's name, let the young Khan's army come,' Gul Mohammad replied, on Nasir Khan's behalf, 'but we cried "Bismillah – in God's name" long before you. We cried it when first we came into this country, and we shall again cry "Bismillah – we are coming" and place our trust in the Almighty.'[20]

Meanwhile, in Mastung, Masson and Loveday were kept in a tumbledown building in a garden, 'unused by the owners but as a place for fuel and rubbish, on account of large and troublesome bugs'. Whenever Masson stepped outside, he was 'pelted with stones and clods of earth', while 'on the tops of the walls, and even on the trees in the gardens, spectators were constantly perched'.[21] With each passing day, he was less and less able to hold himself together.

Too late, Loveday realised that he had been out-thought and outmanoeuvred at every turn. 'I am suffering every privation, and with Mr Masson am shut up in a close room, with a guard who never quit me for a moment, whilst at night chains are put on my feet to prevent – so 'tis said – my escape,' he wrote to Bean. 'In consequence of my suffering from heat, insects, want of clothes, I fear my health has become impaired.'[22] For hours on end, Loveday sat motionless and unresponsive, staring at nothing, while 'jeers, execrations, and menaces'[23] rained down from outside. The cruel, power-drunk young man had become a helpless, frightened boy.

To keep themselves awake during the night, the guards 'told tales and sang songs, without any respect to our rest. At length musical instruments were brought, and kept ringing until morning, so that it was impossible to sleep.'[24] In the middle of one particularly awful night, Masson was sent for by Gul Mohammad. 'My head at the time was distracted and I was scarcely in my senses. As I left the apartment, I said to the Darogha's man, that his master had hit upon a good method of getting us out of the way by his cursed music, and the fellow nearly tumbled over with laughter. On seeing the Darogha he said, "Are you well?" and I asked how I could be well when we were not allowed to sleep by day or night, and complained of the music. I told him further that he had better kill us at once than destroy us in so cowardly a manner.'[25] Shouting at heavily armed, nervous men was not wise, Masson knew, but 'I was too enraged to be able to conceal my feelings'.[26]

When he next saw Gul Mohammad, Masson was calmer, and he tried to get Loveday out while he still could, telling the old man to 'appoint Lt. Loveday your envoy, and despatch him to Quetta. He looked amazed; but I continued, that no one would do his business so well; experience had opened his eyes, and he had become so convinced of former errors, that he was prepared to advocate the cause of the Khan.' 'I am in your hands,' Masson said to him. 'Keep me, dismiss Loveday, and if peace be not the result, cut me to pieces.' Gul Mohammad stared at Masson 'for two or three minutes, when, shaking his head, he said, he would not'.[27]

Instead, a decision was made 'to kill both of us, and advance upon Quetta'.[28] The guards began to argue about who would get their clothes, after they were executed. One claimed Masson's battered, filthy lungi, another Loveday's cloak. There was nothing else left to divide up. All Loveday's gold and silver, and all Masson's papers and treasures were gone. 'The people about us seemed to think the resolution final,' Masson wrote. 'All who dropped in also made no secret of the affair.'[29]

Loveday was shaking with fever and fear, 'nearly unmanned'.[30] He scribbled a piteous note to Bean.[31] 'Your letter to the Khan,' he wrote, 'has had the worst effect possible, and from the harshness of its tone has irritated him and his sirdars [commanders] beyond measure. On its contents being made known, the latter assembled and tumultuously demanded that I should be given into their hands and be put to death, as you had paid no attention whatever to their complaints and were purely playing with them, that you had driven them to despair, and that they were compelled to take arms as their last resource, and having no other place of refuge that they would sacrifice themselves in the endeavour to obtain the restoration of their country. And failing in this, they would occupy the hills and passes, cut off all communication, and make constant attacks, so that it would require a large army to hold their country. Such was their declaration, and each sirdar swore by the Quran to fulfil the compact, and never to cease hostility whilst one Englishman remained.'[32]

Masson and Loveday were brought before Gul Mohammad one last time. The old man could barely look at Loveday: he told one of his advisers 'that his blood boiled at the sight of him, as he had fed his dogs on human flesh'.[33] Loveday collapsed onto his knees, and 'placed his hands on the Darogha's feet, saying he was his prisoner, and at his mercy, but craved his protection. I did not think the Darogha was displeased at the act. He said at first, "It is well"; and finally, Lt. Loveday continuing his hands in their position, he said, "Be at ease." '[34]

At dawn, a man came for Masson. Expecting to be led away to his death, he was instead told 'to get ready for Quetta, and Lt. Loveday to prepare a letter for Captain Bean'. Masson thought this had to be a trick, or a cruel joke. 'I was very doubtful whether I should be permitted to leave, and to get ready gave me no trouble, as I had no other clothes than those I wore.'[35] But, to his amazement, Loveday's supplication had worked. Masson was 'led straight through the gardens and put behind another man on horseback' and was soon riding for Quetta as fast as he could. Nasir Khan and his advisers had decided that it was better to negotiate than to fight, and hoped Masson could make peace for them. 'On taking leave of Lt. Loveday I promised to request Captain Bean to go as far as his instructions permitted him. Lt. Loveday said, "Tell him to go beyond them." '[36] They shook hands, and Masson was taken away.

17

The Spy

Masson reached Quetta in the middle of the night. Soon, he was sitting in front of a half-dressed Captain Bean and his assistant, Lieutenant Hammersley, pouring out his story. Bean looked very unhappy to be awake, and even less happy to see Masson. He read through the letter Loveday had sent. 'My dear Bean,' Loveday had written, 'let me earnestly entreat you to pause before you commence a war to which I see no easy termination. Probably this is the last time I may ever write to you, and therefore I feel no hesitation in offering my opinion … After a massive campaign you can only keep the ground on which you are encamped.'[1] As Bean read, the lamps flickered and cast gigantic shadows across the ceiling. He turned the pages, each rustle and crinkle of paper filling the room. Below Bean's house in the citadel, Quetta slept. 'Farewell,' Loveday's letter ended, 'perhaps for the last time, for these people look upon me as their sacrifice.'[2] Bean put down the letter, grunted with displeasure, muttered 'that the situation of Lt. Loveday only excused his manner of writing'[3] and told Masson he was going back to bed.

The next morning, Bean was more awake, but no more agreeable than he had been the night before. He kept Masson standing while he ate breakfast, and 'gave audience much in the same way as a heavy country magistrate in England would to a poacher'.[4] Masson, who had not even been able to change out of his prison rags, soon saw that Gul Mohammad's hunch was correct: Captain Bean was an idiot. Bean desperately wanted to be a sinister spymaster like Wade. Unfortunately, his self-satisfaction was exceeded only by his stupidity. 'I was,' Masson wrote, 'too plainly addressing a weak man, puffed up with absurd conceptions of his official importance, and so uninformed of the nature of things, that it was wasting words to speak to him.'[5]

Bean's arrogance and incompetence had been an open secret in the East India Company for months. Andrew Ross Bell, his superior, had to warn him to stop 'embarrassing' the government.[6] 'Captain Bean, in a letter which I have just received, states that he has been "misled" from the commencement. He has so quickly altered his opinion, however,' Bell complained, 'that I cannot place much dependence on his judgement, particularly as I know his means of information to be defective.'[7]

Bean interrogated Masson on the siege of Kalat and its aftermath, but was remarkably unconcerned about Loveday himself. He was particularly upset by the letter Masson had written to him during his captivity. Masson had been blunt: Mehrab Khan 'was not the guilty man he was supposed to be', the 'attack and consequent pillage of Kalat' was a colossal mistake, and also happened to be contrary to the confidential instructions of Lord Auckland. Mehrab Khan's 'son, amiable and unoffending, should have been seated on his throne'. It was time, Masson had written, to show 'magnanimity to repair our error when it becomes known that one has been committed'.[8] All in all, it was a letter guaranteed to make Bean boil over: a ragged drifter, some no-account coin collector, was lecturing him on policy, and informing him of the private opinions of the Governor General.[9] Even worse, and even more unforgivably, Masson was right.

Breakfast with Bean, however, was a positive delight for Masson compared to what happened next. After a long interrogation, 'Captain Bean finally informed me, that he had been so good as to provide an abode for me while I might remain at Quetta, and he directed a person to show the way to it. I was conducted to the upper apartment of a Hindu's house, and immediately an armed guard of troopers and chaprassis [attendants] was placed over it.

Beyond doubt I was a prisoner, though Captain Bean had not let fall a word to intimate his intention, and I could but smile at the oddness of a man inviting me to breakfast, and then sending me into confinement.'[10]

Masson had not expected a hero's welcome at Quetta, but he had certainly not expected this. His new prison was even less appealing than his old one. When he asked for bedding, the guards cornered an old man in the street, stripped the felt cloak from his back and threw it at Masson. That night, he discovered it was 'filled with vermin'.[11] He lay there shivering with cold, still reeking from his weeks of confinement, feeling the lice and fleas crawling over him, appalled and penniless and alone.

Bean had little interest in keeping his new prisoner alive. 'His first intention seemed to be literally to starve me, and on one occasion I passed two entire days and three nights without food.'[12] Too stubborn to beg the guards for help, Masson sat staring at the wall for hours on end, without so much as a book to pass the time, 'until one of the guard, untold by me, went to Captain Bean and reported it'. Bean then reluctantly sent a few scraps of 'cold mutton'. 'Two or three more days passed, and no more food was sent.'[13] 'I might have fasted longer,' Masson reflected, 'had not one of the guard, unsolicited by me, gone and reported the circumstance' again. Bean then grudgingly promised 'that I should be kept from dying of hunger, and the consequence was, that two cakes of dry bread were brought to me morning and evening from the bazaar. On this fare I subsisted several days.'[14] No one came to visit him.

Weak and traumatised as he was, Masson knew he had to get to the bottom of what was going on. Surely, after all these years, he could not have been locked up as a deserter? Did Bean think he had been up to something nefarious in Kalat? When he and Loveday had been in prison, a letter from Bean had arrived. 'The mystery attached to the presence of Mr Masson at Kalat,' it ran, 'has impressed me with a conviction that that individual's motives for having clandestinely remained there unknown to you must be anything but favourable to our government.'[15] Even Loveday found this ridiculous, and 'was abashed, and also, to do him justice, apparently much hurt, remarking to me, "Poor fellow, your case is a hard one, to be a sharer in my misfortunes, and, at the same time, to be so ungenerously suspected." I consoled him by expressing the opinion that Captain Bean would have addressed his suspicions to those who would treat them with ridicule.'[16] Loveday's last letter ended with a plea to Bean: 'Do not detain Mr Masson – you must relinquish the prejudice you had. I have the fullest confidence in him. Anything I have omitted he will supply.'[17]

'I can assure you,' Masson now wrote to Bean, 'that I had no other reason for coming to Kalat than those that any other indifferent person would have in passing from one place to another, and expecting that you will favour me with an interview that further explanations, if necessary, may be made.'[18] Whatever the misunderstanding was, Masson was sure it could be cleared up in a few minutes. As always, he had overestimated the East India Company.

While Masson was in the Chamber of Blood, Bean had been busy airing his suspicions about him to anyone who would listen. 'Though I have no direct evidence to the fact, I strongly suspect Mr Masson has been intriguing very deeply in that neighbourhood. The fact,' he wrote to Macnaghten in Kabul, 'that Mr Masson had never quitted Kalat, is strong presumptive evidence against the integrity of his motives. And the tenor and tone of the accompanying letter from him, which came with Lt. Loveday's, clearly evince that he is an advocate and supporter of the young Khan's claim to the chiefship of Kalat, and possessions of his father. May I beg the favour of your instructions with regard to the treatment and disposal of this individual, in the event of his hereafter falling into my hands?'[19] Macnaghten was only too happy to play along. 'The facts which you state regarding Mr Masson are very suspicious,' he wrote, despite Bean's letter containing not a single fact, 'and should that individual happen to fall into your hands, you are authorized to detain him.'[20]

A few days later, Bean – looking very pleased with himself – summoned Masson and told him that 'he ought not to be surprised at suspicion being attached to persons travelling in disguise, particularly when he must be fully aware of the Russian intrigues that had been carrying on in this country'.[21] In fact, said Bean 'very gravely', he had recently received a report from another officer, Major Outram, of a mysterious Russian agent. This Russian had an army of several hundred Arab soldiers with him, and had apparently been 'intending to place the son of the late Mehrab Khan on the musnud [throne] of Kalat'.[22] When Bean put this report together with the 'letter from Mr Masson when at Kalat, breathing so strongly the interest he took in the affairs of the young Khan and the rebel sirdars, I could not avoid recording my suspicion of the integrity of the motives Mr Masson appeared under at Kalat'.[23] Masson was taken back to prison, his head spinning. Bean thought that he had caught a Russian spy.

'God forgive the simple man,' Masson reflected. This was, however, no laughing matter. Bean 'seems to have persuaded himself' that Masson was the mysterious Russian, and 'supplies me with a formidable party of Arabs'[24] besides. That left Masson guilty of high treason, with few witnesses who would be inclined to clear his name with the East India Company. Years after his desertion, was payment about to come due? Having escaped the noose once, was he about to be executed?

'It is by no means my wish to give you trouble,' he wrote to Bean, then added, sardonically, 'or at least any unnecessary trouble, but you must excuse me for demanding of you to state [in writing] the charges under which you detain me.' Masson could not believe that Bean had told him the full story. However, he wrote, 'I must know of what I am charged to be able to refute it. I believe I only require of you, what every individual, under suspicion or accusation, has a right to require.'[25] To this, Bean simply replied: 'You are detained here by authority, which authority has been applied to for further instruction.'[26]

Word of Masson's arrest soon reached Kabul, where Alexander Burnes was living in a style very different from Masson's. Every day, his table was laid with 'my champagne, hock, madeira, sherry, port, claret, sauterne, not forgetting a glass of Curaçao and maraschino, and the hermetically-sealed salmon and hotch-potch (veritable hotch-potch, all the way frae Aberdeen)'. At breakfast, British officers descended on his house and consumed vast quantities of 'smoked fish, salmon grills, devils, and jellies, puff away at their cigars till ten'.[27] Harlan, never one to turn his nose up at free food, had been a regular at the breakfast table until he huffed out of Kabul. He would arrive early and dig in, looking all the while like 'the pride and glory of a Tyrolese Pan-pipes band at Vauxhall [Gardens, London's spectacular pleasure garden]'. Between mouthfuls, he introduced himself as a 'free and enlightened citizen of the greatest and most glorious country in the world'.[28] In the past, Burnes had leaped to Masson's defence no matter the reason, even if that meant staring down the Governor General himself. But when he heard of Masson's imprisonment, he did absolutely nothing. Why would Burnes refuse to help now – unless, of course, he thought Bean's suspicions were correct?

A few months before Masson was imprisoned in Quetta, Burnes had been thinking back on the failure of his mission to Kabul. Something about it kept nagging at him, even after his humiliation had been forgotten. The more he pondered, the more he became convinced that Masson had been playing a double game all along. 'Here is a curious anecdote for you; let me have your opinion,' he wrote secretly to a friend. 'A couple of years before our mission arrived at Kabul, Vikevitch (the true Vikevitch) came to Bukhara, called at Rahim Shah's relative's house, and asked him to send letters to Masson at Kabul for Messrs. Allard and Ventura [Ranjit Singh's European mercenaries]. The king of Bukhara took offence at Vikevitch's presence, and the kush-begi [interior minister] sent him off sharp. So the letters were never sent. This shows an earlier intention to intrigue on the part of Russia; but how came Masson not to report this, and if he reported it, how came he to give, years afterwards, twenty-one reasons for Vikevitch not being what he was? I cannot unravel this. I once spoke of this before to you and to no other man.'[29]

Burnes was right: why would Masson fail to report the arrival of a Russian agent at Bukhara? And why, years later, would he claim so loudly that Vikevitch was an imposter when he must have

The British attack on Kalat

The Asiatic Society of Bombay

Sikandar and the talking tree, from the *Shahnameh*

The steamer *Berenice*, which took Masson away from India, leaving Bombay Harbour

William Brydon, sole
survivor of the Kabul
army, reaches India

The Court Room of
London's East India
House, where support for
Masson was cut off

The Reading Room
of the British
Museum in 1840

Guide to the Panorama of Kabul

Explanation of a View of CABUL, the capital of AFFGHANISTAN, now Exhibiting at the PANORAMA, LEICESTER SQUARE

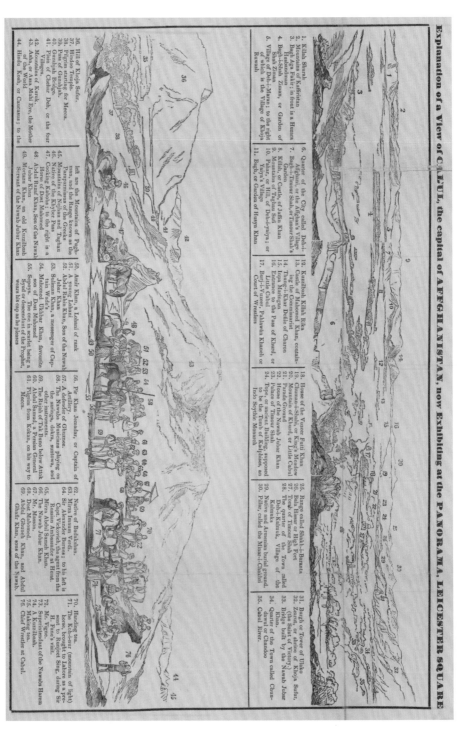

1. Killah Shunk
2. Mountains of Kaffiristan
3. Bagh Aga Fakir: in front is a Huzara
4. Baghaashman
5. Baghaashman Zinan, or Garden of Shah Zinan
6. Village of Deh-i-Meran; to the right of which is the Village of Khoja Ruwah

6. Quarter of the City called Deh-i-Afghani, or the Afghan's Village
7. Bagh-i-Timour Shah, or Timour Shah's Garden
8. Khaun, or Castle of Julin Khan
9. Month, or Castle of Kuful Khan
10. Pahar, or Hill, of Deh-i-yaiya, or Yaiya's Village
11. Bagh, or Garden of Huzyn Khan

12. Kuzelbesh, Killah Rika
13. Castle of Mahomed Khan, containing the Commissariat
14. Thung-i-Khur Defile of Charon
15. Enpa Muringan
16. Little Cabul the Pass of Khord, or Little Cabul
17. Burj-i-Vuzeer, Pahlawin Khaneh or Court of Wrestlers

18. House of the Vuzeer Futti Khan
19. Chumun-i-Shah, or King's Meadow
20. Mountain of Khurd, or Little Cabul
21. Parade Ground
22. House of the Nawab Jubar Khan
23. Palace of Timour Shah
24. Topee, a mound, supposed to be the Tomb of Kaujhuisun, an Indo Scythic Monarch

25. Range called Shikh-i-Busuna
26. Buia Husar or High Fort
27. Tomb of Timour Shah
28. The quarter of the Town called Deh-i-Kalmik, Village of the Kalmuks
29. Native and Armenian burial ground
30. Pillar, called the Minar-i-Chikhri

31. Bargh or Tower of Uluko
32. Zearut, or shrine of Khoja Sufur, (the Saint of Victory)
33. Bridge built by the Nawab Jubar Khan
34. Quarter of the Town called Chundawal or Chandoo
35. Cabul River.

36. Hill of Khoja Sufur
37. Hindoo Temple
38. Pilgrim starting for Mecca
39. Pass of Gurahjik
40. Gurahjik Bridge
41. Pton of Chehir Deh, or the four Villages
42. Mountains of Kurnk
43. Asba, or Awa Mah! Eve, the Mother of the World
44. Hindu Kosh, or Caucasus; to the

left are the Mountains of Pugh-man, and the Range known as the Paropamisus of the Greeks
45. Mountains of Nijbun and Taghun
46. Native of the Khyber Pass
47. Cooking Kabobs; to the right is a tain Wade's
48. Abdul Rul Khan, Son of the Nawab Jubar Khan
49. Mortaza Khan, an old Kuzzilbash Sirdar of the Nawab Jubar Khan

50. Amir Khan, a Lohani of rank
51. A young Lohani
52. Abdul Rahin Khan, Son of the Nawab Jubar Khan
53. Suliman Khan, a messenger of Captain Wade's
54. Mahomed Ukhbar Khan, favourite son of Dost Mahomed
55. Sepoys. The one in saddle being a Syud or descendant of the Prophet, wears his cap as he pleases

56. Pir Khan Jemadar, or Captain of man
57. A defender of Ghuznee
58. The Nawabs Musicians playing on the suringa, dokra, suntoora, and other instruments
59. The Rajah of Fuk Buno below Attuk
60. Hir Samuel, a Persian General
61. Pilgrim from Kokan, on his way to Mecca

62. Native of Budakhian
63. Meer Imam
64. Sir Alexander Burnes; to his left is Capt. Vickovich, the agent from the Russian Ambassador at Herat
65. Mirza Abdul Sameh Khan
66. The Nawab Jubar Khan
67. Mr. Mason
68. Don Mahomed, Khan, and Abdul Ghafir Khan, sons of the Nawab
69. Abdul Ghuneh Khan

70. Handing tea
71. The Koh-i-Nur (mountain of light) the jewel, brought to Lahore as a present to Runjeet Sing, during Sir H. Fane's visit
72. Mr. Vigne
73. Superintendent of the Nawabs Harem
74. Kuzzilbash,
75. Makes
76. Chief Wrestler at Cabul.

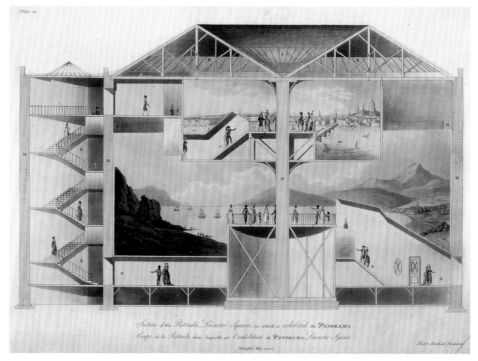

Inside the Panorama, Leicester Square

Masson's only surviving likeness: at the right hand of Dost Mohammad Khan (figures 67 and 68), in the Panorama of Kabul

Josiah Harlan

Joseph Wolff, the
occasionally naked
missionary

Henry Pottinger

Paolo Avitabile

Alexander Burnes, 'the second Alexander'

Dost Mohammad Khan, as painted by Godfrey Vigne

known that to be untrue? The only reasonable explanation, however outlandish, was the one Bean had uncovered in Quetta: Masson had been in the pay of Russia all along.

Years later, historians established how it had happened. In 1833, Johann Martin Honigberger, the Transylvanian treasure hunter, passed through Kabul on his way home to Europe. His road took him straight across Russia. 'Though Honigberger mentions Masson only casually,' concluded Charles Grey and H. L. O. Garrett, 'it appears that the latter accompanied him as far as [the Russian city of] Orenburg.'[30] There, early in 1834, Masson came into contact with Russian officials, Wade's counterparts across the frontier. Even the stupidest Russian intelligence officer could have recruited him, given how much Masson loathed and feared the East India Company. He was a wanted deserter. He had already betrayed the British once, so why would he hesitate to do so again? As a recent biographer of Burnes put it, 'the evidence that Masson was part of the Russian intelligence network seems strong'.[31]

After that, for half a decade, Masson had played a double game in Kabul: feeding the British deliberately misleading information while secretly advancing the interests of his Russian paymasters. His fear in the face of Wade's blackmail and intimidation had been an elaborate act. Instead of being caught in Wade's web, he had caught Wade in his own. For years, he had been working to bring down the East India Company.

The 'definite evidence of Masson's Russian connections'[32] solved puzzles which were otherwise intractable. How else could Burnes have been outmanoeuvred so spectacularly in Kabul, unless his closest adviser was playing for the other side? Why else would a virtuoso traveller, a master of disguise and deception, have been reduced to helpless submission by a self-important bureaucrat like Wade?

Had a ruthless intelligence agent been hiding behind the shy archaeologist all along? Was Masson's search for Alexander just a charade? Vikevitch certainly thought so. 'Masson,' he wrote to St Petersburg, 'lives in Kabul under the pretext of looking for ancient coins.'[33] As Burnes's biographer put it, 'Masson may have been not only a deserter, but a double-agent and traitor'.[34] He had been one step ahead of everyone else all along – but now his secret was out. And, wrote the *Bombay Times*, 'if Mr Masson has for one moment been employed as alleged, no reprobation – no punishment can be too severe for such conduct'.[35]

18

Entrails

There is only one problem with the story of Charles Masson, Russian spy: like many of his own tales about himself, it was not true.

The story stands, unsteadily, on three legs: that Masson met with Russian agents in the frontier town of Orenburg; that he suppressed reports about Vikevitch's visit to Bukhara; and that the rumour about a Russian agent leading an army to Kalat was correct.

Masson never went to Orenburg. Far from travelling there with Honigberger in November 1833, he remained in Kabul until the end of December, then went in the opposite direction.[1] While Honigberger was in Russia, Masson was immersed in excavations hundreds of miles away. Those excavations led to his most spectacular find: the Bimaran Casket.[2] Masson never spent a day of his life in Russia. The first Russian he met was Vikevitch, in Kabul.

Masson did not suppress reports about Vikevitch. 'The Russian gentleman who reached Bukhara was named Ivan Vekterich,' Masson wrote to Wade in June 1836, his spelling leaving something to be desired. 'On arrival at Bukhara, he [Vikevitch] sent for one Nizamuddin, a Kabul merchant, whose name he had learned from M. Honigberger, and told him he should write letters to Messrs. Ventura, Court and myself. For three days he was at large in Bukhara, and went freely about, when it being reported that he took notes, and committed his observations to writing, the Amir directed his seizure, which the kush-begi prevented, by urging that the step would be unwise. He was, however, placed under restraint, all intercourse between him and the townspeople interdicted – and after seven or eight days' stay in the city, was dispatched in charge of an escort of horse.'[3] Masson's report went to the East India Company's Secret Committee in London.[4] Along the way, Burnes heard about it: his account of Vikevitch in Bukhara is too similar to Masson's – from the letter Vikevitch tried to send to Masson in Kabul, to his unceremonious expulsion – for it to be a coincidence. Burnes should have realised that the intelligence came through Masson: the British had no other networks in Bukhara. Instead, he jumped to a conclusion which took considerable chutzpah, even for him: Masson's own report of a Russian agent proved that Masson did not report on Russian agents.

(As for why Masson did not realise that 'the true Vikevitch'[5] was a genuine diplomat, the answer is simple: it was an error of judgement. He thought Vikevitch was a drifter and storyteller, like him. In fact, of course, Vikevitch was the real thing.)

That only left Major Outram's report. But Outram was horrified when he learned of Masson's imprisonment. He wrote a furious letter to Bean, and an apologetic one to Masson, via a mutual acquaintance, Thomas Postans: 'Major Outram desires me at the same time to express to you his great annoyance at your detention at Quetta, in consequence of some misunderstanding on the part of Captain Bean of his (Major Outram's) expressions respecting you, and he begs me to assure you of his being perfectly unconscious of ever having cast the slightest suspicion on your character.'[6]

Masson loathed the East India Company, but he never spied on it. His obsessive, guilt-ridden accounts leave not a rupee of his income unexplained: there is not a drop of Russian gold to be seen amidst his pile of debts. The obsessive, guilt-ridden Russian imperial archives in St Petersburg contain not a word about a British double agent in Kabul. But the best argument against the story of Charles Masson, Russian spy, is also the simplest: Masson hated every moment of his life as a spy. It literally made him sick. He only spied for the British because he believed he had no choice. He would never have given up a second of his excavations to spy for another empire.

Now, in Quetta, watching the shadows move around his prison, listening to the voices and laughter from the street below, Masson's mind wandered back to his first, wild days in Afghanistan. He remembered camping out near the giant Buddhas of Bamiyan, in company with Haji Khan. One dizzying night, he and Haji Khan had sat up late by the fire, with a thousand stars shining over their heads, and told one another their dreams. 'The Khan explained, that he was favoured by visions, and had been instructed in them that he was to become a great man; that the country, whether Afghan or Uzbek, was bi-sahib, or without a master; and he proposed that he and I should benefit by such a state of things, and turn ourselves into padshah [king] and vizier.' That night, Masson, his head spinning, had refused the fearsome Haji Khan with care. 'I forget which of us was to have been the padshah,' he smiled. But, he thought to himself wryly, staring out of the window in Quetta, if he had been trying to start an empire, he would at least have done it properly. 'As I have recently been suspected of being willing to establish a principality at Kalat, by the aid of Arab auxiliaries, justly indignant at the imputation of so paltry a project, I may lament that at this time I did not lend a hand to the vision-seeing Khan, and that I had not revived the old Bactrian empire.'[7]

By now, with no sign of release in sight, Masson was seriously concerned. Gritting his teeth, he composed a letter to Macnaghten, Bean's superior, in Kabul. 'I must crave of you in what mode these unfavourable suspicions have originated, for,' he wrote, 'I still have rights.'[8] Macnaghten blandly informed Masson that he was being detained because he had attempted to travel into Afghanistan 'without permission to do so, either from the British government, or from his Majesty Shah Shujah al-Mulk'.[9] That made no sense: the East India Company did not keep people under armed guard because of potential irregularities in their paperwork. Besides, in all his years of travel, Masson had never asked permission before taking one road or the other. Nor had any of the thousands of merchants, pilgrims and wanderers who criss-crossed northern India and Afghanistan, every year. Burnes himself had invited Masson to Kabul a few months earlier, and had not said a word about asking permission first.[10] Macnaghten's explanation was absurd: clearly he was stalling until Bean had his evidence ready. Bean continued to refer, darkly, to 'whatever causes I may have for suspicion',[11] while refusing to state in writing what those suspicions were. He found it a very convenient way to keep his options open.

There were days when all Masson could feel was regret. Any path he could have taken in the past, it seemed, would have led him to a better place than the one he had chosen.

Then, at his lowest ebb, one of his guards brought in a letter. It was from the last person he had expected to hear from: Colonel Lewis Stacy, the coin-collecting army officer who was one of Masson's most rabid admirers. Stacy's command was attached to the British camp in Quetta. He was waylaid with fever, but had heard a rumour that Masson was in town. 'I hear you have been robbed of everything, but the clothes you wear,' he wrote. 'That must plead my excuse for offering you assistance. I have a tailor, and I dare say could be of use to you otherwise, if you would allow me. I cannot write, the ague has left me quite powerless.'[12] Masson begged pen and paper from the guards and poured out his heart.

It was a shock for Stacy to learn that the man he had looked up to for years was now a penniless prisoner, living on dry bread and sleeping under a lice-ridden cloak. He did not, however, waste a single moment taking Bean's story seriously. 'I have the pleasure to send you a change of linen and a blanket,' he wrote, 'and if you will kindly give me a list of your wants, I will with pleasure assist you if in my power.'[13] Clean clothes. After weeks in his old sweat-stained, filthy rags, Masson pulled them on with inexpressible relief. Still shivering with fever, Stacy staggered over to see Masson. 'I observed your boots torn – excuse my offering such a shabby pair,' he wrote afterwards.[14] 'May I see you walk in with these shoes on.'[15] Stacy also sent him a bundle of newspapers. Opening one, Masson found his own obituary.

'Poor Masson is now known to have been in Kalat at the time of its capture,' the *Bombay Times* wrote. 'Should he have perished, not only a most valuable life will have been lost, but the destruction of the stores of information and the manuscripts he had accumulated through years of indefatigable labour, in reference to the history and customs of this little known region, which have perished with him, may be viewed as a great and irreparable public calamity.'[16]

It was the kindest thing anyone had said about him all year.

The chance to respond to his own obituary was too good to pass up: 'It has not been my destiny to perish,' Masson wrote to the *Bombay Times*. 'It is, however, too true that I have lost all my manuscripts and accumulated stock of literary materials, upon which you have set so high, and possibly, in your favour, an undue value. The loss, such as it may be, is still irreparable to me, and undoubtedly throws some uncertainty over the future, as I find myself suddenly bereft of the greater portion of the results of my labours for some years.'[17]

Stacy, meanwhile, was trying to get Masson fed. 'I mentioned to Lt. Hammersley you had not meat,' he wrote, 'and also requested him to send you a little ink.'[18] Hammersley – nervously self-important at the best of times – did not appreciate that. He made his feelings known by sending Masson 'a platter, much in the manner as a dog would be, with an addition to the bread in the shape of two pice [hundredths of a rupee] worth of sheep's entrails from the bazaar. And when it is considered that this is the food only of the most miserable, the nature of the insult will be imagined.' Looking at the nasty, sludge-coloured heap, Masson almost missed 'the nights I had gone hungry to bed'.[19] It was 'a mess, certainly, which any dog in Quetta might have claimed for his own'.[20] Then he had a slightly wicked idea.

A few minutes later, one of Masson's guards, looking somewhat sheepish, stuck his head into Colonel Stacy's tent, carrying the platter. Stacy took one look at the coiled, slithery intestines, lumps of excrement still clinging to them, gagged, 'shed tears' and murmured, in Hindustani: 'So they want to kill the sahib.' Then he grabbed the platter from the guard, and marched it around the British camp, showing it 'first to the officers in camp, and then to General Nott, after which he took them over to Lt. Hammersley. This officer came running to me.'[21] Panting, Hammersley burst into Masson's room and 'exclaimed, very innocently, "Good God!

Why did you send that mess to Colonel Stacy? Why did you not send it to me?" '²² 'I thought I had no occasion to,' replied Masson. Hammersley 'said that such things were disgraceful. I answered, I should think so.'²³

When the Indian newspapers learned why Masson had been locked up in Quetta, no one could believe their ears. 'Masson,' wrote one journalist, 'has, we observe, ample leisure just now for adjusting his notes, being under detention by Captain Bean, for – you may well smile, gentle reader! – engaging in political intrigues against the British government! Don Quixote's mistaking a kitchen wench for a Duchess is not more absurd than this, nor the trick upon which a play or a farce turns, more ridiculous. Mr Masson is a pure savant, he has sought poverty, danger and obscurity in the pursuit of his favourite researches; no act of his career, as far as it has transpired, shows him either desirous of wealth or distinction, but singularly inattentive to both. But even had he the disposition, he has not the means to work out political intrigues. The idea of a poor man like Masson, unfriended and alone, who has spent years in a humble and dangerous search of old coins, turning traitor, and leading a body of Russians to the relief of Kalat, is one, we believe, which could have entered no head, but that which rules the destinies of Quetta [Bean].'²⁴

Captain Bean, much to his chagrin, swiftly became a national joke. The idea that he should tremble in fear, lest a mild-mannered archaeologist 'pull his 200 Russians from out his breeches pocket, seize the treasure, and hoist the twin eagle of Muscovy over the Union Jack' seemed, to the Indian press, downright hilarious.²⁵ 'Mr Masson's character,' as one writer pointed out, 'was not a doubtful or unknown one.'²⁶ The man currently under arrest for spying on the East India Company was the Company's choice for head of Afghan intelligence, one 'whose genius was admired, and his acquaintance coveted by everyone'.²⁷

It was a rare occasion where India's newspapers agreed on anything, but they agreed on this: when it came to Masson's case, 'a more monstrously one-sided one it never was our lot to see'.²⁸ It 'has been discussed by the newspaper press in every part of India, and the idea that one particle of well-grounded suspicion can, for a moment, justly attach to his character, has been universally and contemptuously scorned'.[29] 'The Delhi and Agra papers make you the lion of the day,' Stacy wrote to Masson.[30]

Bean, now well established as a national joke, was soon on his way to becoming a worldwide one. Masson's accusers, the *Bombay Times* wrote, 'have worked out, after a fashion, celebrity for themselves, which by other means, or with a less happy selection of the object of oppression, they might have failed to secure. How the members of the Institute of France will scorn the system which could advance men to places of authority, who could thus suffer themselves to be led astray. How the students in Petersburg will scoff; how the learned in Germany, who have filled volumes with disquisitions on the discoveries of Masson, will deride.'[31]

All this was very satisfactory to Masson, but it did not change the fact that he was still locked up. Days turned into weeks, and weeks turned into months. Guards were 'stationed over me day and night. The orders given to them I am not aware of, for I take no pains to learn, but among them I know are those of reporting to Captain Bean what persons come to visit me, and when I send a letter to the dak [post] or to anyone, of bringing it to the same worthy official, that he may note to whom it is addressed.'[32] Bean and Macnaghten kept fishing for anything to support their suspicions, instructing the East India Company's clerks in Bombay to root through their archives for evidence to incriminate Masson.[33] 'It was with much disgust,' Masson wrote, 'I found myself doomed to exist for an indefinite period, in captivity, with the political agent of Quetta as my jailer.'[34]

19

Frontiers

Snow began to fall on the mountains that loomed over Quetta. It was early November 1840, and Masson shivered in his 'rank smelling'[1] prison, barely holding back his tears. Once, he had been able to weave his stories through the world, and make it his own. Now, he was tangled up in other people's lies: try as he might, he could not find a way out. Charles Masson had been created by stories. Now he was being destroyed by them.

On 3 November, Kalat awoke to find a British army bearing down on the town. Inside the walls, people buried the few valuables they had left and prayed that they would live through the day. Then something strange happened. The British did not attack. Instead, the commanders, Stacy and General Nott, 'sent in proclamations, assuring the inhabitants that if they remained quietly in their houses, their persons and property should be protected, that no plunder or violence should occur, and that every article should be paid for'.[2] After a few hours of negotiation, the gates were opened, and Kalat was captured without a shot being fired. The quiet, scholarly Stacy had always been scorned by his fellow officers. 'It was supposed that his military talents were of an indifferent order. Opportunity established the reverse.'[3]

From his prison in Quetta, Masson had planned the whole campaign. To Masson, Stacy wrote in his report, 'I consider I owe much of the success which has attended my exertions.'[4]

After he had secured the town, Stacy set to work recovering Masson's lost papers. By nightfall, he had already tracked down one of his friend's notebooks. 'I have put it by carefully,' he wrote. 'I will do all I can to ferret out the books.'[5]

Loveday had been killed by his guards a few days earlier. He was found by the British 'naked save a pair of drawers', an emaciated wreck, his almost severed head lolling from his neck.[6] Memories of his reign still hung over Kalat like a nightmare. 'Every mouth,' Stacy told Masson, 'is filled with his abuse of power.'[7] At least two people had died from 'the wounds or bites of his dog'.[8] One of Loveday's other amusements had been to invite the most influential men of Kalat to his house, welcome them warmly, then grab them by their beards and drag them from room to room, giggling all the while.[9]

The East India Company had a long history of atrocities, and an equally long history of hushing them up. 'If you had seen as much of public life behind the scenes as I have done since becoming a quill driver,' Jephson had once written to Masson, 'you would be still more surprised at the want of principle amongst men of education, and pretensions to high and honourable feelings.'[10] But Stacy and Nott did not quash the stories about Loveday. Their reports spelled out his monstrous record in lurid detail.[11] In Calcutta, no one could decide which was worse: Loveday's cruelty, or the fact that it was now widely known. 'His Lordship,' wrote Thomas Maddock, Secretary to the Government of India, 'is most anxious.'[12]

The East India Company tried to get ahead of the stories by spreading a rumour 'amongst newspaper conductors and government functionaries that Loveday was insane and that there is a predisposition to insanity in the family'.[13] Macnaghten, swift to cover his own back, was soon eager to tell anyone who would listen that 'I had always heard that the chief defect in the deceased officer's [Loveday's] character was an excessive partiality to the natives of the country, and if the allegations of Colonel Stacy are well founded, I should be led to apprehend that the ill-fated officer's intellect must have been disordered for some time previous to his death.'[14] 'The story,' Jephson wrote to a friend, 'has been got up in anticipation of Masson's exposé of the management of affairs at Kalat – and the death of the two men who were worried by Loveday's dogs.'[15]

Masson pleaded for permission to go back to Kalat to look for his papers. He would be surrounded by a British army, and in the middle of the desert: there was no danger of him escaping. Bean refused point-blank. Stacy could not understand it. 'Are they afraid,' he wrote, 'you would bribe your guards, raise an army of Arabs and seize the principality of Kalat? 'Tis strange!'[16] One scrap at a time, he was reassembling Masson's papers. But much of his friend's work seemed to be lost for ever. Stacy broke the news as gently as he could. 'I fear your books are gone – at any rate for a time,' he wrote. 'I have left promises of reward and friendship to whomsoever shall bring them to you or me.'[17]

The threads that held Masson's hopes together were fraying and breaking. By now, very few were left.

It was now deep winter, almost Christmas. Masson wondered, desperately, how many more seasons he would have to see from inside his prison. He still had no idea what he was charged with: was it being a Russian spy, or travelling without the correct papers, or something else entirely? His guards huddled outside the door and continued to take all his letters straight to Bean. The one piece of good news was that his case had been turned over to Andrew Ross Bell, Bean's superior, to investigate. Bell wrote to Masson with silky formality, asking him 'whether you placed the enemy of the British government in possession of any information which could be useful to them in the offensive operations which they were carrying on, or which could have induced them to treat Lt. Loveday, then their prisoner, with increased rigour'. 'I would point out to you,' his letter continued, menacingly, 'how important the question above referred to is to your own character as a loyal subject of the British government.'[18] Stacy, back in Quetta, visited Masson daily and helped him pen his defence. He also tried to keep Masson warm. 'I send you a bit of broadcloth,' he wrote. 'I am sorry I have no better – but I only thought of the cold.'[19]

Stacy was determined to clear his friend's name. 'Will you kindly give me a copy of the memoir you wrote on the back of a book, which

I read in your prison house?' he wrote to Masson. 'It is too forcible to be thrown away.'[20] 'I feel ashamed to think of the disrespect heaped upon Mr Masson so wantonly,' he wrote to Bell. 'He has been most miserably treated.'[21] 'I have spoken as I know you would have done for me,' he wrote to Masson. 'I have asked no favour, but fair play.'[22] Privately, Stacy was sure that 'Bean and Hammersley are now both convinced of the mistake, on which Mr Masson has not only suffered detention but the most disgusting imprisonment'[23] and were trying to wriggle out of responsibility for it.

Masson spent Christmas alone, watched over by his guards.[24] 'I only wish you could exchange your prison for a seat by my fire,' Stacy wrote to him from Kalat. Masson's friends in Kalat, even the men who had guarded him in the Chamber of Blood, could not believe he had been locked up again. One asked Stacy 'to release you – poor fellow, I told him that it was not in my power – but they could not detain you for ever. I think I have a scent of your books.'[25] The people of Kalat were starving and Bean refused to help Stacy buy food.[26] 'I am not prepared to send any,' he wrote, 'nor would such disbursement be warranted under present circumstances, nor do I recognize anyone in charge there.'[27] It was enough to make Stacy despair. 'I am not half up to these people,' he wrote to Masson. 'I wish you were here.'[28]

Bean, finally obliged to put his evidence down on paper, spent the new year sweating. Having lost control of his district so comprehensively a few months earlier, he was already in hot water.[29] 'That fool Bean,' went the whispers in Calcutta, 'has already done Mr Masson all the injury he possibly could and seems mightily vexed at the turn which the affair has at last taken.'[30]

Deprived of any other outlet, Masson had discovered a taste for long letters to the newspapers: sad, sardonic epistles, which 'gibbetted'[31] the East India Company. 'I am determined,' he seethed to the *Bombay Times*, 'to the extent of my power, to resent the insolence and villainy which have emboldened bad or foolish men to entertain suspicions of my honour and honesty.'[32] Stacy tried, in vain, to turn the temperature down. 'I think every fact might be introduced and all angry expressions avoided,' he wrote to Masson.

'It may be difficult to speak of your imprisonment and its style without painful feelings, still to give way to them in words would not better your case.'[33]

Finally, after keeping Masson locked up for months, after the platter of sheep guts and the flea-infested bedding, Bean reluctantly admitted that 'nothing further had transpired by which the disloyalty of Mr Masson as a British subject could be established'.[34] There was, in other words, no case for Masson to answer. 'Let anyone read Captain Bean's letter,' wrote the *Bombay Times*, 'and if he can conscientiously aver that a more unsatisfactory or unbusinesslike public document ever met his eye, his experience in the imbecilities of diplomacy must be more than usually extensive.'[35]

Masson had been an inconvenience to the East India Company from the moment he appeared in Quetta. As more and more newspapers took up his story, he was rapidly turning into a threat.[36] A secretary in Calcutta murmured suspiciously to Jephson that 'you [Masson] once remarked that "you would not be anybody's servant"'.[37] Even in prison, Masson's intelligence network did not fail him. Embarrassing facts about Bean started appearing in the press. 'The grain contractor at Quetta,' Masson reported, 'a bankrupt when taken under Captain Bean's wing, was notoriously known to have discharged all his prior debts and to have netted above three lakhs [300,000] of rupees.'[38] Half of India was soon gossiping about Bean's incompetence. The idea of Masson wandering around Afghanistan, asking awkward questions and writing awkward letters, was positively horrifying. Even if he was cleared of all charges, 'it will be advantageous, even for himself,' the Company's Court of Directors in London wrote, 'that he should be removed, for the present at least, within our frontiers, without any constraint or appearance of punishment'.[39] 'This individual is I believe much discontented, however unreasonably, with the treatment he has received at the hands of the British government,' Macnaghten wrote, separately, 'and I would submit for consideration of His Lordship in Council whether it would not be prudent to prevent the possibility of mischief that he should be interdicted from travelling.'[40]

Bell interviewed every single eyewitness to the siege of Kalat he could find, from Nawaz Khan to Loveday's servants. 'All,' Bell wrote in his report, 'agree in their accounts as to Mr Masson's statement being perfectly correct, and absolve him from having been in the slightest degree connected with any political event which occurred in Kalat, further than his having been made prisoner along with Lt. Loveday and eventually released for the purpose of carrying letters.'[41] 'I consider you entirely freed from the suspicion,' Bell wrote to Masson. 'I regret that any misapprehension should have caused you to be so long detained.'[42]

'Should you not require the further attendance of the chaprassis who are with you,' Hammersley wrote, as if Masson had been placed under guard by his own request, 'I am desired to withdraw them.'[43] From Bean, there was complete silence. He was a great believer in delegation.

Masson was free.

But the world he walked out into was very different. It had boundaries and frontiers, places he could not go. Afghanistan was barred to him. The horizon was not so wide, or so open, any more.

Masson left Quetta on foot, penniless, carrying his few remaining books with him. 'So entirely had the country been devastated,' he wrote, 'that I could no longer recognize it to be the same I traversed some fourteen years before. Villages, then flourishing, had ceased to exist; those remaining were destitute of their attendant groves of trees, and even the very waste had been denuded of the jungle of small trees and shrubs, once spreading over its surface. There was no fear, indeed, of losing the road, as formerly, for that was now well marked by the skeletons of camels and other animals, whose bleached and bleaching bones too well described it.'[44]

Masson trudged down the road of bones. Occasionally, he looked back over his shoulder, 'paralyzed',[45] watching Quetta and the mountain passes to Afghanistan slowly sinking into the horizon. Alexander had slipped through his fingers again.

'There was one good thing in the world,' runs a riddle, much told among the people of Kalat and Quetta. 'An enemy has pursued it and driven it out. In the morning light, it passed along the road. Now, neither prayers nor entreaties will bring it back.'

The enemy is time.

The good thing which has been driven from the world, never to return, is hope.[46]

20

The Man Who Would be King

On 9 March 1841, towards the end of the afternoon, a strange-looking figure began to climb the steps of the Asiatic Society of Bombay. His head was shaved and wrapped in a turban. His clothes were uncertain: Turkish, some thought.[1] People stopped to stare as Masson passed through the white Doric columns and into the hushed cool of the Society's monstrous neoclassical building, which loomed over Bombay harbour.

Masson quickly realised that behind the grand façade, little more than dust and gossip hung in the air. 'The Society has indeed possessed a room in which are shelves, upon which have been placed a few mummies, two or three bottled snakes, and a Hindu god or so,' sighed the *Bombay Times*. 'It need excite no wonder that museums in London, Calcutta, and perhaps many a county museum in England or Scotland can supply more information on the products, antiquities, and natural history of western India than its own capital.'[2] By the time Masson emerged into the evening air, having sat through some exquisitely dull bureaucratic discussion, and been shown around the room of battered bottled snakes, he felt as if he too had been pickled and stuffed in a jar.

Sunset turns Bombay golden. For a moment, the sweat and strain of the day fade away, the ocean breeze blows cool and clear and the city fills with laughter and possibility. While Masson feigned polite interest in the Asiatic Society's decaying mummies, Bombay's Parsi community gathered a few blocks away on Marine

Drive, as the sun began to sink beneath the waves. They were dressed all in white, 'riding, driving, walking, and sitting on the grass or on the sea-shore'.³ The Parsis had arrived in India from Persia over a thousand years earlier. They brought with them stories about Alexander: fearful tales, legends of a violent, ruthless king, who brought nothing but death and destruction in his wake.⁴ For the Parsi community and their fellow Zoroastrians, Alexander was evil incarnate. He did not care how many bodies he had to climb over, as long as he could follow his dreams.

Even Greek and Roman authors knew that Alexander did terrible things. He razed the city of Thebes to the ground, leaving it a smoking ruin with only a single house standing. After the capture of Tyre, he massacred all the men of military age and sold the women and children into slavery. 'If you wonder how great the bloodshed was,' wrote Quintus Curtius Rufus, 'consider this: six thousand warriors were trapped and slaughtered inside the city. Then Alexander's army had to witness the true, mad anger of their king. Two thousand Tyrians had survived the blood-lust of the exhausted Macedonians. Two thousand Tyrians now writhed and died, nailed to crosses all along the vast empty beach.'⁵ The same thing happened at Gaza: all the men of military age were killed, and the women and children were sold into slavery. The Persian governor of Gaza, Batis, refused to plead for his life, even when he saw everyone around him fall. 'I shall,' Alexander said, 'make him speak – or at least make him scream.'⁶ So Batis was held down, and holes were bored through his ankles. Strips of leather were looped through the holes, and Batis, still living, was tied to the back of Alexander's chariot. 'Then Alexander's horses dragged Batis around and around the walls of Gaza. Alexander could not have been happier: he had punished his enemy in the same way as Achilles once had.'⁷ When Achilles dragged Hector around the walls of Troy in the *Iliad*, there was one important difference: Hector was already dead.

For the Zoroastrians, Alexander's story was defined by one atrocity, above all. The great city of Persepolis, capital of the Persian Empire, lay on a windblown plateau at the foot of the Mountains of Mercy. No hostile army had ever seen it, or dared to dream of capturing it. For generations, the wealth of the vast Persian Empire had flowed into Persepolis. 'The sun,' wrote the Greek historian Diodorus, 'never shone on a richer city.'[8] Alexander captured it, looted it and burned the royal palace, the ceremonial heart of the empire, to the ground.

Zoroastrian legend had it that their religion's sacred texts were stored in the palace library at Persepolis. And the library was lost to Alexander's fire. 'Our religion spread across the world for three hundred years. Then Evil tempted Alexander the Accursed,' ran the Zoroastrian tale. 'The Fortress of Archives kept safe our religion, our tradition and our sacred texts, written on ox-hides in golden ink. The enemy, the evil-doer, the unbeliever, Alexander the Accursed, stole them, and burnt them … And so the tradition was shattered, and doubt, and uncertainty and disagreement came into the world.'[9]

Many British historians celebrated the burning of Persepolis. Sir Mortimer Wheeler stood in its ruins and called Alexander's fire 'a beacon in the history of Asia'.[10] 'To trace the sequel of Persepolis,' he wrote, 'is to explore two of Alexander's greatest achievements: the systematic civilization of the wild eastern regions of the old Persian Empire; and the resultant creation of a civilized continuum through a multitude of nations and cultures from the Mediterranean to the Ganges. That continuum has never been completely broken.'[11] When archaeologists came to excavate Persepolis, they found that the palace floor was covered by a layer of ash three feet deep. This was the 'civilized continuum' of Alexander: fire and ruin.

Two thousand years after Alexander's sack of Persepolis, the Parsis of Bombay are still telling stories of that day. For generations, they have seen the shadows behind Alexander's greatness, even when others did not. 'Go to bed,' a Parsi bedtime story runs, 'or Alexander will get you.'

***

In Kabul, 'the second Alexander' was ill at ease. Burnes knew that the British occupation was not going well. 'I ought never to have come here, or allowed myself to be pleased with fair though false words,'[12] he wrote. 'It appears to have been his mission in

Afghanistan to draw a large salary every month, and to give advice that was never taken,' wrote the historian John Kaye. 'This might have satisfied many men. It did not satisfy Burnes. He said that he wanted responsibility; and under Macnaghten he had none.'[13] Burnes feared that Shah Shujah's rule was faltering, but no one cared to listen to him. 'If they really wanted truth, I would give it cordially, but it is a chiming-in, a coincidence of views which they seek; and I can go a good way, but my conscience has not so much stretch as to approve of this dynasty. But, mum – let that be between ourselves.'[14] 'Be silent,' he said to himself, 'pocket your pay, do nothing but what you are ordered, and you will give high satisfaction. They will sacrifice you and me, or anyone, without caring a straw.'[15]

For over a year, Masson had been waiting for news about his book. In his darkest moments, those pages, which he had parcelled up so carefully in early 1840 and sent off to London with Pottinger, had given him hope. 'On them I must depend, for the means of continuing my travels,' he reflected.[16] Pottinger had assured him that the publisher John Murray would take him under his wing. 'It would be of the first consequence to me, to be on such an understanding with so eminent a publisher as Mr Murray,' Masson had replied, 'that I might be confident that my future papers, on transmission to England would be received by him, while from his known high character I could feel assured he would do as justly by me, as if I were present to advocate my own interests.'[17] Murray had made Burnes a fortune a few years earlier, and, with even a fraction of those resources, Masson could return to Afghanistan and pick up Alexander's trail again.

Masson's manuscript arrived in Murray's office on 11 July 1840,[18] carrying his hopes with it. Murray sat on it for months, then rejected it.[19]

Masson had written a hair-raising, mud-slinging attack on the invasion of Afghanistan and the men behind it. With the occupation seemingly successful, neither Murray nor Pottinger thought there was a market for an angry anti-war book.[20] When Murray's rejection finally arrived in early 1841, Pottinger wrote that it would devastate

Masson, 'though I think my communication will in some degree have prepared him for it, as I have, from the first, pointed out to him that the style and contents of the greater portion of his book are ill suited to the taste of the reading public of this country'.[21] At the height of Britain's obsession with Afghanistan, Murray had silenced one of the fiercest critics of the war.

Masson knew nothing about any of this until he reached Bombay. There, instead of the handsome sum of money and freshly printed books he had hoped would be waiting for him, he found a rejection letter instead. 'No one of the respectable booksellers in England will publish any work (on their own risk) animadverting on public men or measures,' he was told. 'They justly say, that that is the duty of the daily press, and that such criticisms are quite out of place in books of travels.'[22]

Masson had spent more time in Afghanistan than everyone else in Britain combined, but he had no way to make his voice heard. Stacy urged him not to wait a moment longer, and work with the first publisher he could find in Bombay. 'This delay in publishing your papers robs them of half their value – still I hope they will appear. I would have printed them in Bombay – I mean your detention by the Brahuis and imprisonment by the English – fed on bazaar bread and sheep's entrails!!!!!'[23]

Whispers about him seemed to be everywhere.[24] 'Bell's report is just come in,' wrote one East India Company official, 'fully acquitting Masson – declaring that no ground of suspicion ever existed against him and recommending he be remunerated for the trouble and annoyance to which he has been so unjustly subjected.'[25]

Whenever he could, Masson slipped away from Bombay's British community. Wrapping a turban around his head, he would take a boat across the harbour, away from the pale buildings and tended lawns of the colonial city, to the wild green hills of Elephanta Island. He scrambled up the slopes, through woods of tamarind and palm, past troops of brazen monkeys, to his refuge: the ancient Hindu cave temples which crowned Elephanta's summit.

Elephanta's temples are one of the wonders of India. Inside the caves, it takes a moment for your eyes to adjust to the darkness.

Then its treasures come into focus around you: sculptures of Shiva carved out of the rock walls of the caves, looking so alive that they seem to have been completed only yesterday, yet dating from 1,500 years ago, when Justinian still reigned over the Roman Empire from Constantinople. (The carved stone elephant which gave Elephanta its name has now been hauled across the water to a museum, where it silently presents its backside to a headless statue of Lord Cornwallis.) Masson would sit in the caves for hours on end, sketching and dreaming. Colonial Bombay, with its cricket pitches and ballrooms, was built to ease nostalgia for Britain. But Masson was trying to ease a very different kind of nostalgia: for the world the East India Company called 'foreign and uncivilized',[26] and he called home.

Masson felt profoundly lost and alone. He had no idea what the future held for him. He had barely a rupee to his name and Afghanistan was closed to him. 'I was lowly – I wished to be high,' he scribbled sadly, one day. 'I found that my object was vain. I lamented the loss of content. And I wished to be lowly again.'[27] Ten years ago, he had set out in pursuit of Alexander. His quest had cost him everything.

For the Greeks, pursuing your wildest dreams meant risking everything. Pothos was not just your deepest desire. It was also your most dangerous one. Alexander's pothos destroyed him. At the age of thirty-two, the lord of the world died a broken man in Babylon. Now, Masson wondered if his dreams had consumed him, too.

In Kalat, Stacy was still hunting for Masson's lost papers. The peace was increasingly fragile: Nasir Khan was a fugitive and the East India Company was growing impatient. 'Between you and I,' Stacy wrote to Masson, 'I shall go to the poor boy all alone.'[28] At the end of June, in defiance of his orders, half-expecting a bullet in the head at any moment, Stacy rode into the village where Nasir Khan was taking shelter. 'We do not distrust you,' one of Nasir Khan's attendants said to Stacy, after they were finally persuaded that a British army was not hiding over the horizon. 'You have left a comfortable house and your friends, and come amongst us in rain and cold to suffer privations like ourselves. You have come amongst us alone without a single sepoy – we therefore feel you are an honest man and our friend.'[29] When Stacy was alone with the heir of Kalat, Nasir Khan, exhausted and grief-stricken, broke down and 'gave vent to his tears'.[30]

A few days later, Nasir Khan set out for Kalat, alone. 'When he was on his horse they [his attendants] seized the bridle and said – go anywhere but to the Feringhis. But it would not do. He told them,' Stacy wrote to Masson, ' "I shall go direct to Kalat. If the Colonel kills me – Kabul (be it so) – if he imprisons me – Kabul – if he puts me on my father's throne – Kabul – I go to my fate." '[31]

Later, when it was all over, and Nasir Khan was on his father's throne, an old grey-bearded warrior took Stacy aside. 'If you had not sent for the Khan,' he told him, 'we should have all gone to our hills, and as we could not fight you on equal terms, we resolved to stop all the daks [couriers], attack all convoys and annoy your camps in every way – not a sepoy at Kalat should have shit outside the gates.'[32]

'Now the Khan is come,' the people of Kalat said to one another, 'Masson sahib will return.'[33] At least, that was what Stacy told Masson. The hint was no more subtle than the Himalayas. Stacy knew where the credit for his success lay. 'Let me thank you for your kind advice,' he wrote to Masson. 'I am grateful for it, and you must be gratified that, acting on it, I have accomplished what the world said was impossible.'[34] He thought that it was time his friend stepped out into the limelight. 'If they should appoint me to Kalat,' he wrote, 'will you "take office" under me? May I ask government to appoint you? On what terms? What salary?'[35] 'It would be poor pay – poor remuneration – but you would be amongst friends, and I hope happy with me.'[36]

From Bombay, there was no answer. Stacy's letters – increasingly anxious and puzzled – had been piling up for months. 'How long will you remain silent?' he wrote to Masson. 'All your friends here are most anxious you should return to them. Never a day passes but they ask news of you – pray write.'[37] 'Are you in the same blessed state of uncertainty that I am,' he tried again, weeks later, 'that you have never written to me? God knows if this will find you in

Bombay. If it should let me beg of you to write and let me know your present intentions.'[38] But Masson could not bring himself to reply.

He was sinking ever more deeply into depression. His claims against the East India Company had gone nowhere. 'Month after month passed and no notice whatever was taken',[39] then he was finally, stuffily, told that 'any person who without a proper passport, and credentials, thinks fit to risk his own safety in foreign and uncivilized countries must abide by the chances ... of his own unauthorised and imprudent proceedings'.[40] No money would be arriving from London. His misadventures in Kalat had left him destitute, and destitute he remained. Without funds, further excavations were impossible: even if he managed to reach Afghanistan on foot, how could he make any progress without the means to buy a shovel, or pen and paper, or a roof to cover his head? He felt 'paralyzed'.[41]

Each day reminded Masson, in a dozen heart-breaking ways, how little power he had.[42] He saw only one chance to reclaim his story. It lay half a world away, in London. There, he might find a publisher who would take a chance on his work. And there, he might have a chance of shaming the East India Company into covering at least some of his losses in Kalat.[43] 'I feel assured that the Court [of Directors of the Company] will, if you choose to seek for it, render you the fullest compensation,' Jephson wrote to him. 'Now don't forget this, nor allow the fruits of your long labours to be lost through the freaks of a madman and a fool.'[44]

Since he could not afford a voyage to Britain by sea, Masson made plans to set off by land, despite being in no condition to attempt the impossibly long and arduous journey. One of his few remaining friends in government interceded and found him a berth on one of the East India Company's ships. 'I should myself be disposed to extend further aid to this enterprising traveller,' his friend wrote, 'but I fear we could not do this.'[45] Masson was only told about this plan a few days before his ship was due to sail. Through gritted teeth, he was 'grateful'[46] one last time.

After two decades in India, he now had a week to say his farewells.

Masson had almost nothing to pack. He would be leaving India with little more than when he first arrived as Private James Lewis, stumbling off the *Duchess of Athol* onto the docks in 1822.

In Kabul, Macnaghten was packing, too. He was being shuffled off to Bombay, and Burnes had been appointed his successor. Much of the occupying army had orders to return to India as well. 'Supreme at last,' Burnes gloated. 'I fear, however, that I shall be confirmed as Resident, and not as Envoy, which is a bore; but as long as I have power and drive the coach, I do not much care.'[47] In his excitement, his doubts and fears were quite forgotten.

Even hundreds of miles away in Bombay, Masson could see that things were going wrong in Afghanistan. A few days before his ship was due to leave, he and the editor of the *Bombay Times*, George Buist, tried to make sense of the latest reports. Masson 'pointed out to Dr Buist the improbability that Burnes could remain at Kabul without troops – and how assured I was that he would find reasons, in spite of all he had said, to detain them. I even asserted that it would surprise me if he would be tolerated in Kabul with troops.' Rumours of a coming uprising against the British were everywhere, and Masson said to Buist that 'if such an event should take place, he might take my word that it would lead to the ruin of the force'.[48]

Masson had no way of knowing it, but the uprising was already breaking out. At its head was his old friend and supporter, Dost Mohammad's son, Akbar Khan. Once, Masson and Akbar Khan had taken tea in the palace of Kabul, and told one another stories. High above the city, they had slipped into the past together, turning over one find after another from Bagram, delighting in the quiet beauty of this or that finely sculpted piece. Now, Akbar Khan meant to take his country back from the East India Company:

If you have one true story left in you,
Pull up a seat for yourself,
And tell the tale.
Tell us of the battles of the young lion.
Tell of Akbar the hero,
Who smashed the foreigners to dust.[49]

On 1 November 1841, the East India Company's steamer *Berenice* prepared to leave Bombay. The last packets of mail were hurried aboard, the boilers stoked with coal, the ropes cast off, and the two huge paddle wheels began to turn. Masson watched the land fall away behind him. The fort and dockyards. The long curve of Marine Drive. The tomb of Pir Haji Ali Shah, perched on an island, the waves breaking over the long, impossibly thin causeway which connected it to the mainland. (Haji Ali's tomb, now augmented by the Haji Ali Juice Centre, still bids farewell to travellers speeding north to the airport.) The Towers of Silence, where generations of Bombay's Parsis have left their dead, to be taken by the wind and sun and vultures, returning their elements to the earth in a final act of charity.

Masson feared that his story would soon be over. There were just a few lines left. 'Repress your desires and know,' he wrote, 'The bliss you seek through them is vain. He is happy who thinks himself so. Go home and be lowly again.'[50]

In Kabul, 'the second Alexander' was preparing for the glorious culmination of his own story. Yet, in spite of himself, Burnes was uneasy. 'I have been asking myself,' he wrote, 'if I am altogether so well fitted for the supreme control here as I am disposed to believe. I sometimes think not, but I have never found myself fail in power when unshackled. On one point I am, however, fully convinced, I am unfit for the second place.'[51] That evening, as Masson's steamer was leaving the coast behind, Burnes met with his old friend the Indian scholar Mohan Lal, who warned him that anger against the British was growing dangerously strong. Burnes 'stood up from his chair, sighed, and said he knows nothing, but the time has arrived that we should leave this country'.[52] 'I grow very tired of praise,' he confessed to his diary, 'and I suppose that I shall get tired of censure in time.'[53]

A few hours later, Burnes was woken in the middle of the night. Revolts were breaking out across Kabul, and no one knew what to do. Rather than marching into the city, the British army sat tight in their barracks outside the walls and let Kabul burn. Burnes's house in the old city was quickly surrounded by an angry crowd. Fires were kindled and soon the gates were ablaze. Burnes tried to slip away through a side gate, wrapped in a lungi. But within seconds he was recognised and 'was rushed on by hundreds, and cut to pieces with their knives'. As he fell, and the world spun around him, the cry went up: 'Here is Sikandar!'[54]

That morning, when Masson woke aboard the *Berenice*, India had disappeared over the horizon.

21

The Lamp-Lighter

Dusk smelled of dead leaves.

Church Street, Edmonton, is an unremarkable road in north London, lined with thin Victorian houses, their white paint fading to grey. In the last of the light, children hurry home, hunched over and wrapped up, passing the stone tower of All Saints' Church without a second glance. Behind a line of trees in the churchyard, in an unmarked grave, is the final resting place of Charles Masson.

When he left Bombay in 1841, Masson had no idea he was heading towards an anonymous grave on the outskirts of London. He planned to travel slowly back to Britain, gather his resources, then return to Afghanistan and finish his work. The *Berenice* took him from Bombay to Suez. From there, he rode north through Egypt towards another Alexandria: the most famous of Alexander's cities, on the Mediterranean coast, from where he would sail to Britain.

Time and history look different in Egypt. Masson had spent the last decade uncovering what, for him, was the distant past: tracing tales and kings all the way back to Alexander. But by the time Alexander reached Egypt, the Great Pyramid of Giza was over 2,000 years old. It was as distant from Alexander's time as Alexander is from our own. Greek writers, sure of the great antiquity of their culture, often had a rude awakening in Egypt. Herodotus told gleefully of how one of his rivals, Hecataeus of Miletus, was humiliated by the priests of Thebes. Hecataeus unwisely boasted to

the priests that he could trace his family back sixteen generations to
a god. The priests invited Hecataeus into their temple, Herodotus
wrote, 'just as they did me, later on, though I certainly did not
boast about my ancestors to them. They led me into the vast inner
sanctum of the temple. There they showed me a huge number of
giant wooden statues.' Each statue was of a previous high priest
of the temple, 'since the custom was that each high priest should,
while he lived, set up his own statue there. We went from one
statue to another, counting as we went. Each high priest, they told
me, was the son of his predecessor. On and on we went, starting
with the most recently deceased high priest, then working further
and further backwards in time, until we came to the last statue.
Now when Hecataeus told the story of his ancestors, he insisted
that, sixteen generations back, he was descended from a god. The
priests had a better story than him: they had no need for gods.
Each one of those giant statues was, they said, a man. And each of
them was fathered by a man. We counted the statues up: there were
three hundred and forty-five of them.'[1]

In Cairo, Masson wandered the old city's bazaars: a warren of
shouting merchants and heaps of cloth, spices and gold, camels and
donkeys and lost-looking travellers. Almost everything that can be
imagined – along with several things which have never officially
existed – has been offered for sale here, at one time or another.
Masson slipped into the crowds like a fish slipping back into the
water. Soon, he was gossiping with stallholders and asking, just
as he always had in Kabul, if they knew of any ancient coins for
sale. A coin of Alexander the Great was promptly dropped into
his hands. The traders of Cairo and Giza have been in business
for more than 4,000 years: they know how to give people what
they want.

Masson held the coin up to the light, as he had long ago in
Bagram, on the day of his first discoveries, when an old man had
brought out a single copper coin and his life had changed for ever.
The years of disappointment had not changed his instincts one
bit: he left Cairo not just with Alexander's coin, but with 259
others.[2]

While Masson was haggling in Cairo, Afghanistan was in flames.
On 23 December 1841, Akbar Khan killed Macnaghten and led
a general revolt, besieging Kabul. The British forces, stationed
outside the city, had the misfortune to be commanded by one of
the worst soldiers in the country's history: the anxious, mumbling,
hypochondriac General William Elphinstone. Elphinstone fretted
and fussed for a week then, instead of marching into Kabul, where
the army might have waited out the winter from behind the city
walls, he ordered a retreat to India. Men and women, soldiers
and their families, the sick and the wounded, set out through the
winter snows, in a long, helplessly vulnerable column. Years earlier,
when Masson had crossed Afghanistan in the winter, on his way
back to Kabul from Bamiyan, the journey had nearly killed him,
and that was with Afghan hospitality along the way. Stumbling
towards India, Elphinstone's army was easy prey. Within days, of
the thousands who had set out from Kabul, all but one man had
been killed or taken prisoner.

Masson arrived back in Britain to find the country in turmoil.
Dispatches from Afghanistan, each worse than the last, were
splashed across the newspapers. 'It has never yet fallen to our lot to
communicate to our home readers such disastrous intelligence as
that which we are now about to lay before them,' wrote *The Times*.
'Our worst fears regarding the results of the Afghanistan expedition
have been realised. Disaster has trodden upon the heels of disaster
rapidly within the last two months, and we are even now in a state
of the utmost anxiety and suspense, fearing that the worst has yet
to be told.'[3] News of Burnes's death had reached Britain, but, after
that, nothing had been heard from Kabul. For weeks, the country
waited for news. No one knew whether Elphinstone and his men
were alive or dead, victors or prisoners. 'Day after day, week after
week, of the time which has passed since I last wrote have I looked
for news of an authentic character from Kabul, but in vain. Report
after report has arrived, each differing from that of its predecessor,'
wrote a newspaper correspondent in Bombay. 'We watch with
anxiety which has probably had no parallel in Indian history.'[4]
On 13 January 1842, the sole survivor of Elphinstone's army, Dr

William Brydon, reached India. The truth, as it turned out, was far worse than anyone had imagined.

Cold, grey British reality engulfed Masson.

There was no way back to Kabul. Bloody vengeance was being sworn on Afghanistan from every corner of Britain and India. The days of him being able to live quietly among his Afghan friends were over. The life of travel and discovery he had dreamed of was out of reach. He was stranded.

Masson had walked into Afghanistan as a wandering storyteller, but he walked out of it as one of the most respected scholars in Asia. Across the world, people were waiting to hear about his discoveries. But after losing years of notes in Kalat, telling that story was easier said than done. All of Masson's most spectacular finds were in the hands of the East India Company. And H. H. Wilson, the Company's Librarian, was keeping them to himself. When Masson got back to London, he found that Wilson had already published.

Wilson thought that Masson's story should be told the way it always had been: from an armchair in Oxford, by someone like himself. While Masson had been escaping Kalat and surviving Captain Bean, Wilson had been writing. 'I am wicked enough to suppose you may find many of your remarks embodied in Professor Wilson's outcoming work,' Stacy had written to Masson in the summer of 1841. 'I suspect you have been told.'[5] Pottinger, a few years earlier, had given Masson a similar warning. 'Wilson offers to embody any part of your journal and sketches that may be suitable in the work,' he had written. 'I am still of the opinion that no-one can do it as well as yourself.'[6]

A few pages into Wilson's book, Masson began to think the same thing. The book, called *Ariana Antiqua*, was huge and lavish: the East India Company had paid for everything. But almost everything else about it was wrong. His years in Kabul had taught Masson one thing: straightforward distinctions between East and West never worked. Wilson, on the other hand, saw everything in terms of Greeks versus 'barbarians'.[7] 'I commend the institutions of those you stigmatise as barbarians,' Masson wrote.[8] He had seen cultures reaching out for each other, and learning from each other, and trying to understand each other. Wilson saw a world where Asia submitted to 'the superior civilization and the purer faith' of British imperialism.[9]

Masson's copy of *Ariana Antiqua* is covered in pencilled annotations. They start out shocked. They become incredulous. They end up furious. The further he read, the angrier Masson became. 'Whether any ruins exist in it,' Wilson wrote of one region, 'there has been no opportunity of enquiring.' Masson: 'Ruins are in it.'[10] Wilson: 'A very extensive tract of country, which is yet but imperfectly known to us, never having been traversed by Europeans.' Masson: 'Ah Wilson, you are an old rogue.'[11] Wilson: 'Found by Mr Masson at Bagram.' Masson: 'Not found at Bagram.'[12] Wilson: 'One of two coins in the Masson collection.' Masson: 'I had many of these coins.'[13] Wilson: 'Readily identifiable.' Masson: 'Stop, Wilson.'[14] Wilson: 'In consistency with classical notices.' Masson: 'What a lie!!!'[15]

As he turned the pages, Masson saw his years of painstaking scholarship tossed aside. 'Did he,' Masson wrote, with a mix of sadness and injured pride, 'learn anything from C.M.?'[16] With a sinking heart, he realised that Wilson had stolen his story.

In April 1842, Masson finally found a publisher willing to take a chance on his own book. But Richard Bentley's offer would not cover Masson's fare home on the horse-drawn bus, let alone allow him to continue his travels. He received not a penny up front. Any share of the profits would come only 'after deducting, from the produce of the sale thereof, the charges for printing, paper, advertisements, embellishments, if any, and any other incidental expenses, including the allowance of ten per cent on the gross amount of the sale, for commission and risk of bad debts'.[17] It was a bad bargain, in exchange for his life's work.

Still, Masson hoped that he might spin his words into gold. But literary alchemy, like other kinds of alchemy, is harder than it first appears. However precious the materials, however earnestly they are blended together, however carefully they are muttered over, the result is all too often tinged with regret. Masson's book was published in the autumn of 1842. His *Narrative of various journeys* bore little resemblance to the work he had imagined, and his friends had anticipated, for so many years. In a feat of reverse alchemy which would have driven even the mystics of Kabul to despair, he had spun the gold of his adventures into sludge.

Masson's imagination had kept him alive for a decade: his stories had turned suspicion into kindness and doubt into faith. They had fed him and clothed him in some of the wildest corners of the world. They had conjured gold out of the ground and had led him to a lost city. But now, his words had lost their power. 'His apparent total want of imagination,' complained *The Times*, 'renders his journeys somewhat wearisome.'[18]

One door after another was closed in Masson's face. The East India Company refused to consider any compensation for his wrongful imprisonment in Quetta.[19] 'We are glad that Mr Masson is acquitted,' the Company wrote to the Governor General in India, 'but we agree with you in the opinion that he is not entitled to remuneration.'[20] (Jephson, Masson's old friend, had been certain that the East India Company would do the right thing.[21] But Christmas Day of 1844 found 'George Jephson of Bankshall Street, in Calcutta, lately of the firm of Jephson and Company' a 'prisoner in Calcutta gaol',[22] locked up for unpaid debts and begging for forgiveness.)

One of Masson's friends wrote to the British Museum suggesting that, as it was struggling to make sense of its Asian collections, 'the Trustees of the Museum might perhaps have it in their power to confer a real benefit upon the public by the employment of a most deserving and remarkable man, Charles Masson':

Since he has been in England, all his time and thoughts are given to the same pursuits, and from the study of a few damaged and duplicate [coin] specimens, of which, by dint of solicitation, he has obtained the return from the East India Company, he has been able to compile various papers which have been read by him before the Asiatic and I believe other societies. And it is the confident opinion of those who know him that in the knowledge of the ancient coins of that portion of Aria [modern-day Afghanistan and Pakistan], and generally of its ancient history, there is no man in England who will be found to surpass him.

If therefore the British Museum could find employment for him in this time, I believe they would afford great pleasure to Mr Masson. If they cannot find it, I will venture to say they ought to make it. It is no favour that I ask for Mr Masson, for there is never any favour in picking out the best man. At the same time, Mr Masson is not, I believe, in affluent circumstances, and mainly depends on a pitiful pension ... He is a very modest retiring man, of a very rare character nowadays; one who seeks knowledge for its own sake.[23]

The Museum blandly replied 'that Mr Masson's services were not required'.[24]

Ever since Masson first put on the East India Company's uniform as Private James Lewis, he had known one thing: powerful men did not appreciate having their power questioned.[25] Masson's book did just that: his hope 'that those who have so wilfully abused the power confided to them and whose rashness and folly in plunging the country into wars ruinous to its reputation may yet be punished'[26] was not well received in the drawing rooms of Britain's great houses. 'He [Masson] adds that Sir A. Burnes retired from Kabul with disgrace,' Burnes's brother David seethed. 'I would beg to ask Mr Masson, under what circumstances he himself *retired* from the Bengal artillery?'[27]

Masson was too late. He had condemned the Afghan war, and the men responsible for it, when the war was popular and the men were heroes. But his book came out after the war had ended and the bodies were buried. It looked like one more piece of peevish, perfect hindsight. The British press changed its tune the moment Macnaghten's head was separated from his body. 'We reminded Englishmen of the terrible account they were running up in India,' wrote *The Times*, after news of the Afghan disaster reached London, 'We warned them that such things could not last – that there were such things as universal national risings, never to be trifled with.'[28]

Of course, Masson's hindsight was actually foresight: he had seen the disaster coming. But no one had listened.

Historians dismissed Masson as 'in a small way one of the first actors in the great Central Asian drama; something, perhaps, in the lamp-trimming way, a thrower of light upon the proscenium and the stage – one of those functionaries who bustle about before the curtain is drawn up and win a little derisive applause from hands eager to begin the noisy labours of the night'.[29] J. A. Norris banished him even more cruelly: an insignificant little man, 'tormented by personal spite'[30] and 'clinging to the skirts of the Army of the Indus'.[31] 'He has,' remarked Norris contemptuously, 'done great damage to the reputation of better men.'[32]

In America, Harlan had been pushed aside, too. He never saw it coming. He had blustered his way through Egypt and Russia on the way back to the United States. Before leaving India, he gathered up a sheaf of letters of introduction from American missionaries, proclaiming the fine Quaker morals and steadfast honesty of 'Colonel Harlan'. 'As missionaries and representatives of American Christians in foreign countries,' one wrote, 'we feel a confidence in thus addressing you, and recommending to your kind attention our friend Colonel J. Harlan of Philadelphia ... aide de camp and general of brigade to Dost Mohammad, ex-Amir of Kabul.'[33] Before he reached Cairo, Harlan had given himself a promotion, and presented himself to the American consul as 'General Harlan'. 'Stature: six feet. Forehead: high', Harlan's new passport read. 'Chin: prominent. Hair: dark brown. Complexion: sallow'.[34] In St Petersburg, Harlan pestered Russian princesses[35] and ingratiated himself with American temperance campaigners. Preaching 'total abstinence'[36] from alcohol in nineteenth-century St Petersburg was, if anything, a more Quixotic mission than setting oneself up as an Afghan prince.

Harlan landed in the United States anticipating great things. He gloated over the wreck of the British expedition: the men who had boasted of their 'feats of valour rivalling the victories of Alexander'[37] were all dead or humiliated. 'The calamities of England,' he wrote, 'are blessings to America.'[38] Yet stories of 'retracing the steps of

Alexander'[39] in Afghanistan did not pay the bills in West Chester, Pennsylvania, and Harlan became tangled up in one money-making scheme after another, each more dubious than the last (camels! machinery! grapes! a regiment of his own in the American Civil War! the litigation which followed its mutiny!).[40] He died in October 1871. Among his possessions, his executors found a ticket for the Kentucky State Lottery.[41] Right to the end, he had still believed in his luck.

As the months turned into years, Masson settled into the age-old pattern of London poverty: battles with the landlord; a home too far away from the centre to be comfortable; friends who always seemed to be richer and more successful than he was; budgets which never quite balanced.[42] Richard Bentley, his publisher, developed a sudden shyness whenever Masson brought up the subject of royalties. After more than a year, Masson pointed out that 'an adjustment of accounts between us, so far as could be made, would not be unreasonable. Having received no reply to my communication, I again bring these matters to your notice.'[43] Poverty forced him into a permanent apologetic crouch. One day, sitting down to write a letter, he began 'With apologies', crossed it out, wrote 'Apologizing for', crossed that out, and wrote, with barely concealed exasperation, 'Begging to apologize (if it is necessary so to do)'.[44]

In 1844, after years of extreme anxiety around any woman who was not several hundred years old and currently being dug up, Masson suddenly married. His wife, Mary Ann Kilby, took the name he had plucked out of the air so long ago in India, and became Mary Ann Masson.[45] It may have taken Masson some time to get past his coyness about anything to do with sex, but their first child was born six years later in 1850: a son, Charles Lewis Masson. A daughter, Adelaide Masson, followed in 1853. Suburban family life was rather a shock for Masson. When he was trying to write, he was obliged to hang a large and probably fruitless notice: 'Silence to be observed here'.[46]

Masson would occasionally climb onto the horse-drawn bus, and rattle into the centre of London, nine miles south of Edmonton.

The bus dropped him at Holborn, just around the corner from the British Museum. He could sit in the book-lined reading room, with the starving scholars of London's intellectual underclass, and wander the galleries. Even in London, Alexander's shadow was hard to escape. One of the glories of the British Museum's collection was the sarcophagus of Pharaoh Nectanebo II. When it was first discovered, many believed that the sarcophagus was actually Alexander's own.[47]

As darkness fell, Masson would reluctantly leave the Museum behind, and clamber back onto the horse-drawn bus, crammed with small-time clerks and office workers, for the long ride home.

His dreams were always the same: his old house in Kabul, and the summer fruits of Afghanistan. 'Is there a way to forget the happiness of that place?' Babur, the first Mughal emperor, wrote sadly of his beloved city. 'I was brought, recently, a single melon from Kabul. And as I cut into it, and began to eat it, I was moved in a way I can barely describe. With every bite, I wept.'[48] Babur longed for his gardens in Kabul. Masson had spent joyful summer evenings in those gardens, by then long ruined and overgrown, with the scent of roses heavy in the air, watching the young men playing leapfrog, and listening to the singers and the storytellers. In the freezing London winters, Masson remembered the songs he used to sing – those sweet, sad verses from Hafiz – in castles and cities on the far side of the world:

Love taught me how to speak.

And since then
Every tale
Every word of mine
Has been heard across the world.

But don't call me wise
Or brilliant
Or true.
I know myself.

I know Hafiz all too well.
He doesn't know a thing.

Masson never returned to Afghanistan.

He died on 5 November 1853, of 'disease of the brain, uncertain':[49] as close as the English language comes to pothos.

People who discover lost cities are not supposed to end up in lost graves. Heinrich Schliemann, who uncovered the ancient city of Troy, looms over modern-day Athens even in death. His tomb dominates the city's First Cemetery: a neoclassical pastiche of one of the temples on the Acropolis. Schliemann's temple is fronted by a gigantic bust of Schliemann himself, and covered with friezes depicting his excavations: Schliemann in a floppy hat, waving the *Iliad* and loading artefacts onto a cart. It has become one of the city's most bizarre tourist attractions. Atop Schliemann's tomb, his message to the world is spelled out in ancient Greek: 'Schliemann the Hero'.

Heinrich Schliemann loved a tall tale even more than Charles Masson did. Today, scholars are divided between those who think he was a liar, and those who think he was a 'pathological liar'.[50] He swindled the Rothschilds with dodgy shipments of gold-dust.[51] He wrote a horrifying account of surviving the great San Francisco fire of 1851, despite being nowhere near San Francisco at the time.[52] When he discovered a cache of gold and precious objects in Troy, he dubbed them 'Priam's Treasure' after the legendary king of Troy (they had nothing to do with Priam). A diadem and some gold became the 'Jewels of Helen' (they had nothing to do with Helen). Schliemann draped his wife, Sophia, in the jewels, and posed her in front of a camera: the photograph became iconic.

Schliemann was not a subtle excavator. He favoured dynamite. Like Bagram, ancient Troy was a site of many layers: one city built on top of another. Schliemann was sure that the oldest layers were Homer's city, and blasted straight through anything in his way. Unfortunately, the oldest layers of Troy turned out to be from the early Bronze Age, 1,000 years before any historical Trojan War could have happened. It was not a small error: equivalent to dating

Queen Victoria's reign to 2837, rather than 1837. Today, Schliemann is celebrated for discovering Homer's Troy. He actually destroyed it. The layer closest in time to Homer's city was reduced to dust and rubble.

Today, in Berlin's Neues Museum, Schliemann's tiny bronze head surveys proceedings from a place of honour. His plagiarised doctorate is forgotten. His lies and looting are brushed aside. The Trojan gold is still labelled 'Priam's Treasure'. The photograph of Sophia Schliemann in her jewels still stares down from the wall. The galleries are titled not 'Troy', but 'Schliemann's Troy'.

Many heroic stories of archaeological discovery are also stories of humbug. Each year, over a million visitors flock to the palace of Knossos in Crete: home of the Minotaur, the fearsome half-man, half-bull of Greek mythology, and the impossible labyrinth of Daedalus. No one tells the tourists that the site is not the work of Daedalus and his artisans, but of Sir Arthur Evans and his team of twentieth-century workmen.[53] Hardly anything is original. Evans and his men, as Evelyn Waugh put it, 'tempered their zeal for reconstruction with a predilection for covers of *Vogue*'.[54] The palace of Minos is a masterpiece of Art Deco and reinforced concrete.[55]

Evans is another of history's great archaeological stars, celebrated across the world for his discoveries. It is rarely mentioned that many of his craftsmen worked two shifts: the first, restoring Minoan antiquities, and the second, faking Minoan antiquities. One man, much to Evans's discomfort, made a spectacular deathbed confession:

> 'I'm going to die, so I'm all right, but for years I've been in partnership with George Antoniou, the young fellow who works with me for Evans, and we have been forging antiquities … George is a scoundrel and I hate the fellow, and I've been waiting for this moment to give him away. Go straight to his house and you'll find all the forgeries and all our manufacturing plant there.'
>
> The police went, they raided, and they found exactly what he said, and they asked Evans to come and look, and I never saw

so magnificent a collection of forgeries as those fellows had put together.

There were things in every stage of manufacture. For instance, people had been recently astounded at getting what they call chryselephantine statuettes from Crete; statuettes of ivory decked out with gold ... These men were determined to do that sort of thing, and they had got everything, from plain ivory tusk and then the figure rudely carved out, then beautifully finished, then picked out with gold. And then the whole thing was put into acid, which ate away the soft parts of the ivory giving it the effect of having been buried for centuries. And I didn't see anyone could tell the difference![56]

The freshly poured ruin of Knossos may be no more authentic than a theme-park Minotaur ride, but Evans's heroic status endures. His bronze statue greets visitors to his 'concrete labyrinth'.[57] The statue wears the half-smile of a man who has got away with it.

No statues were ever set up to Masson. No marble mausoleums were erected. Not even a portrait of him survives. One was painted in 1836 by Godfrey Vigne, the English traveller who drank brandy with Masson in Kabul. But as soon as Vigne's portrait was complete, Akbar Khan insisted that he had to have it. Vigne sent a scribbled note to Masson's house in Kabul: 'The Amir's son is here and swears you must come. He took possession of your portrait directly he saw it.'[58] In the chaos which followed the British invasion of Afghanistan, the portrait was lost. It has never been recovered.

Masson sometimes wondered if his years of travelling had been for nothing: had it all been a fool's errand – was he the fool? Had he followed Alexander for years, only to come away empty-handed? Was Bagram Alexandria or not? Masson died with the story of his pursuit of Alexander, his last story, unfinished.

**

But the story of Alexander will always be unfinished.

Today, Alexandria beneath the Mountains is still an enigma: buried, perhaps, beneath Bagram Airbase, beneath the ruins of Soviet barracks, an abandoned CIA torture site, and a mountain of Pizza Hut boxes from today's American base. Certainly, if Alexandria is not at Bagram, it must be very close by.[59] 'The prodigious number of coins and relics,' wrote the nineteenth-century historian George Grote, 'discovered by Mr Masson at Bagram, supply better evidence for identifying the site with that of Alexandria ... than can be pleaded on behalf of any other locality.'[60]

Alexander still haunts the dreams of many in Afghanistan. 'A half hour's drive from where I sit at Task Force Warrior headquarters on Bagram Air Field,' wrote an American official in 2009, 'there lies a literal empire's graveyard of rusting Soviet tanks, BMP armored troop carriers, trucks, guns and other dead armor, stretching out for miles across the skirt of the Hindu Kush where it meets the Shomali Plain. Somewhere nearby, buried deep in the dust, lies the base camp Alexander the Great used for his invasions of Central Asia and India.'[61]

How does history get written? Look closely and you'll realise something important. Often, it's not because of a professor sitting in a library, but because of someone like Masson: a strange and wonderful character fighting through the snows, chasing an impossible dream. Knowledge, as we hold it in our hands today, is formed not just from scholarship and experiments, facts and equations. It is also made of stories.

The British Museum's Hotung Gallery is a high, luminous space, full of impossibly beautiful Hindu goddesses, Chinese ceramics and delicately carved Buddhas. It tells what the Museum's director calls 'the interconnected story of the world',[62] the story that Masson devoted his life to making possible. In one corner, the Greek Titan Atlas holds up a Buddhist stupa. Beneath a window, Vajrapani, a Bodhisattva or follower of the Buddha, is dressed in Hercules's lion-skin.[63] Coins from across Asia, many of them Masson's finds, mingle with Greek and Indian gods. In pride of place, gleaming in the afternoon sunlight, sits the tiny golden reliquary which Masson uncovered on one of his happiest days in Afghanistan, and which the curator Dr Sushma Jansari recently called 'one of the most

important objects in the entire British Museum':[64] the Bimaran
Casket.

For much of the nineteenth century, Masson's finds sat neglected
in the store rooms and cabinets of the East India Company. In 1878,
years after power in India had passed from the Company to the
British government, Masson's collection was finally transferred to the
British Museum.[65] Expecting to find a treasure trove, the Museum's
curators discovered, with sinking hearts, that many of the most
important items were missing, labels were 'rarely in the trays to which
they belong', and everything was hopelessly jumbled. Thousands of
Masson's finds had been lost. Thousands more had been auctioned off
by the East India Company. 'It is much to be regretted that portions
of Masson's collection seem to have been dispersed,' the Museum
reported, 'as they are of great historical value.'[66] 'Some of these objects
may turn up,' one of the curators wrote, hopefully. 'I think they must
be in some drawer.'[67] In 1995, 6,500 coins from Bagram were found
unexpectedly in the British Library. In 2007, 500 more turned up.[68]

Reassembling Masson's collection has taken over a century,[69] but
today, thanks to the British Museum's curators, Masson's discoveries
have at last been catalogued, and are understood more fully than
ever before. Uncovering his life's work has become the life's work of
others.[70] The 'lowly' lamp-lighter shed more light than he dared to
imagine – and his lamps are burning brighter every day.[71]

Alexander never quite reached the ends of the earth. Masson
never quite found his lost city. Not every quest will reach its goal.
But both Alexander and Masson discovered one thing: in pursuit
of our wildest dreams, we hold it in our power to change the world.

***

In the summer of 1842, all eyes in London turned to Robert Burford's
Panorama. It was one of the weird wonders of the age: a gigantic
rotunda, looming over the alleys and theatres of Leicester Square.
Visitors to the Panorama would enter the building through a long,
dark tunnel, which curved upwards until it reached a platform
in the middle of the rotunda. Then, all of a sudden, they would
emerge into another world: looking down on a strange city, or a

mountain range, or a bloody battle. Light flickered on a gigantic painting, covering the circular wall in every direction. It was like nothing anyone had experienced before: like walking into a frame, and finding yourself inside the picture. Some visitors immediately vomited.[72]

That summer, Afghanistan came to London. Stepping out of the darkness, visitors to the Panorama found the ramparts of Kabul towering over them. Londoners were overawed: 'We have never been more gratified by any panorama than by that of Kabul, painted by Mr Burford,' wrote one journalist. 'The city is seen as from an eminence, with its suburbs at the feet of the spectator; the mountains, ascending to an awful height around, with the Hindu Kush, capped with snow, in the distance.'[73] At the foot of the mountains, beside the Kabul River, Dost Mohammad and his court were gathered. Burnes was there, as was Vikevitch, along with Akbar Khan – whose 'handsome person, and open manly expression' left the ladies of London swooning[74] – and the 'Chief Wrestler of Kabul',[75] posing atop a rock. Pilgrims, soldiers and tea-drinkers crowded in every direction. Seated at Dost Mohammad's right hand, resplendent in his turban, was Masson.[76]

Burford had brought Masson in to advise on the Panorama, along with Godfrey Vigne, whose portrait of Masson had once been claimed by Akbar Khan. Burford wanted the definitive story of Kabul: rich and poor, living and dead, everyone was going on the wall. Vigne and Masson built the scene out of a patchwork of smaller paintings and sketches.[77] For Dost Mohammad, they used a watercolour by James Atkinson: in it, the Amir reclined on a carpet under a parasol, speaking to three members of his court. Masson and Vigne kept Dost Mohammad, the carpet, the parasol and one of the courtiers.[78] In place of the other two courtiers, they put Masson, lounging on a cushion.

Burford sold visitors an 'explanation' of his Panorama: a guidebook with a key to the scene. Figure 67 is 'Mr Masson'.[79] It is Masson's only surviving likeness: an ample turban, a slash of beard. But unlike in the Panorama itself, the faces in the guidebook are blank. The closer you look at Masson, the less you see.

When the Panorama opened to the public, Masson stood on the viewing platform, unnoticed by the chattering, excited crowds around him. The past two years had brought him little but disappointment. But for one last time, looking up at the mountains and the rooftops of Kabul, he was home.

On the wall of the Panorama, inside his story, Masson was smiling.[80]

Notes

I THE RUNAWAY

1 Anon., *A Brief Memoir of an Officer of the Bengal Artillery*, L. B. Seely, London, 1834, p. 29.
2 British Library, Or.16805.
3 Guildhall Library (London), Microfilm MSS 3572/2.
4 Pierce Egan, *Life in London: Or, The Day and Night Scenes of Jerry Hawthorne, Esq., and His Elegant Friend Corinthian Tom*, Sherwood, Neely, and Jones, London, 1822, p. 23.
5 William Wordsworth, 'Prelude,' book 7, 'Residence in London', in William Wordsworth, *The Poetical Works of William Wordsworth*, Edward Moxon, London, 1869, p. 488.
6 Egan, *Life in London*, p. 36.
7 *The Examiner*, 1816, p. 283.
8 George Gordon, Lord Byron, *The Works of Lord Byron: Including the Suppressed Poems*, A. & W. Galignani, Paris, 1828, p. 554. This was Byron's maiden speech in the House of Lords.
9 Walpole to Sir Horace Mann, 4 November 1772. *The Yale Edition of Horace Walpole's Correspondence*, ed. W. S. Lewis, Yale University Press, New Haven, CT, 1937–83, vol. 23, p. 451.
10 William Dalrymple, *The Anarchy: The Relentless Rise of the East India Company*, Bloomsbury, London, 2019.
11 Cobbett to William Creevey, 24 September 1810. *The Creevey Papers: A selection from the correspondence and diaries of the late Thomas Creevey, M.P.*, ed. Sir Herbert Maxwell, John Murray, London, 1903, vol. 1, p. 134.

12 British Library, Bengal Secret Consultations, IOR/P/BEN/SEC/380, 19 June 1834.

13 J. N. Creighton, *Narrative of the Siege and Capture of Bhurtpore*, Parbury, Allen and Co., London, 1830, p. 148.

14 This is based on a conversion rate of 10 rupees to 1 GBP. See Anon., *Return to an order of the Honourable the House of Commons, dated 24 June 1839: Accounts of all monies supplied from the revenues of India*, London, 1839, p. 6, for the contemporary exchange rate, and for inflation rates see Bank of England Inflation Calculator [online]: https://www.bankofengland.co.uk/monetary-policy/inflation/inflation-calculator.

15 Charles Masson, *Narrative of Various Journeys in Balochistan, Afghanistan and the Panjab Including a Residence in Those Countries from 1826 to 1838*, Richard Bentley, London 1842, vol. 1, pp. 309–10.

16 John Blakiston, *Twelve Years' Military Adventure in Three Quarters of the Globe*, Henry Colburn, London, 1829, vol. 1, p. 309.

17 *Blackwood's Edinburgh Magazine*, vol. 23 (January–June 1828), p. 449.

18 Creighton, *Narrative*, p. 17.

19 Ibid., pp. 52–3.

20 Ibid., p. 29.

21 Ibid., pp. 52–3.

22 Masson, *Various Journeys*, vol. 1, p. 19.

23 Ibid., p. 3.

24 Chester County Historical Society (West Chester, PA), Harlan Papers, 'Oriental Sketches', 76.

25 Ibid.

26 Ben Macintyre, *Josiah the Great: The True Story of the Man Who Would Be King*, HarperCollins, London, 2004, p. 9.

27 Chester County Historical Society, Harlan Papers, 'Oriental Sketches', 76.

28 Ibid., 78.

29 Ibid., 24.

30 Ibid., 46.

31 Ibid., 46–7.

32 Ibid., 42.

33 *The Calcutta Review*, vol. 86 (1888), p. 350.

34 Masson, *Various Journeys*, vol. 3, pp. 85–6.

35 Chester County Historical Society, Harlan Papers, 'Oriental Sketches', 78.
36 Ibid.
37 Masson, *Various Journeys*, vol. I, p. 41.
38 Chester County Historical Society, Harlan Papers, 'Oriental Sketches', 48.
39 Ibid., 78.
40 Masson, *Various Journeys*, vol. I, p. 32.
41 Chester County Historical Society, Harlan Papers, 'Oriental Sketches', 10.
42 Ibid., 9.
43 Ibid., 'Shah Shujah', 3.
44 Ibid., 'Oriental Sketches', 34.
45 Ibid., 'Shah Shujah', 6–7.
46 Ibid., 'Oriental Sketches', 179.
47 Ibid., 151.
48 Ibid., 93.
49 Ibid., 92–3.
50 Macintyre, *Josiah the Great*, p. 73.
51 Chester County Historical Society, Harlan Papers, 'Oriental Sketches', 96.
52 Ibid.
53 Ibid., 95.
54 Ibid., 99.
55 Macintyre, *Josiah the Great*, p. 73.
56 Chester County Historical Society, Harlan Papers, 'Oriental Sketches', 29.
57 Ibid.
58 Ibid., 28–9.
59 Masson, *Various Journeys*, vol. I, p. 42.

2 THE ILLUSIONISTS

1 John F. Riddick, *The History of British India*, Praeger, Westport, CT, 2006, p. 292.
2 *The Asiatic Journal and Monthly Miscellany*, vol. 34 (March 1841), p. 194.

3 George W. Forrest, ed., *Selections from the Travels and Journals preserved in the Bombay Secretariat*, Government Central Press, Bombay, 1906, p. 103.

4 Gordon Whitteridge, *Charles Masson of Afghanistan: Explorer, Archaeologist, Numismatist, and Intelligence Agent*, Orchid Press, Warminster, 1986, p. 11.

5 J. W. Kaye, 'The Poetry of Recent Indian Warfare', *The Calcutta Review*, vol. 11 (1848), p. 223.

6 Masson, *Various Journeys*, vol. 1, p. 1.

7 'Lewis, James, Private' appears on the Muster Rolls of the Bengal Artillery for 1 July 1827, but not for 1 July 1828. British Library, IOR/L/MIL/10/147 (1827) and IOR/L/MIL/10/148 (1828).

8 British Library, MSS Eur. E.163, 3.

9 *The Calcutta Review*, vol. 2 (1844), p. 474.

10 C. Grey and H. L. O. Garrett, *European Adventurers of Northern India, 1785 to 1849*, Languages Department, Patiala, 1970, p. 211.

11 Masson, *Various Journeys*, vol. 1, p. 45.

12 Ibid., p. 54.

13 Ibid., p. 55.

14 Ibid., p. 56.

15 Adapted from Paul Smith, *The Divan of Hafiz*, New Humanity Books, Melbourne, 1986, Ghazal 10.

16 Masson, *Various Journeys*, vol. 1, pp. 58–9.

17 Adapted from Thomas Rain Crowe, *Drunk on the Wine of the Beloved: 100 Poems of Hafiz*, Shambhala, London, 2001, p. 8.

18 Masson, *Various Journeys*, vol. 1, p. 60.

19 Ibid., p. 63.

20 Ibid., p. 73.

21 Ibid., p. 82.

22 Ibid., p. 70.

23 Ibid., p. 76.

24 Ibid., pp. 77–8.

25 Ibid., p. 87.

26 Ibid., p. 260.

27 Ibid., p. 94.

28 Ibid., p. 303.

29 Ibid., pp. 303–4.

30 Ibid., p. 304.

31 Ibid., pp. 304–5.

32 Ibid., p. 305.

33 Ibid., p. 306.

34 Ibid., p. 305.

35 Ibid., p. 309.

36 Ibid., p. 343.

37 Ibid., p. 313.

38 Ibid., p. 314.

39 Ibid., p. 316.

40 Ibid., p. 402.

41 Ibid., p. 74.

42 Ibid., p. 312.

43 Forrest, ed., *Travels*, p. 137.

44 Masson, *Various Journeys*, vol. 1, p. 372.

45 Ibid., pp. 345–6.

3 THE STORYTELLER

1 Masson, *Various Journeys*, vol. 2, p. 62.

2 Ibid., vol. 1, pp. 446–7.

3 Forrest, ed., *Travels*, p. 103.

4 British Library, MSS Eur. E.163/5, 25.

5 Ibid., 26.

6 Ibid., 25.

7 Ibid., 26.

8 Plutarch, *Life of Alexander*, 55.4–5. Unless otherwise indicated, quotes from ancient sources throughout the book are from my own translations; references to these works in the notes are to the original texts.

9 Plato, *Timaeus*, 25a–d.

10 Forrest, ed., *Travels*, p. 166.

11 Ibid.

12 Ibid.

13 Ibid.

14 Ibid., p. 105.

15 National Archives (UK), FO 705/32, Masson to Pottinger, 16 January 1837.

16 Masson, *Various Journeys*, vol. 1, p. 452.

17 Ibid., vol. 2, pp. 7–8.

18 Ibid., p. 22.

19 Ibid.
20 Ibid., p. 23.
21 Ibid., vol. 1, pp. 52–3.
22 Ibid., vol. 2, p. 91.
23 Ibid., p. 90.
24 Ibid., p. 179.
25 Ibid., vol. 2, p. 226.
26 British Library, MSS Eur. E.165, 43.
27 Masson, *Various Journeys*, vol. 2, pp. 231–3.

4 THE WILD EAST

1 Joseph Wolff, *Travels and adventures of the Rev. Joseph Wolff*, Saunders, Otley and Company, London, 1861, p. 358.
2 Ibid.
3 Ibid., p. 373.
4 Ibid., p. 357.
5 Fanny Parkes, *Wanderings of a Pilgrim in Search of the Picturesque*, Manchester University Press, Manchester, 2001, p. 191.
6 Wolff, *Travels*, p. 361.
7 Ibid., p. 518.
8 Parkes, *Wanderings*, p. 191.
9 Ibid.
10 Wolff, *Travels*, p. 368.
11 Ibid., p. 369.
12 British Library, MSS Eur. E.163/7, 12.
13 Ibid.
14 Chester County Historical Society, Harlan Papers, 'Oriental Sketches', 156.
15 British Library, MSS Eur. E.163/7, 12.
16 Ibid.
17 Ibid.
18 Wolff, *Travels*, p. 369.
19 Ibid.
20 Johann Martin Honigberger, *Thirty Five Years in the East: Adventures, Discoveries, Experiments, and Historical Sketches, Relating to the Punjab and Cashmere*, H. Ballière, London, 1852, p. 57.
21 British Library, MSS Eur. E.163/7, 12.
22 Joseph Wolff, *Researches and Missionary Labours Among the Jews, Mohammedans, and Other Sects*, Orrin Rogers, Philadelphia, 1837, p. 180.

23 National Archives of India, Foreign/Secret/19 March 1833/30–1.
24 Ibid.
25 British Library, MSS Eur. E.163/7, 12.
26 Alexander Burnes, *Travels Into Bokhara: Being the Account of a Journey from India to Cabool, Tartary, and Persia*, John Murray, London, 1834, vol. 1, p. 137.
27 Ibid., p. 117.
28 Masson, *Various Journeys*, vol. 2, p. 353.
29 Ibid., p. 316.
30 Ibid., p. 317.
31 Ibid.
32 Ibid., p. 305.
33 Ibid., p. 383.
34 Ibid., p. 322.
35 Ibid., p. 332.
36 Ibid., p. 337.
37 Ibid.
38 Ibid., pp. 337–8.
39 Ibid., p. 338.
40 Ibid., p. 341.
41 Ibid., p. 343.
42 Ibid., p. 319.
43 Ibid., p. 316.
44 Ibid., p. 322.
45 Ibid., pp. 344–5.
46 Ibid., p. 363.
47 Ibid., p. 358.
48 Ibid., p. 359.
49 Ibid., p. 360.
50 Ibid., pp. 360–1.
51 Ibid., p. 361.
52 Ibid.
53 Ibid., p. 345.
54 Ibid., p. 361.
55 Burnes, *Travels*, vol. 1, p. 182.
56 Vincent Eyre, *Military Operations at Cabul, which Ended in the Retreat and Destruction of the British Army, January 1842*, John Murray, London, 1843, p. 344.

57 Masson, *Various Journeys*, vol. 2, p. 380.

58 Ibid., p. 371.

59 Yahyā ibn Khālid, adapted via Abu Yūsuf Ya'qūb ibn 'Isḥāq aṣ-Ṣabbāḥ al-Kind into Ibn al-Nadim, trans. B. Dodge, *The Fihrist of al-Nadīm: a tenth-century survey of Muslim culture*, Columbia University Press, New York, 1970, vol. 2, p. 829.

60 Masson, *Various Journeys*, vol. 2, p. 382.

61 Ibid., p. 362.

62 British Library, MSS Eur. G.42, 32.

63 Masson, *Various Journeys*, vol. 2, p. 427.

64 British Library, MSS Eur. E.165, 191.

65 Masson, *Various Journeys*, vol. 2, pp. 392–3.

66 Alā' al-Dīn 'Aṭā Malik Ata-Malik Juvaini, trans. J. A. Boyle, *Genghis Khan: The History of the World Conqueror* [*Tarīkh-i Jahān-gushā*], Manchester University Press, Manchester, 1997, pp. 132–3.

67 Masson, *Various Journeys*, vol. 2, pp. 392–3.

68 Burnes, *Travels*, vol. 1, p. 183.

69 British Library, MSS Eur. E.165, 191.

70 Masson, *Various Journeys*, vol. 2, p. 393.

71 British Library, MSS Eur. G.42, 32.

72 Charles Masson, 'Notes on the antiquities of Bamian', *Journal of the Asiatic Society of Bengal*, vol. 5 (1836), p. 709.

73 British Library, MSS Eur. G.42, 32.

74 The fullest account of the wonders of Bamiyan can be found in Takayasu Higuchi, バーミヤーン: 京都大学中央アジア学術調査報告: アフガニスタンにおける仏教石窟寺院の美術考古学的調査 1970-1978年 / 樋口隆康編 [*Bāmiyān: Kyōto daigaku chūō ajia gakujutsu chōsa hōkoku: Afuganisutan niokeru bukkyō sekkutsu jīn no bijutsu kōkogakuteki chōsa 1970 1978nen*], Dōhōsha Shuppan, Kyōto, 1983–4.

75 Masson, 'Antiquities of Bamian', p. 720.

76 British Library, MSS Eur. F.65, 202.

77 Masson, *Various Journeys*, vol. 2, p. 420.

78 Ibid., p. 433.

79 Ibid., p. 437.

80 Ibid., p. 464.

81 Ibid.

82 J. Hackin and J. Carl, *Nouvelles recherches archéologiques à Bâmiyân. Mémoires de la Délégation Archéologique Française en Afghanistan*, G. Van Oest, Paris, 1933, p. 2.

5 THE CITY BENEATH THE MOUNTAINS

1 Masson, *Various Journeys*, vol. 3, p. 4.

2 Ibid., vol. 2, p. 243.

3 Ibid., p. 244.

4 Ibid., p. 246.

5 Ibid.

6 British Library, MSS Eur. E.163/11, 11.

7 Mohan Lal, *Travels in the Panjab, Afghanistan, Turkistan, to Balk, Bokhara, and Herat*, W. H. Allen, London, 1846, p. 71.

8 Masson, *Various Journeys*, vol. 3, p. 5.

9 National Archives of India, Foreign/Secret/19 March 1833/30–1.

10 John William Burgon, *Petra, a Poem: To which a Few Short Poems are Now Added*, F. Macpherson, Oxford, 1846, p. 23.

11 P. M. Fraser, *Cities of Alexander the Great*, Clarendon Press, Oxford, 1996, p. 192.

12 Arrian, *Anabasis*, 3.28.

13 There are almost as many names for this city as there are accounts of it. It has been known as Alexandria ad Caucasum, Alexandria ad calcem Caucasi, Alexandria in the Caucasus, Alexandria on the Caucasus, Alexandrie du Caucase, and many other names besides. For the sake of clarity, it will be referred to as Alexandria beneath the Mountains throughout.

14 Xuanzang, trans. Samuel Beal, *Si-Yu-Ki: Buddhist Records of the Western World: Translated from the Chinese of Hiuen Tsiang*, Kegan, Paul, Trench and Company, London, 1884, p. 646.

15 Masson, *Various Journeys*, vol. 2, p. 161.

16 Arrian, *Anabasis*, 7.13.

17 Ibid., 5.1.

18 Burnes, *Travels*, vol. 1, p. 146.

19 Adapted from Idries Shah, *The Pleasantries of the Incredible Mulla Nasrudin*, Octagon Press, London, 1983, p. 27.

20 British Library, MSS Eur. E.163/11, 16–17.

21 Masson, *Various Journeys*, vol. 3, p. 140.

22 Ibid., p. 5.

23 British Library, MSS Eur. E.163/11, 14.

24 Masson, *Various Journeys*, vol. 3, p. 5.

25 British Library, MSS Eur. E.163/11, 16.

26 National Archives of India, Foreign/Secret/19 March 1833/30–1.

27 Ibid.

28 Masson, *Various Journeys*, vol. 3, pp. 92–3.

29 Ibid., p. 3.

30 British Library, MSS Eur. E.163/11, 20.

31 Masson, *Various Journeys*, vol. 3, p. 94.

32 Ibid.

33 Ibid., p. 117.

34 Ibid., p. 96.

35 Ibid., p. 97.

36 Ibid.

37 Ibid., vol. 2, p. 234.

38 Chester County Historical Society, Harlan Papers, 'Oriental Sketches', 179.

39 Masson, *Various Journeys*, vol. 3, p. 140.

40 Chester County Historical Society, Harlan Papers, 'Oriental Sketches', 166.

41 Ibid.

42 British Library, MSS Eur. E.165, 226.

43 Masson, *Various Journeys*, vol. 3, p. 123.

44 Ibid., p. 138.

45 Ibid., p. 141.

46 Ibid.

47 Ibid., p. 142.

48 Ibid.

49 Ibid., pp. 142–3.

50 Ibid., p. 143.

51 Ibid., p. 157.

6 THE GOLDEN CASKET

1 National Archives (UK), FO 705/32, Masson to Pottinger, 1 January 1833.

2 Ibid.

3 Masson, *Various Journeys*, vol. 3, p. 117.

4 Ibid., p. 13.

5 British Library, MSS Eur. E.163/11, 20.

6 Ibid.

7 Masson, *Various Journeys*, vol. 3, p. 13.

8 National Archives (UK), FO 705/32, Masson to Pottinger, 1 July 1833.

9 Masson, *Various Journeys*, vol. 3, p. 2.

10 Ibid., p. 1.

11 Ibid., p. 4.

12 National Archives (UK), FO 705/32, Masson to Pottinger, 1 January 1833.

13 Frank Holt, *Into the Land of Bones: Alexander the Great in Afghanistan*, University of California Press, Berkeley, 2005, p. 108.

14 National Archives (UK), FO 705/32, Masson to Pottinger, 17 August 1833.

15 British Library, MSS Eur. E.163/11, 22.

16 Wolff, *Travels*, p. 375.

17 National Archives (UK), FO 705/32, Masson to Pottinger, 17 August 1833.

18 Ibid., Masson to Pottinger, 23 April 1834.

19 Ibid., Masson to Pottinger, 1 July 1833.

20 British Library, MSS Eur. E.163/12, 1.

21 Ibid.

22 Burnes, *Travels*, vol. 1, p. 117.

23 British Library, IOR/P/BEN/SEC/380, Bengal Secret Consultations, 19 June 1834, Gerard to Government, 8 April 1834.

24 Ibid.

25 Masson, *Various Journeys*, vol. 2, p. 253.

26 Burnes, *Travels*, vol. 1, p. 149.

27 Ibid., pp. 149–50.

28 Chester County Historical Society, Harlan Papers, 'Oriental Sketches', 176.

29 Masson, *Various Journeys*, vol. 3, p. 148.

30 British Library, IOR/P/BEN/SEC/380, Bengal Secret Consultations, 19 June 1834, Gerard to Government, 8 April 1834.

31 National Archives (UK), FO 705/32, Masson to Pottinger, 17 August 1833.

32 British Library, IOR/P/BEN/SEC/380, Bengal Secret Consultations, 19 June 1834, Gerard to Government, 8 April 1834.

33 Masson, *Various Journeys*, vol. 3, p. 98.

34 *Journal of the Asiatic Society of Bengal*, vol. 3 (1834), p. 363.

35 National Archives (UK), FO 705/32, Masson to Pottinger, 17 August 1833.

36 *Journal of the Asiatic Society of Bengal*, vol. 3 (1834), p. 363.

37 National Archives (UK), FO 705/32, Masson to Pottinger, 17 August 1833.
38 Ibid.
39 Ibid.
40 British Library, IOR/P/BEN/SEC/380, Bengal Secret Consultations, 25 March 1834, Karamat Ali to Wade, 31 October 1833.
41 Ibid.
42 Ibid., Karamat Ali to Wade, 2 November 1833.
43 Ibid.
44 Ibid.
45 British Library, IOR/P/BEN/SEC/380, Bengal Secret Consultations, 25 March 1834.
46 Horace Hayman Wilson, *Ariana Antiqua: a descriptive account of the antiquities and coins of Afghanistan*, Published Under the Authority of the Honourable The Court of Directors of The East India Company, London, 1841, p. 69.
47 Ibid., pp. 69–70.
48 Ibid., p. 70.

7 POTHOS

1 Demosthenes, *Philippic* 3, 9.31.
2 Richard van Leeuwen, *The Thousand and One Nights: Space, Travel and Transformation*, Routledge, New York, 2007, p. 86.
3 E. Badian, *Alexandre le Grand, image et réalité*, Fondation Hardt, Geneva, 1976, p. 280.
4 Arrian, *Anabasis*, 3.20–1.
5 Firdausi, *The Shahnama of Firdausi*, Kegan, Paul, London, 1905, vol. 6, pp. 53–4.
6 Phiroze Vasunia, *The Classics and Colonial India*, Oxford University Press, Oxford, 2013, p. 105.
7 Ibid., p. 108.
8 Quoted in Barbara Schmitz, *Islamic Manuscripts in the New York Public Library*, Oxford University Press, New York and Oxford, 1992, vol. 1, p. 160.
9 Richard Stoneman, *Alexander the Great: A Life in Legend*, Yale University Press, New Haven, CT, 2010, p. 108.
10 Adapted from Pseudo-Callisthenes, trans. Richard Stoneman, *The Greek Alexander Romance*, Penguin Books, London, 1991, pp. 118–19.

11 'Faulty ACs endanger 4000-year-old Egyptian mummy at Kolkata Museum', *Times of India*, 9 June 2014.

12 British Library, MSS Eur. E.165, 183.

13 *Journal of the Asiatic Society of Bengal*, vol. 3 (1834), p. 154.

14 Ibid.

15 Ibid., p. 161.

16 National Archives, London, FO 705/32, Masson to Pottinger, 1 July 1833.

17 British Library, MSS Eur. E.165/11, 12.

18 British Library, IOR/P/BEN/SEC/380, Bengal Secret Consultations, 10 April 1834, Extract of Intelligence from Shikarpore.

19 Punjab Archives (Lahore), Case 106, 9/II/665, Chief Secretary, Calcutta, to David Ochterlony, 17 December 1816.

20 National Archives (UK), FO 705/32, Masson to Pottinger, 3 October 1833.

21 British Library, IOR/P/BEN/SEC/379, Bengal Secret Consultations, 3 January 1834, Shah Shujah to Wade, received 24 December 1833.

22 British Library, IOR/P/BEN/SEC/380, Bengal Secret Consultations, 19 April 1834, Wade to the Secretary of Government, 17 March 1834.

23 British Library, IOR/P/SEC/BOM/82, Secret Consultations, 26 August 1834, Wade to Government, 27 July 1834.

24 British Library, IOR/P/BEN/SEC/380, Bengal Secret Consultations, 25 March 1834, Wade to Karamat Ali, 3 January 1834.

25 Ibid.

26 National Archives, London, FO 705/32, Masson to Pottinger, 9 October 1834.

27 British Library MSS Eur. E.161, 11, Masson to Pottinger, 23 April 1834.

28 British Library MSS Eur. E.161/6–7, 4, Pottinger to Masson, 1 January 1834.

29 National Archives, London, FO 705/32, Masson to Pottinger, 23 April 1834.

30 British Library, MSS Eur. E.161/1, 3, Pottinger to Charles Norris, Chief Secretary to Government, Bombay, 27 November 1833.

31 Wilson, *Ariana Antiqua*, p. 109.

32 National Archives (UK), FO 705/32, Masson to Pottinger, 15 July 1834.

33 British Library, MSS Eur. E.161/6–7, 6.

34 Masson, *Various Journeys*, vol. 1, p. 402.

35 National Archives (UK), FO 705/32, Masson to Pottinger, 9 October 1834.

36 Ibid.

37 Ibid., Masson to Pottinger, 15 July 1834.

38 British Library, MSS Eur. E.161/6–7, 10a, Pottinger to Masson, 4 November 1834.

39 Wilson, *Ariana Antiqua*, p. 114.

40 Masson, *Various Journeys*, vol. 3, p. 138.

41 Ibid., pp. 98–9.

42 National Archives (UK), FO 705/32, Pottinger to Masson, 6 September 1834.

8 OUR MAN IN KABUL

1 M. E. Yapp, *Strategies of British India: Britain, Iran and Afghanistan 1798–1850*, Clarendon Press, Oxford, 1980, p. 227.

2 Victor Jacquemont, *Letters from India: Describing a Journey in the British Dominions of India, Tibet, Lahore, and Cashmere*, Edward Churton, London, 1834, p. 370.

3 William Barr, *Journal of a March from Delhi to Peshâwur: And from Thence to Câbul, with the Mission of Lieut.-Colonel Sir C.M. Wade*, J. Madden, London, 1844, p. 101.

4 Chester County Historical Society, Harlan Papers, 'Oriental Sketches', 70.

5 Ibid., 76.

6 Ibid., 179.

7 British Library, Bengal Secret Consultations, IOR/P/BEN/SEC/380, 10 April 1834.

8 National Archives of India, Foreign/Secret/19 March 1833/30–1.

9 British Library, Bengal Secret Consultations, IOR/P/BEN/SEC/380, 19 June 1834, Wade to Macnaghten, 9 April 1834.

10 National Archives of India, Foreign/Secret/19 March 1833/30–1, 'Abstract of intelligence from Kabul from the 3rd to the 25th of December 1832'.

11 British Library, IOR/P/BEN/SEC/380, Bengal Secret Consultations, 19 June 1834, Gerard to Government, 8 April 1834.

12 Ibid.

13 Ibid.

14 Ibid., Wade to Macnaghten, 9 April 1834.

15 Ibid., Gerard to Government, 8 April 1834.

16 Ibid., Wade to Macnaghten, 9 April 1834.

17 Ibid., Wade to Masson, 6 April 1834.

18 Ibid., Wade to Macnaghten, 9 April 1834.

19 British Library, MSS Eur. E.161/7, 6.

20 National Archives (UK), FO 705/32, Masson to Pottinger, 9 October 1834.

21 Emily Eden, quoted in Henry Morris, *The Governors-General of India*, Christian Literature Society for India, London, 1896, p. 53.

22 British Library, IOR/P/BEN/SEC/380, Bengal Secret Consultations, 19 June 1834, Macnaghten to Wade, 26 May 1834.

23 British Library, MSS Eur. E.161/2, Wade to Masson, 11 February 1835.

24 Ibid., Wade to Masson, 5 December 1834.

25 Anon., *The Law Relating to India and the East India Company*, W. H. Allen, London, 1842, p. 485.

26 *The Asiatic Journal and Monthly Miscellany*, vol. 11 (September–December 1833), pp. 174–5.

27 Ibid., p. 84.

28 British Library, MSS Eur. E.165, 133.

29 Masson, *Various Journeys*, vol. 3, p. 322.

30 British Library, MSS Eur. E.164, 50.

31 Masson, *Various Journeys*, vol. 3, p. 252.

32 Ibid., p. 87.

33 Burnes, *Travels*, vol. 1, pp. 330–1.

34 Christine Noelle-Karimi, *The Interaction Between State and Tribe in Nineteenth-century Afghanistan*, University of California, Berkeley, CA, 1995, p. 38.

35 Mohan Lal, *Life of the Amir Dost Mohammed Khan of Kabul: With His Political Proceedings Towards the English, Russian, and Persian Governments, Including the Victory and Disasters of the British Army in Afghanistan*, Longman, London, 1846, p. 72.

36 Josiah Harlan, *A memoir of India and Avghanistaun, with observations on the present exciting and critical state and future prospects of those countries*, J. Dobson, Philadelphia, 1842, p. 154.

37 Ibid., p. 152.

38 Lal, *Life of the Amir*, p. 71.

39 Masson, *Various Journeys*, vol. 3, p. 86.

40 Burnes, *Travels*, vol. 1, pp. 134–5.

41 British Library, MSS Eur. E.164, 50.

42 Chester County Historical Society, Harlan Papers, 'Oriental Sketches', 178.

43 British Library, MSS Eur. E.164, 50.

44 National Archives of India, Foreign/Political/4 May 1835/117–18.

45 British Library, IOR/P/SEC/BOM/82, Secret Consultations, 26 August 1834, Wade to Government, 27 July 1834.

46 Masson, *Various Journeys*, vol. 3, p. 334.

47 British Library, MSS Eur. E.164, 48.

48 Ibid., 19.

49 Ibid.

50 Ibid.

51 Masson, *Various Journeys*, vol. 3, p. 335.

52 Ibid., p. 338.

53 Richard Hartley Kennedy, *Narrative of the campaign of the Indus, in Sind and Kaubool in 1838–9*, Richard Bentley, London, 1840, vol. 2, p. 118.

54 Masson, *Various Journeys*, vol. 3, p. 337.

55 Harlan, *Memoir*, pp. 158–9.

56 Masson, *Various Journeys*, vol. 3, p. 342.

57 Ibid., p. 344.

58 Ibid., p. 347.

59 Ibid., p. 350.

60 British Library MSS Eur. E.161, 15, Masson to Pottinger, 11 December 1834.

61 National Archives (UK), FO 705/32, Masson to Pottinger, 20 September 1834.

62 British Library, MSS Eur. E.165, 234.

63 Ibid.

64 Ibid., 234–5.

65 Marcus Aurelius, *Meditations*, 3.12. Adapted from George Long, *The Thoughts of the Emperor Marcus Aurelius Antoninus*, Lee and Shepard, Boston, 1876, p. 118.

9 STRANGER THAN FICTION

1 British Library, MSS Eur. E.161/5, Brownlow to Masson, 11 April 1835.

2 Ibid.
3 British Library, MSS Eur. E.165, 9.
4 Masson, *Various Journeys*, vol. 3, p. 353.
5 Ibid.
6 British Library, MSS Eur. E.164, 15.
7 British Library, MSS Eur. E.161/2, Wade to Masson, 5 March 1835.
8 Ibid., Wade to Masson, 25 July 1835.
9 *Morning Post*, 24 June 1842, p. 2.
10 National Archives of India, Foreign/Secret/27 July 1835/28.
11 Ibid., Foreign/Secret/27 July 1835/27.
12 British Library, Bengal Secret Consultations, IOR/P/BEN/SEC/380, 19 June 1834, Wade to Macnaghten, 9 April 1834.
13 National Archives (UK), Ellenborough Papers, PRO 30/12/29/1, 54.
14 Ibid.
15 Ibid., 69.
16 British Library, MSS Eur. E.161/2, Wade to Masson, 19 August 1835.
17 National Archives (UK), FO 705/32, Masson to Macnaghten, 6 November 1837.
18 Ibid., Masson to Pottinger, 30 November 1835.
19 Ibid., Masson to Pottinger, 20 September 1834.
20 British Library MSS Eur. E.161, 5, Masson to Pottinger, 6 July 1834.
21 British Library, MSS Eur. E.165, 227.
22 Ibid., 176.
23 National Archives (UK), FO 705/32, Masson to Pottinger, 11 December 1834.
24 British Museum, Original Papers, OP 21/8/1835, Honigberger to Forshall, 21 August 1835.
25 Ibid., Hawkins to Forshall, 20 August 1835.
26 Ibid., Hawkins to Forshall, 26 August 1835.
27 Ibid., Hawkins to Forshall, 31 August 1835.
28 British Library, MSS Eur. E.161/7, 68.
29 British Library, MSS Eur. E.161/2, Wade to Pottinger, 3 September 1835.
30 National Archives (UK), FO 705/32, Pottinger to J. P. Riach, 5 March 1836.
31 Ibid., Masson to Pottinger, 30 September 1835.
32 Ibid.
33 Ibid.

34 British Library, MSS Eur. E.161/2, Wade to Masson, 25 December 1835.

35 National Archives (UK), FO 705/32, Masson to Pottinger, 30 September 1835.

36 British Library, MSS Eur. E.165, 129.

37 Getzel M. Cohen, *The Hellenistic Settlements in the East from Armenia and Mesopotamia to Bactria and India*, University of California Press, Berkeley, CA, 2013, p. 267.

38 William Fordyce Mavor, *Universal History, Ancient and Modern: From the Earliest Records of Time, to the General Peace of 1801*, Collins and Sons, Philadelphia, 1803, vol. 4, p. 357.

39 William Mitford, *The History of Greece*, Cadell and Davies, London, 1818, vol. 5, p. 343.

40 Connop Thirlwall, *History of Greece*, Longman, London, 1840, vol. 7, p. 369.

41 National Archives (UK), London, FO 705/32, Masson to Pottinger, 23 April 1834.

42 British Library MSS Eur. E.165, 218.

43 National Archives (UK), FO 705/32, Masson to Pottinger, 26 May 1836.

44 James Prinsep, 'Further notes and drawings of Bactrian and Indo-Scythic Coins', *Journal of the Asiatic Society of Bengal*, vol. 4 (1835), p. 329.

45 Ibid., pp. 349–50.

46 Ibid., p. 290.

47 Ibid., p. 329.

48 Firdausi, *Shahnama*, vol. 6, p. 143.

49 *The British Critic*, vol. 13 (1833), p. 387.

50 *Milinda Pañha*, 39.

51 *Mahāvaṃsa*, 29.7.

52 Athenaeus of Naucratis, *Deipnosophistae*, 3.14.

53 Tim Whitmarsh and Stuart Thomson, *The Romance Between Greece and the East*, Cambridge University Press, Cambridge, 2013, p. 6.

54 British Library, MSS Eur. E.161/5, Brownlow to Masson, 28 March 1836.

55 Masson, *Various Journeys*, vol. 3, p. 362.

10 THE AGE OF EVERYTHING

1 Masson, *Various Journeys*, vol. 3, p. 362.

2 British Library, MSS Eur. E.165, 225.

3 Masson, *Various Journeys*, vol. 3, p. 367.

4 British Library, MSS Eur. E.165, 224.

5 British Library, MSS Eur. E.161/5, Brownlow to Masson, 28 March 1836.

6 Richard Hartley Kennedy, *Various Journeys of the campaign of the Indus, in Sind and Kaubool in 1838–9*, Richard Bentley, London, 1840, vol. 2, p. 118.

7 Honigberger, *Thirty Five Years*, p. 55.

8 Lal Sohan Lal Suri, *Umdat-ut-tawarikh*, S. Chand, Delhi, 1961, vol. 3, p. 286.

9 *The Calcutta Review*, vol. 7 (January–June 1847), p. 285.

10 Suri, *Umdat-ut-tawarikh*, vol. 3, p. 289.

11 *The Calcutta Review*, vol. 7 (January–June 1847), p. 285.

12 Punjab Archives (Lahore), Punjab Records, Book 142, letter 78.

13 Harlan, *Memoir*, frontispiece.

14 Grey and Garrett, *European Adventurers*, p. 261.

15 Ibid., p. 241.

16 National Archives (UK), FO 705/32, Pottinger to J. P. Riach, 5 March 1836.

17 Ibid., Pottinger to Masson, 7 April 1836.

18 Ibid., Pottinger to Masson, 8 March 1836.

19 British Library, MSS Eur. E.165, 129–30.

20 National Archives (UK), FO 705/32, Masson to Pottinger, 13 July 1836.

21 Ibid., Masson to Pottinger, 26 May 1836.

22 Anon., *Correspondence Relating to Persia and Affghanistan*, J. Harrison, London, 1839, pp. 395–6. Dost Mohammad to Government, 31 May 1836.

23 Masson, *Various Journeys*, vol. 3, pp. 362–3.

24 Ibid., pp. 395–6.

25 British Library, MSS Eur. E.165, 20.

26 National Archives (UK), London, FO 705/32, Masson to Pottinger, 9 October 1834.

27 Ibid., Pottinger to Masson, 15 January 1837.

28 National Archives (UK), FO 705/32, Masson to Pottinger, 18 October 1836.

29 British Library, MSS Eur. E.161/5, Masson to Brownlow, 26 June 1836.

30 Ibid., Brownlow to Masson, 28 March 1836.

31 British Library, MSS Eur. E.165, 223.

32 National Archives (UK), FO 705/32, Masson to Trevelyan, 15 February 1836.

33 Ibid., Masson to Pottinger, 18 October 1836.

34 National Archives (UK), FO 705/32, Masson to Trevelyan, 15 February 1836.

35 British Library, MSS Eur. E.161/2, Wade to Masson, 10 April 1836.

36 Godfrey Vigne, *A personal narrative of a visit to Ghuzni, Kabul and Afghanistan, and of a residence at the court of Dost Mohamed*, George Routledge, London, 1843, pp. 140–1.

37 National Archives (UK), FO 705/32, Masson to Pottinger, 13 July 1836.

38 Vigne, *Various Journeys*, p. 153.

39 Ibid., p. 382.

40 Ibid.

41 Ibid., p. 160.

42 British Library, MSS Eur. E.161/4, 14.

43 Vigne, *Various Journeys*, p. 212.

44 British Library, MSS Eur. E.165, 232–3.

45 Smooth, flat disc of ivory, British Museum, 1880.3828.u.

46 Cast copper alloy coin (AD 618–906), British Museum, IOLC.4641.

47 Oval, amber-coloured chalcedony intaglio, showing a female bust in profile (first–second century AD), British Museum, 1880.3548.

48 Fredrik Hiebert and Pierre Cambon, *Afghanistan: Crossroads of the Ancient World*, British Museum Press, London, 2011.

49 Translucent glass beaker, found at Bagram in 1937, exhibited at the Musée Guimet, Paris, in 1976, published in *Afghanistan: Ancient Land with Modern Ways*, Ministry of Planning of the Royal Government of Afghanistan, Kabul, 1961, p. 34.

50 Muḥammad ibn Aḥmad Ibn Jubayr, trans. J. C. Broadhurst, *The Travels of Ibn Jubayr*, Jonathan Cape, London, 1952, p. 33.

51 National Archives, London, FO 705/32, Pottinger to Masson, 27 April 1837.

52 Wilson, *Ariana Antiqua*, p. 118.

53 British Library, MSS Eur. E.165, 219.

54 Firdausi, *Shahnameh*, vol. 6, p. 168.

55 Ibid., pp. 168–9.

56 British Library, MSS Eur. E.169, 103.

57 Masson, *Various Journeys*, vol. 3, p. 379.

58 National Archives (UK), FO 705/32, Masson to Pottinger, 16 January 1837.

59 Ibid., Masson to Pottinger, 18 October 1836.

60 British Library, MSS Eur. E.161/5, Brownlow to Masson, 22 September 1836.

61 National Archives (UK), FO 705/32, Masson to Pottinger, 18 October 1836.

62 British Library, MSS Eur. E.161/5, Brownlow to Masson, 22 September 1836.

II THE SECOND ALEXANDER

 1 Burnes, *Travels*, vol. 1, p. 117.

 2 British Library, MSS Eur. E.161/5, Brownlow to Masson, 22 September 1836.

 3 Burnes, *Travels*, vol. 1, p. vii.

 4 John Kaye, *Lives of Indian Officers: illustrative of the history of the civil and military service of India*, A. Strahan, London, 1867, vol. 2, p. 232.

 5 Ibid., p. 233.

 6 Ibid., pp. 237–8.

 7 National Library of Scotland, John Murray Archive, MS.42048, Burnes to Murray, 28 December 1834.

 8 Ibid., Burnes to Murray, 25 January 1834.

 9 National Library of Scotland, John Murray Archive, MS.42050.

10 National Library of Scotland, John Murray Archive, MS.42048, Burnes to Murray, 7 November 1834.

11 *The Gentleman's Magazine*, vol. 17 (1842), p. 435.

12 Burnes, *Travels*, vol. 1, p. 117.

13 Ibid., vol. 2, p. 214.

14 Henry Miers Elliot, *The History of India, as Told by Its Own Historians*, Trübner and Co., London, 1871, vol. 3, pp. 170–1.

15 Rudyard Kipling, *Under the Deodars*, Doubleday, Garden City, NY, 1914, pp. 189–236.
16 National Archives (UK), FO 705/32, Pottinger to Masson, 16 September 1838.
17 Ibid., Pottinger to Masson, 15 January 1837.
18 Ibid., Masson to Pottinger, 16 January 1837.
19 Masson, *Various Journeys*, vol. 3, p. 425.
20 Vigne, *Narrative*, pp. 158–9.
21 Masson, *Various Journeys*, vol. 3, pp. 425–6.
22 British Library, MSS Eur. E.161/3, Burnes to Masson, 2 June 1837.
23 National Archives (UK), FO 705/32, Pottinger to Masson, 5 October 1837.
24 *The Literary Gazette and Journal of Belles Lettres*, vol. 18 (1834), p. 707.
25 *The Manchester Times and Gazette*, 9 January 1841.
26 British Library, MSS Eur. E.169/1, 81.
27 National Archives (UK), FO 705/32, Masson to Wade, 6 November 1837.
28 British Library, MSS Eur. E.165, Burnes to Masson, 9 March 1836.
29 Worcester College, Oxford, MS.109, Journal of Alexander Burnes, 18 September 1837.
30 British Library, MSS Eur. E161/3, Burnes to Masson, 22 August 1837.
31 Masson, *Various Journeys*, vol. 3, p. 445.
32 Worcester College, Oxford, MS.109, 20 September 1837.
33 Ibid., 21 September 1837.
34 British Library, MSS Eur. E.161/3, Burnes to Masson, 2 June 1837.
35 Harlan, *Memoir*, p. 138.
36 National Archives of India, Foreign/Political/20 December 1837/34, Burnes to Macnaghten, 24 September 1837.
37 Harlan, *Memoir*, p. 139.
38 Worcester College, Oxford, MS.109, 25 September 1837.
39 Ibid.
40 National Archives (UK), FO 705/32, Masson to Pottinger, 7 November 1837.
41 Kaye, *Lives*, vol. 2, p. 219.
42 Masson, *Various Journeys*, vol. 3, p. 439, Burnes to Masson, 6 August 1837.

43 British Library, MSS Eur. E.161/3, Burnes to Macnaghten, 9 October 1837.

44 National Archives of India, Foreign/Political/31 July 1837/81–3.

45 National Archives (UK), FO 705/32, Pottinger to Masson, 27 March 1837.

46 British Library, MSS Eur. E.161/3, Burnes to Colvin, 12 May 1837.

47 National Archives (UK), FO 705/32, Masson to Pottinger, 24 June 1838.

48 British Library, MSS Eur. E.161/3, Burnes to Masson, 2 June 1837.

49 Alexander Burnes, *Cabool: A Personal Various Journeys of a Journey To, and Residence in that City, in the Years 1836, 7, and 8*, John Murray, London, 1843, p. 245.

50 Masson, *Various Journeys*, vol. 3, p. 452.

51 National Archives of India, Foreign/Secret/15 May 1837/8, Dost Mohammad Khan to Wade, 25 February 1837.

52 Masson, *Various Journeys*, vol. 3, p. 455.

53 Ibid., p. 459.

54 Worcester College, Oxford, MS.109, 15 November 1837.

55 Masson, *Various Journeys*, vol. 3, p. 457.

56 Ibid., p. 456.

57 Ibid., p. 460.

58 Ibid., p. 456.

59 National Archives of India, Foreign/Secret/28 September 1842/43, Burnes to Holland, 30 October 1837.

60 William Dalrymple, *Return of a King: The Battle for Afghanistan*, Bloomsbury, London, 2013, pp. 82–4.

61 National Archives (UK), FO 705/32, Masson to Pottinger, 7 November 1837.

62 British Library, MSS Eur. E.161/3, 125, Burnes to Masson, undated.

63 National Archives of India, Foreign/Secret/28 September 1842/43, Burnes to Holland, 9 January 1838.

64 Worcester College, Oxford, MS.109, 30 December 1837.

65 Masson, *Various Journeys*, vol. 3, p. 464.

66 British Library, MSS Eur. E.165, Burnes to Masson, 9 March 1836.

67 British Library, MSS Eur. E.161/3, Burnes to Masson, 12 December 1837.

68 Harlan, *Memoir*, pp. 155–6.

69 Masson, *Various Journeys*, vol. 3, p. 459.

70 Worcester College, Oxford, MS.109, 17 January 1838.

71 Ibid., 2 January 1838.

72 National Archives of India, Foreign/Secret/28 September 1842/43, Burnes to Holland, 9 January 1838.

73 British Library, Add. MSS 37691, Colvin to Burnes, 13 September 1837.

74 Worcester College, Oxford, MS.109, 27 January 1838.

75 Ibid., 5 February 1838.

76 Ibid., 18 January 1838.

77 Anon., *Parliamentary Papers, Session 2, 31 May–13 August 1859*, House of Commons, London, 1859, vol. 25, p. 115, Macnaghten to Burnes, 20 January 1838.

78 Anon., *Accounts and Papers of the House of Commons, Session, 5 February–27 August 1839*, House of Commons, London, 1839, vol. 40, p. 31, Burnes to Macnaghten, 13 March 1838.

79 Harlan, *Memoir*, p. 171.

80 Anon., *Accounts and Papers*, p. 37.

81 Masson, *Various Journeys*, vol. 3, p. 469.

82 Ibid., p. 463.

83 Worcester College, Oxford, MS.109, 19 February 1838.

84 Masson, *Various Journeys*, vol. 3, p. 475.

85 Lal, *Life of the Amir*, p. 312.

86 Worcester College, Oxford, MS.109, 5 February 1838.

87 Masson, *Various Journeys*, vol. 3, p. 477.

88 Worcester College, Oxford, MS.109, 3–4 March 1838.

89 Anon., *Accounts and Papers*, 41, Burnes to Dost Mohammad Khan, 22 April 1838.

90 Ibid., Dost Mohammad Khan to Burnes, 23 April 1838.

91 Masson, *Various Journeys*, vol. 3, p. 476.

92 Burnes, *Cabool*, pp. 269–70.

93 Worcester College, Oxford, MS.109, 22 April 1838.

94 Masson, *Various Journeys*, vol. 3, p. 478.

95 Worcester College, Oxford, MS.109, 24 April 1838.

96 Ibid., 25 April 1838.

97 Gertrude Landa (pseud. Aunt Naomi), *Jewish Fairy Tales and Legends*, Shapiro, Valentine & Co., London, 1900, pp. 286–8. Adapted from Talmud, *Tamid*, 32a–b.

98 National Archives (UK), FO 705/32, Masson to Pottinger, 8 May 1838.

12 LAST RESORT

1 Walter Thornberry, *Old and New London: the city ancient and modern*, Cassell, London, 1887, p. 184.

2 National Archives (UK), FO 705/32, H. H. Wilson to James Prinsep, 21 May 1836.

3 British Library MSS E/4/1062, Bombay Dispatches, 5 January–31 May 1838, 67.

4 Ibid.

5 Grey and Garrett, *European Adventurers*, p. 130.

6 Herbert Benjamin Edwardes, *Life of Sir Henry Lawrence*, Smith, Elder, London, 1872, pp. 295–6.

7 Julian James Cotton, *General Avitabile*, Edinburgh Press, Calcutta, 1906, p. 16.

8 Ibid., pp. 19–20.

9 Grey and Garrett, *European Adventurers*, pp. 130–1.

10 Cotton, *General Avitabile*, p. 25.

11 Daniel Henry MacKinnon, *Military Service and Adventures in the Far East*, Charles Oliver, London, 1847, vol. 1, pp. 247–8.

12 Ibid., pp. 245–6.

13 Cotton, *General Avitabile*, pp. 21–2.

14 MacKinnon, *Military Service*, vol. 1, p. 249.

15 Ibid., pp. 248–50.

16 Erich Von Schonberg, *Travels In India And Kashmir*, Hurst and Blackett, London, 1853, vol. 1, pp. 310–11.

17 Edwardes, *Life of Sir Henry Lawrence*, p. 292.

18 Cotton, *General Avitabile*, p. 59.

19 Edwardes, *Life of Sir Henry Lawrence*, pp. 295–6.

20 Cotton, *General Avitabile*, p. 16: 'Per amore di Dio, fatemi partire da questo paese.'

21 National Archives of India, Foreign/Secret/28 September 1842/43, Burnes to Holland, 6 May 1838.

22 Ibid.

23 Worcester College, Oxford, MS.109, 6 May 1838.

24 National Archives (UK), FO 705/32, Masson to Pottinger, 8 May 1838.

25 Ibid., Pottinger to Masson, 4 June 1838.

26 Ibid., Masson to Pottinger, 18 October 1838.

27 Ibid., Masson to Pottinger, 8 May 1838.

28 Ibid.

29 British Library, MSS Eur. E.161/3, Macnaghten to Masson, 23 May 1838.

30 Ibid., Burnes to Masson, 2 June 1838.

31 Ibid., Burnes to Masson, 22 June 1838.

32 Worcester College, Oxford, MS.109, 8 June 1838.

33 Craig Murray, *Sikunder Burnes: Master of the Great Game*, Birlinn, Edinburgh, 2016, p. 135.

34 Emily Eden, *Up the Country*, Richard Bentley, London, 1867, p. 148.

35 William Osborne, *The court and camp of Runjeet Singh*, Henry Colburn, London, 1840, p. 73.

36 Ibid., pp. 79–80.

37 Ibid., p. 90.

38 Ibid., p. 198.

39 National Archives of India, Foreign/Secret/3 October 1838/104, Torrens to Macnaghten, 15 May 1838.

40 National Archives of India, Foreign/Secret/17 October 1838/71, Burnes to Macnaghten, 2 June 1838.

41 John Kaye, *History of the War in Afghanistan*, W. R. Allen, London, 1874, vol. 1, p. 356.

42 National Archives of India, Foreign/Secret/28 September 1842/43, Burnes to Holland, 8 June 1838.

43 National Archives of India, Foreign/Secret/17 Oct 1838/72.

44 British Library, MSS Eur. E.161/3, 16.

45 Eden, *Up the Country*, p. 140.

46 George Buist, *Outline of the operations of the British troops in Scinde and Afghanistan*, Times Office, Bombay, 1843, p. 21.

47 Eden, *Up the Country*, p. 145.

48 National Archives of India, Foreign/Secret/28 September 1842/43, Burnes to Holland, 8 June 1838.

49 Ibid., Burnes to Holland, 27 June 1838.

50 British Library, MSS Eur. E.161/3, Burnes to Masson, 27 June 1838.

51 Cotton, *General Avitabile*, p. 24.
52 Ibid., p. 26.
53 *The Calcutta Review*, vol. 123 (July 1906), p. 549. See also British Library, F/4/2034/92125, F/4/1992/88327.
54 National Archives (UK), FO 705/32, Masson to Pottinger, 22 July 1838.
55 Ibid., Masson to Pottinger, 24 June 1838.

13 NO RETURN

1 British Library, MSS Eur. E.162, 8.
2 Kaye, *History of the War*, pp. 366–7.
3 British Library, MSS Eur. E.359/6, Colvin Diaries, 12 July 1838.
4 Masson, *Various Journeys*, vol. 3, p. 490.
5 British Library, MSS Eur. E.359/6, Colvin Diaries, 4 July 1838.
6 National Archives of India, Foreign/Secret/28 September 1842/43, Burnes to Holland, 6 May 1838.
7 British Library, MSS Eur. E.359/6, Colvin Diaries, 13 July 1838.
8 Kaye, *Lives*, vol. 2, p. 37.
9 British Library, MSS Eur. E.162, 11.
10 Eden, *Up the Country*, p. 157.
11 National Archives (UK), FO 705/32, Masson to Pottinger, 22 July 1838.
12 Cotton, *General Avitabile*, p. 25.
13 British Library, MSS Eur. E.165, 127.
14 National Archives (UK), FO 705/32, Burnes to Masson, 4 August 1838.
15 Ibid.
16 Ibid.
17 British Library, MSS Eur. E.165, 122.
18 National Archives (UK), FO 705/32, Burnes to Masson, 4 August 1838.
19 British Library, MSS Eur. E.161/3, Burnes to Masson, 13 September 1838.
20 National Archives (UK), FO 705/32, Masson to Pottinger, 10 September 1838.
21 Ibid., Pottinger to Masson, 16 September 1838.
22 Ibid., Masson to Pottinger, 10 September 1838.
23 Ibid., Masson to Pottinger, 18 October 1838.

24 British Library, MSS Eur. E.161/3, Burnes to Masson, 5 September 1838.
25 British Library, MSS Eur. E.162, 4.
26 Anon., *The Bengal and Agra Annual Guide and Gazetteer for 1841*, William Rushton and Co., Calcutta, 1841, p. 274.
27 National Archives, London, FO 705/32, Jephson to Masson, 23 August 1838.
28 Ibid.
29 British Library, MSS Eur. E.165, 134.
30 British Library, IOR/P/BEN/SEC/380, Bengal Secret Consultations, 19 June 1834, Macnaghten to Wade, 26 May 1834.
31 British Library, MSS Eur. E.161/2, Wade to Masson, 11 February 1835.
32 British Library, MSS Eur. E.165, 134.
33 Ibid., 136.
34 National Archives, London, FO 705/32, Jephson to Masson, 23 August 1838.
35 British Library, MSS Eur. E.165, 122.
36 National Archives of India, Foreign/Secret/28 September 1842/35, Burnes to Jacob, 5 August 1838.
37 Ibid., Burnes to Holland, 6 May 1838.
38 Ibid., Burnes to Jacob, 5 August 1838.
39 Ibid.
40 National Archives, London, FO 705/32, Masson to Pottinger, 18 October 1838.
41 Ibid.
42 Ibid.
43 Ibid., Masson to the Government of India, 16 October 1838.

14 WORLDS TO CONQUER

1 Eden, *Up the Country*, p. 175.
2 Ibid., p. 169.
3 National Archives of India, Foreign/Political/24 October 1838/8.
4 Adapted from E. Hultzsch, *Inscriptions of Asoka*, Clarendon Press for the Government of India, Oxford, 1925, p. 44.
5 Charles Masson, 'Narrative of an Excursion from Pesháwer to Sháh-Báz Ghari', *Journal of the Royal Asiatic Society*, vol. 8 (1846), p. 295.
6 Ibid., p. 296.
7 Ibid., p. 298.

8 Ibid., p. 301.

9 Anon., *The Policy of the Government of British India, as exhibited in Official Documents*, W. H. Allen, London, 1839, pp. 39–41.

10 Masson, *Various Journeys*, vol. 3, p. 489.

11 British Library, MSS Eur. E.161/6, 16.

12 National Archives of India, Foreign/Political/6 July 1835/16, Wade to Macnaghten, 10 June 1835.

13 Ibid.

14 British Library, MSS Eur. E.165, 43.

15 National Archives of India/Foreign/Secret/11 June 1838/74.

16 British Library, MSS Eur. E.165, 123.

17 *The Dublin University Magazine: A Literary and Political Journal*, vol. 22 (1843), p. 292.

18 British Library, MSS Eur. E.165, 128.

19 Eden, *Up the Country*, p. 209.

20 Ibid., pp. 208–9.

21 Ibid., p. 199.

22 British Library, MSS Eur. E.161/4, Stacy to Masson, 13 December 1838.

23 *Journal of the Asiatic Society of Bengal*, vol. 4 (1835), p. 622.

24 British Library, MSS Eur. E.161/4, Stacy to Masson, 19 December 1838.

25 National Archives (UK), FO 705/32, Masson to Pottinger, 18 October 1838.

26 British Library, MSS Eur. E.162, 9.

27 British Library, MSS Eur. E.165, 66.

28 *The Times*, 4 November 1842, p. 3.

29 James Elroy Flecker, 'The Ballad of Iskander', quoted in *Bulletin of the John Rylands University Library of Manchester*, vol. 69 (1986), p. 372.

30 C. A. Bloss, *Ancient History, illustrated by colored maps, and a chronological chart, for the use of families and schools*, Clark and Maynard, New York, 1869, p. 263.

31 Plutarch, *On tranquillity of mind*, 4.

32 National Archives (UK), FO 705/32, Masson to Jephson, quoted in Masson to Pottinger, 18 October 1838.

33 British Library, MSS Eur. E.165, 135.

34 National Archives of India, Foreign/Secret/28 September 1842/43, Burnes to Holland, 29 November 1838.

35 Kaye, *History of the War*, vol. 2, p. 172.

36 Eden, *Up the Country*, p. 233.

37 William Nott, *Memoirs and correspondence of Major-General Sir William Nott*, Hurst and Blackett, London, 1854, vol. 1, pp. 90–1.

38 Ibid., p. 91.

39 Ibid.

40 *The Eclectic Magazine*, vol. 9 (1846), p. 364.

41 Punjab Archives (Lahore), Punjab Records, book 139, letter 8.

42 British Library, MSS Eur. E.165, 135.

43 Ibid.

44 Josiah Harlan, 'Personal Narrative of General Harlan's Eighteen Years' Residence in Asia', appendix to Harlan, *Memoir*, pp. 4–5.

45 Ibid., p. 4.

46 Ibid., p. 6.

47 Chester County Historical Society, Harlan Papers, email from Eckart Schiewek to the Chester County Historical Society, 11 January 2008.

48 Ibid., unnumbered folio, dated 16 October 1839. Based on a translation by Eckart Schiewek.

49 Harlan, *Central Asia*, p. 145.

50 *United States Gazette*, quoted in Harlan, *Memoir*, p. 1.

51 Harlan, 'Personal Narrative', p. 6.

52 Ibid., p. 5.

53 Chester County Historical Society, Harlan Papers, Miscellaneous Papers/1830s Folder, Stacy to Harlan, 17 December 1838.

54 Ibid., 10 August 1839.

55 Ibid., 'Oriental Sketches', 6.

56 Ibid., Miscellaneous Papers/1830s Folder, Harlan to G. H. Macgregor, Superintendent of Police, 19 October 1839.

57 British Library, MSS Eur. E.161/1, 193, Pottinger to Masson, 15 October 1839.

58 Ibid., Pottinger to Masson, 25 October 1839.

59 British Library, MSS Eur. E.161/3, 34, Burnes to Masson, 20 September 1838.

60 Royal Geographical Society, Henry Rawlinson Papers, 4, Journal, 1 December 1839.

61 British Library, MSS Eur. E.165, 108.

62 Royal Geographical Society, Henry Rawlinson Papers, 4, Journal, 1 December 1839.

63 British Library, MSS Eur. E.165, 20.

64 National Archives (UK), FO 705/32, Masson to Pottinger, 3 November 1839.

65 Ibid., Masson to Pottinger, 2 October 1839.

66 Ibid., Masson to Pottinger, 21 February 1840.

67 British Library, MSS Eur. E.165, 20.

68 National Archives (UK), FO 705/32, Masson to Pottinger, 18 October 1838.

69 Ibid., Masson to Pottinger, 21 February 1840.

70 Royal Geographical Society, Henry Rawlinson Papers, 4, Journal, 1 December 1839.

71 National Archives (UK), FO 705/32, Masson to Pottinger, 3 November 1839.

72 Royal Geographical Society, Henry Rawlinson Papers, 4, Journal, 1 December 1839.

73 British Library, MSS Eur. E.165, 189.

74 Ibid., 165.

75 Quoted in *The Caledonian Mercury*, 7 November 1842, p. 2.

76 National Archives (UK), FO 705/32, Masson to Pottinger, 2 October 1839.

77 Ibid., Masson to Pottinger, 21 February 1840.

78 Ibid., Masson to Pottinger, 3 November 1839.

79 Ibid., Masson to Pottinger, 20 February 1840.

80 Royal Geographical Society, Henry Rawlinson Papers, 4, Journal, 1 December 1839.

81 Ibid.

82 National Archives (UK), FO 705/32, Masson to Pottinger, 21 February 1840.

15 THE CHAMBER OF BLOOD

1 James Atkinson, *Sketches in Afghaunistan*, H. Graves, London, 1842, pp. xi–xii.

2 James Rattray, *The costumes of the various tribes, portraits of ladies of rank, celebrated princes and chiefs, views of the principal fortresses and cities, and interior of the cities and temples of Afghaunistaun*, Hering & Remington, London, 1848, p. 13.

3 *Illustrated London News*, 3 September 1910, p. 353.

4 Rattray, *Costumes*, p. 13.

5 British Library, MSS Eur. E.165, 226.

6 Ibid., 137.

7 Ibid.

8 Ibid.

9 Ibid.

10 *Bombay Times*, 31 March 1841, p. 203.

11 Charles Masson, *Various Journeys of a Journey to Kalât, Including an Insurrection at that Place in 1840: And a Memoir on Eastern Balochistan*, Richard Bentley, London, 1843, p. 10.

12 Masson, *Various Journeys*, vol. 2, p. 111.

13 Ibid., p. 91.

14 Ibid., p. 90.

15 Adapted from H. T. Lambrick, 'Observations on Baloch Poetry of the Sind Border', *Journal of the Sind Historical Society*, vol. 5 (1942), p. 180.

16 British Library, MSS Eur. E.165, 106.

17 *The Asiatic Journal*, vol. 34 (January–April 1841), p. 190, Loveday to family members, 25 January 1840.

18 Masson, *Kalât*, pp. 117–18.

19 British Library, MSS Eur. E.165, 106.

20 Masson, *Kalât*, p. 69.

21 British Library, MSS Eur. E.165, 106.

22 Masson, *Kalât*, p. 68.

23 *The London Quarterly Review*, October 1846, p. 264.

24 Ibid.

25 James Burnes, *Notes on his name and family*, printed for private circulation, Edinburgh, 1851, p. 64.

26 *The Asiatic Journal*, vol. 34 (January–April 1841), p. 186, Loveday to family members, 27 January 1839.

27 Ibid., p. 187, Loveday to family members, 9 May 1839.

28 Ibid., p. 190, Loveday to family members, 25 November 1839.

29 Masson, *Kalât*, pp. 77–8.

30 Ibid., p. 71.

31 Ibid.

32 British Library, MSS Eur. E.165, 107.

33 Ibid., 106.

34 Ibid., 107.
35 Ibid., 75; *The Calcutta Englishman*, 14 January 1841, p. 3.
36 Masson, *Kalât*, pp. 117–18.
37 Ibid.
38 *The Asiatic Journal*, vol. 34 (January–April 1841), p. 187, Loveday to family members, 9 May 1839.
39 National Archives, London, FO 705/32, Masson to Pottinger, 3 November 1839.
40 Adapted from Gholam Mahomed Khan Mazari, ed. T. L. J. Mayer, *Baloch Classics*, CMS Mission Press, Sikandra, Agra, 1906, pp. 1–2.
41 British Library, MSS Eur. E.165, 107.
42 Ibid., 108.
43 Masson, *Kalât*, p. 133.
44 British Library, MSS Eur. E.165, 109.
45 Masson, *Kalât*, p. 137.
46 British Library, IOR/L/PS/5/154, 5, Rawlinson to Macnaghten, 21 October 1840.
47 *Bombay Times*, 13 March 1841, pp. 164–5.
48 *The Asiatic Journal*, vol. 35 (May–August 1841), p. 185.
49 *Bombay Times*, 13 March 1841, pp. 164–5, Loveday to Captain J. D. D. Bean, quoted in Bean to Bell, 2 January 1841.
50 *Bombay Times*, 13 March 1841, pp. 164–5.
51 Ibid.
52 British Library, MSS Eur. E.165, 110.
53 Masson, *Kalât*, p. 143.
54 Ibid., p. 150.
55 Ibid., p. 148.
56 Ibid., pp. 150–1.
57 British Library, MSS Eur. E.165, 112.
58 Masson, *Kalât*, pp. 151–2.
59 Ibid., p. 154.
60 British Library, MSS Eur. E.165, 110.
61 Masson, *Kalât*, p. 154.
62 Ibid., p. 150.
63 *The Asiatic Journal*, vol. 34 (January–April 1841), p. 190, Loveday to family members, August 1840.
64 Masson, *Kalât*, p. 156.
65 Ibid., p. 157.

66 Ibid.
67 Ibid., p. 166.
68 Ibid., p. 167.
69 Ibid., p. 165.
70 *Bombay Times*, 2 January 1841, p. 4.
71 Masson, *Kalât*, p. 165.
72 British Library, MSS Eur. E.165, 110.
73 Ibid., 115.
74 Ibid., 201–2.
75 *The Asiatic Journal*, vol. 34 (January–April 1841), p. 190, Loveday to family members, August 1840.
76 Ibid., vol. 35 (May–August 1841), p. 127, Loveday to Major Griffiths, 11 August 1840.
77 Masson, *Kalât*, p. 169.
78 Ibid., p. 176.
79 Ibid., p. 182.
80 British Library, MSS Eur. E.165, 116; British Library, IOR/L/PS/5/154, 24, Loveday to Bean, 26 August 1840.
81 Masson, *Kalât*, pp. 193–4.
82 Ibid., pp. 174–5.
83 Ibid., p. 197.
84 Ibid., p. 196.
85 Ibid., p. 198.
86 Ibid., pp. 200–1.
87 Ibid., p. 203.
88 Adapted from Mazari, *Baloch Classics*, pp. 10–12.

16 THE PRISONER

1   Masson, *Kalât*, p. 206.
2   British Library, MSS Eur. E.165, 117.
3   Masson, *Kalât*, p. 203.
4   Ibid., p. 204.
5   Ibid., p. 208.
6   Ibid., pp. 208–9.
7   British Library, MSS Eur. E.165, 120.
8   Masson, *Kalât*, p. 214.
9   British Library, IOR/L/PS/5/154, 25.
10 Masson, *Kalât*, p. 214.
11 British Library, MSS Eur. E.165, 124.

12 Masson, *Kalât*, p. 221.

13 Ibid., p. 228.

14 British Library, IOR/F/4/2009/89688, 11.

15 British Library, IOR/L/PS/5/154, 25.

16 Ibid., 26, Bean to Gul Mohammad, 31 August 1840.

17 British Library, IOR/L/PS/5/154, 31.

18 British Library, MSS Eur. E.165, 154.

19 British Library, IOR/L/PS/5/154, 45.

20 Ibid., 31.

21 Masson, *Kalât*, 230.

22 British Library, IOR/L/PS/5/154, 31, Loveday to Bean, 14 September 1840.

23 Masson, *Kalât*, p. 229.

24 Ibid., p. 237.

25 British Library, MSS Eur. E.165, 120.

26 Masson, *Kalât*, p. 234.

27 Ibid., p. 236.

28 Ibid., p. 246.

29 Ibid.

30 Ibid., p. 247.

31 Loveday to Bean, 27 September 1840, quoted in Anon., *Alphabetical catalogue of the contents of the pre-mutiny records of the commissioner in Sind*, Commissioner's Printing Press, Karachi, 1857, p. 213.

32 British Library, IOR/L/PS/5/154, 43, Loveday to Bean, 24 September 1840.

33 Masson, *Kalât*, p. 238.

34 Ibid., p. 249.

35 Ibid.

36 Ibid., p. 250.

17 THE SPY

1 British Library, IOR/L/PS/5/154, 43–4, Loveday to Bean, 24 September 1840.

2 Ibid., 43, Loveday to Bean, 24 September 1840.

3 Masson, *Kalât*, p. 252.

4 Ibid., p. 254.

5 Ibid., pp. 254–5.

6 British Library, IOR/H/797, Bell to Bean, 29 September 1840.

7 Ibid., Bell to Colvin, 19 October 1840.

8 British Library, MSS Eur. E.195, 36–7.
9 British Library, IOR/L/PS/5/550, 33.
10 Masson, *Kalât*, p. 255.
11 British Library, MSS Eur. E.165, 123.
12 Masson, *Kalât*, p. 259.
13 British Library, IOR/F/4/2009/89688, 64–5.
14 Masson, *Kalât*, p. 259.
15 British Library, IOR/L/PS/5/154, 26, Bean to Loveday, 21 August 1840.
16 Masson, *Kalât*, pp. 226–7.
17 British Library, IOR/L/PS/5/154, 43, Loveday to Bean, 24 September 1840.
18 British Library, MSS Eur. E.195, 29–31, Masson to Bean, 25 September 1840.
19 British Library, IOR/L/PS/5/154, 24, Bean to Macnaghten, 31 August 1840.
20 Ibid., 29, Macnaghten to Bean, 10 September 1840.
21 *Bombay Times*, 13 March 1841, pp. 164–5, Bean to Bell, 2 January 1841.
22 Ibid., 13 March 1841, pp. 164–5.
23 Ibid., Bean to Bell, 2 January 1841.
24 British Library, MSS Eur. E.165, 106.
25 British Library, MSS Eur. E.195, 33.
26 Masson, *Kalât*, p. 257, Bean to Masson, 29 September 1840.
27 Burnes, *Notes*, p. 58.
28 Kennedy, *Various Journeys*, vol. 2, p. 118.
29 Kaye, *Lives*, pp. 46–7, Burnes to Lord, 22 November 1839.
30 Grey and Garrett, *European Adventurers*, p. 236.
31 Murray, *Sikunder Burnes*, p. 213.
32 Ibid., p. 158.
33 Quoted in Dalrymple, *Return of a King*, p. 86.
34 Murray, *Sikunder Burnes*, p. 344.
35 *Bombay Times*, 18 November 1840, pp. 738–9.

18 ENTRAILS

1 British Library, MSS Eur. E.163, 16.
2 British Library, MSS Eur. E.161/7, 1–2.
3 Ibid., 49, Masson to Wade, June 1836.
4 British Library, IOR/L/PS/5/126.

5 Kaye, *Lives*, pp. 46–7, Burnes to Lord, 22 November 1839.
6 British Library, MSS Eur. E.161/6, 23, T. Postans to Masson, 28 November 1840.
7 Masson, *Various Journeys*, vol. 2, pp. 360–1.
8 British Library, MSS Eur. E.195, 34–5, Masson to Macnaghten, 25 September 1840.
9 Masson, *Kalât*, p. 262, Macnaghten to Masson, 10 October 1840.
10 Quoted in British Library, MSS Eur. E.165, 137.
11 Quoted in H. T. Lambrick, 'Charles Masson's detention in Quetta, September 1840–January 1841', *Journal of the Sind Historical Society*, vols 5–6 (1941–2), p. 80, Bean to Masson, 25 September 1840.
12 British Library, MSS Eur. E.161/4, 15.
13 Ibid., 16.
14 Ibid., 26.
15 Ibid., 27.
16 *Bombay Times*, 14 August 1840, p. 522.
17 Ibid., 14 November 1838, p. 730.
18 British Library, MSS Eur. E.161/4, 17.
19 British Library, MSS Eur. E.165, 123.
20 Masson, *Kalât*, pp. 259–60.
21 British Library, IOR/F/4/2009/89688, 65–6.
22 Masson, *Kalât*, p. 259.
23 British Library, MSS Eur. E.165, 123.
24 British Library, MSS Eur. E.162, 76.
25 *Bombay Times*, 13 March 1841, pp. 162–3.
26 Ibid.
27 Ibid.
28 Ibid.
29 *The Calcutta Englishman*, 14 January 1841, p. 3.
30 British Library, MSS Eur. E.161/4, 49, Stacy to Masson, 29 December 1840.
31 *Bombay Times*, 13 March 1841, pp. 162–3.
32 British Library, MSS Eur. E.165, 124.
33 British Library, MSS Eur. E.195, 23.
34 Masson, *Kalât*, p. 263.

19 FRONTIERS

1 British Library, MSS Eur. E161/6, 31, Stacy to Masson, 26 June 1841.

2 Nott, *Memoirs*, p. 268.

3 Ibid., p. 248.

4 British Library, MSS Eur. E.161/6, 37–8.

5 British Library, MSS Eur. E.161/4, 35, Stacy to Masson, 4 November 1840.

6 British Library, IOR/L/PS/5/154, 386.

7 British Library, MSS Eur. E.161/4, 35, Stacy to Masson, 4 November 1840.

8 British Library, IOR/L/PS/5/154, 950, Stacy to Bell, 27 December 1840.

9 Ibid.

10 National Archives, London, FO 705/32, Jephson to Masson, 23 August 1838.

11 British Library, IOR/L/PS/5/154, 950, Stacy to Bell, 27 December 1840; British Library, IOR/L/PS/5/154, Nott to Bell, 3 November 1840.

12 British Library, IOR/L/PS/5/155, 357, Maddock to Bell, 11 January 1841.

13 British Library, MSS Eur. E.161/6, 42.

14 Lambrick, 'Charles Masson's detention', p. 83.

15 British Library, MSS Eur. E.161/6, 42.

16 British Library, MSS Eur. E.161/4, 42, Stacy to Masson, 23 November 1840.

17 Ibid., 36, Stacy to Masson, 14 November 1840.

18 *Bombay Times*, 13 March 1841, pp. 164–5, Bell to Masson, 14 December 1840.

19 British Library, MSS Eur. E.161/6, 44.

20 Ibid.

21 British Library, IOR/L/PS/5/154, 950, Stacy to Bell, 27 December 1840.

22 British Library, MSS Eur. E.161/6, 25, Stacy to Masson, 27 December 1840.

23 Ibid.

24 British Library, MSS Eur. E.165, 123.

25 British Library, MSS Eur. E.161/6, 45, Stacy to Masson, 18 December 1840.

26 British Library, IOR/L/PS/5/155, 916, Stacy to Bell, 17 December 1840.

27 Ibid., 923.

28 British Library, MSS Eur. E.161/4, 55.

29 British Library, IOR/L/PS/5/155, 930, Maddock to Macnaghten, 23 January 1841.

30 British Library, MSS Eur. E.161/6, 42.

31 Ibid., 40, Jephson to Masson, 27 March 1841.

32 British Library, MSS Eur. E.161/7, 65.

33 British Library, MSS Eur. E.161/4, 42, Stacy to Masson, 23 November 1840.

34 Masson, *Kalât*, p. 267, Bean to Bell, 2 January 1841.

35 *Bombay Times*, 13 March 1841, pp. 162–3.

36 British Library, MSS Eur. E.161/6, 33, Jephson to Masson, 12 December 1840.

37 Ibid.

38 British Library, MSS Eur. E.165, 154.

39 British Library, IOR/L/PS/5/552, 34–5.

40 British Library, IOR/L/PS/5/154, 47, Macnaghten to Torrens, 8 October 1840.

41 British Library, MSS Eur. E.195, 47–8, Bell to Maddock, 9 January 1841.

42 Ibid., 46, Bell to Masson, 9 January 1841.

43 British Library, MSS Eur. E.161/5, 29, Hammersley to Masson, 29 December 1840.

44 Masson, *Kalât*, pp. 272–3.

45 *Bombay Times*, 13 March 1841, pp. 164–5, Masson to Bell, 24 December 1840.

46 Adapted from M. Longworth Dames, *Popular Poetry of the Baloches*, Royal Asiatic Society, London, 1907, vol. 1, pp. 272–3.

20 THE MAN WHO WOULD BE KING

1 *Bombay Courier*, 13 March 1841, p. 82.

2 *Bombay Times*, 13 March 1841, p. 162.

3 Lal, *Travels*, p. 485.

4 Jivanji Jamshedji Modi, *Oriental Conference Papers*, The Fort Printing Press, Bombay, 1932, p. 59.

5 Quintus Curtius Rufus, *History of Alexander*, 4.4.16–17.

6 Ibid., 4.6.28.

7 Ibid., 4.6.29.

8 Diodorus Siculus, *The Library of History*, 17.70.

9 Adapted from the *Book of Arda Viraf*, 1.1–7.

10 Sir Robert Eric Mortimer Wheeler, *Flames over Persepolis: Turning point in History*, Weidenfeld & Nicolson, London, 1968, p. 23.

11 Ibid., p. 64.

12 Kaye, *Lives*, vol. 3, p. 49.

13 Kaye, *History of the War*, vol. 1, p. 137.

14 Kaye, *Lives*, vol. 3, p. 49.

15 Ibid., p. 48.

16 British Library, MSS Eur. E.165, Masson to Pottinger, 2 October 1839.

17 Ibid.

18 National Library of Scotland, John Murray Archive, MS.42633, Ledger of Manuscripts Returned and Received, 11 July 1840.

19 Ibid., MS.40970, Pottinger to Murray, 4 February 1841.

20 British Library, MSS Eur. E.161/1, 205, Pottinger to Mrs Lewis [Masson's mother], 4 January 1841.

21 National Library of Scotland, John Murray Archive, MS.40970, Pottinger to Murray, 4 February 1841.

22 British Library, MSS Eur. E.161/1, 207, Pottinger to Masson, 25 July 1841.

23 British Library, MSS Eur. E.161/6, 35, Stacy to Masson, 12 July 1841.

24 Ibid., 41, unknown author to Jephson, 11 March 1841.

25 Ibid., 41, unknown author to Jephson, 26 January 1841.

26 British Library, MSS Eur. E.195, Maddock to Bell, 1 February 1841.

27 British Library, MSS Eur. E.165, 190–1.

28 British Library, MSS Eur. E.161/6, 34, Stacy to Masson, 28 June 1841.

29 Ibid.

30 Ibid., 31–2, Stacy to Masson, 26 June 1841.

31 Ibid., 35, Stacy to Masson, 12 July 1841.

32 Ibid., Stacy to Masson, 7 July 1841.

33 Ibid.

34 Ibid., 36, Stacy to Masson, 26 July 1841.

35 Ibid., 35, Stacy to Masson, 7 July 1841.

36 Ibid., 29–30, Stacy to Masson, 24 June 1841.

37 Ibid., 18, Stacy to Masson, 6 May 1841.

38 Ibid., 29–30, Stacy to Masson, 24 June 1841.

39 British Library, MSS Eur. E.165, 156.

40 British Library, MSS Eur. E.195, Maddock to Bell, 1 February 1841.

41 *Bombay Times*, 13 March 1841, pp. 164–5, Masson to Bell, 24 December 1840.
42 British Library, MSS Eur. E.167, 58.
43 Masson, *Kalât*, p. 276.
44 British Library, MSS Eur. E161/6, 40, Jephson to Masson, 7 April 1841.
45 British Library, Bombay Political Consultations, IOR/F/4/1944/ 84442, 11.
46 Ibid., Masson to Willoughby, 24 October 1841.
47 *The Calcutta Review*, vol. 2 (October–December 1844), 248.
48 British Library, MSS Eur. E.162, 6.
49 Maulana Hamid Kashmiri, *Akbarnama*, 1.
50 British Library, MSS Eur. E.165, 190–1.
51 Kaye, *Lives*, vol. 2, p. 61.
52 Kaye, *History of the War*, vol. 2, p. 3.
53 Kaye, *Lives*, vol. 2, p. 62.
54 *The Asiatic Journal*, vol. 38 (May–August 1842), p. 177.

21 THE LAMP-LIGHTER

1 Herodotus, *Histories* II.143.
2 E. Errington, 'Rediscovering the collections of Charles Masson', in M. Alram and D. E. Klimburg-Salter, *Coins, Art and Chronology: Essays on the pre-Islamic History of the Indo-Iranian Borderlands*, Österreichische Akademie der Wissenschaften, Vienna, 1999, p. 211.
3 *The Times*, 7 February 1842, p. 4.
4 Ibid., 10 March 1842, p. 5.
5 British Library, MSS Eur. E.161/6, 31–2, Stacy to Masson, 26 June 1841.
6 British Library, MSS Eur. E.161/1, 90, Pottinger to Masson, 27 September 1839.
7 Wilson, *Ariana Antiqua*, p. 439.
8 British Library, MSS Eur. E.161/7, 14.
9 Wilson, *Ariana Antiqua*, p. 441.
10 Bodleian Library, Oxford, Afghan.1.d.1, 203.
11 Ibid., 139.
12 Ibid., 347.
13 Ibid., 400.
14 Ibid., 429.

15 Ibid., 123.
16 Ibid., 119.
17 British Library, Add. MS 46614, vol. 60, 118.
18 *The Times*, 4 November 1842, p. 3.
19 British Library, MSS Eur. E.165, 156.
20 British Library, IOR/L/PS/5/552, 209–10.
21 British Library, MSS Eur. E.161/6, 40, Jephson to Masson, 7 April 1841.
22 *The London Gazette for the Year 1845*, vol. 1 (1845), p. 985.
23 British Museum, BM-OP 20.6.1847, J. M. Ludlow to H. B. Ker, 20 June 1847.
24 British Museum, BM-TM 24.7.1847, Standing Committee Papers, 24 July 1847, 7301.2.
25 British Library, IOR/F/4/2009/89688, IOR/F/4/2009/89689.
26 Masson, *Various Journeys*, vol. 1, pp. vii–xii.
27 *The Caledonian Mercury*, 7 November 1842, p. 2.
28 *The Times*, 8 February 1842, p. 4.
29 *The Calcutta Review*, vol. 10 (1848), p. 220.
30 J. A. Norris, *The First Afghan War*, Cambridge University Press, Cambridge, 1967, p. 200.
31 Ibid., p. 252.
32 Ibid., p. 188.
33 Chester County Historical Society, Harlan Papers, Miscellaneous Papers/1850s and 1860s, 2981.
34 Ibid., 3004.
35 Ibid., 2988.
36 Ibid., 2986–7.
37 Harlan, *Memoir*, p. 2.
38 Ibid., p. 2.
39 Quoted in ibid., p. 1.
40 Chester County Historical Society, Harlan Papers, Miscellaneous Papers/1880s.
41 Ibid., Miscellaneous Papers/1840s, unnumbered folio.
42 British Library, MSS Eur. F.526.
43 British Library, MSS Eur. E.161/7, 16.
44 Ibid., 22.
45 National Archives (UK), Family Records, FR.1, Marriage Certificate 167, Stoke Newington, 19 February 1844.
46 British Library, MSS Eur. F.526, unnumbered folio.

47 Edward Daniel Clarke, *The Tomb of Alexander, a Dissertation on the Sarcophagus brought from Alexandria, and now in the British Museum*, Cambridge University Press, Cambridge, 1805.

48 Zahiruddin Muhammad Babur, *Baburnama*, Folio Society, London, 2013, p. 761.

49 National Archives (UK), Family Records, FR.4, Death Certificate 224, Edmonton, Middlesex, 5 November 1853.

50 David Traill, *Schliemann of Troy: Treasure and Deceit*, John Murray, London, 1995, p. 3.

51 Ibid., p. 6.

52 Ibid., pp. 10–13.

53 Edmund Richardson, 'Seven Lost Cities Swallowed Up By Time', Atlas Obscura, 8 October 2013 [online]: https://www.atlasobscura.com/articles/seven-lost-cities-swallowed-up-by-time.

54 Evelyn Waugh, *Labels*, Duckworth, London, 1974, p. 136.

55 Cathy Gere, *Knossos and the Prophets of Modernism*, University of Chicago Press, Chicago, 2010.

56 Leonard Woolley, *As I Seem to Remember*, Allen & Unwin, London, 1962, pp. 21–3.

57 Gere, *Knossos*, p. 105.

58 British Library, MSS Eur. E.161/4, 14.

59 P. M. Fraser, *Cities of Alexander the Great*, Clarendon Press, Oxford, 1996, pp. 147–8.

60 George Grote, *History of Greece*, John Murray, London, 1856, vol. 12, p. 201.

61 Todd Greentree, 'A Letter from Bagram' [online]: http://www.the-american-interest.com/2009/07/01/a-letter-from-bagram/.

62 'British Museum to open three new galleries to tell "interconnected story of the world"'. *Evening Standard* (London), 4 July 2017 [online]: https://www.standard.co.uk/go/london/arts/british-museum-to-open-three-new-galleries-to-tell-interconnected-story-of-the-world-a3579101.html.

63 Gandhara School relief (Kushan period), British Museum, 1970,0718.1.

64 Sushma Jansari, 'The oldest, dateable depiction of the Buddha in human form', 20 November 2018 [online]: https://www.youtube.com/watch?v=NZMqY3d-dQA.

65 British Museum, Trustees' Minutes, BM.TM.13.12.1879. Elizabeth Errington, head of the Museum's Masson Project, whose work has

led to Masson's collections being understood more fully than ever before, has traced the afterlives of Masson's finds, and the debt to her research is gratefully acknowledged: Elizabeth Errington, *The Charles Masson Archive: British Library, British Museum and Other Documents Relating to the 1832–1838 Masson Collection from Afghanistan*, British Museum Press, London, 2017.

66 British Museum, Department of Asia, BM.Asia.6.1.1880.

67 Ibid.

68 Errington, *Charles Masson*, p. 25.

69 British Museum, Department of Asia, BM.Asia.1.8.1882.

70 Wilson, *Ariana Antiqua*, p. 26.

71 British Library, MSS Eur. E.165, 190–1.

72 Denise Blake Oleksijczuk, *The First Panoramas: Visions of British Imperialism*, University of Minnesota Press, Minneapolis, 2011, p. 12.

73 *The Asiatic Journal and Monthly Miscellany*, vol. 38 (June 1842), pp. 174–5.

74 Ibid.

75 Robert Burford, *Description of a view of the city of Cabul, the capital of Affghanistan, with the surrounding country, now exhibiting at the Panorama, Leicester Square*, G. Nichols, London, 1842, frontispiece.

76 *The Times*, 4 November 1842, p. 3.

77 G. T. Vigne, 'Chief wrestler at Kabul' (watercolour, 1835–8), Victoria and Albert Museum, SD.1109.

78 James Atkinson, 'Umeer Dost Mahomed Khan', in Atkinson, *Character and Costume*, p. 15.

79 Burford, *The city of Cabul*, frontispiece.

80 *The Times*, 4 November 1842, p. 3.

Sources and References

One winter's day in London, I was in a library. That was normal. I was fighting back tears. That was not.

This being London, I was soon being glared at. A man tutted under his breath. A lady whispered something which sounded a lot like: 'Some people.' There are few greater British sins than showing emotion in a library. If I'd walked in stark naked, they would probably have been less disapproving.

I had been chasing a story for years, about Alexander the Great, an explorer and a lost city. I'd haunted archives, everywhere from New Delhi to Pennsylvania. Then, that day in London, I opened a dusty box much like any other, and finally saw Charles Masson clearly: drunk in a Karachi back street, cursing the world at the top of his voice, and writing, and writing, and writing.

Much of Masson's world still lives and breathes today, in ways which defy footnotes. The desert dust covers the same houses, camels chew and spit on the same street corners, and the same tales of Alexander are told by soldiers on the plains of Afghanistan. The traces of Masson's pursuit of Alexander stretch across the world. The sources listed here are some of the footprints which remain.

Despite the best efforts of almost everyone involved, this has been a true story.

NAMES

There are very few things that people agreed on in the nineteenth century, and how to spell Afghan names was not one of them.

Kabul may, depending on the author, be rendered Kabul, Cabool, Cabul or Kabal (among other possibilities). Individuals do not fare any better: Shah Shujah endured more different attempts to spell his name than he did failed attempts to retake his throne. For the sake of clarity, in consequence, names have been standardised throughout the text.

ARCHIVES

The vast majority of Masson's surviving archaeological finds are now in the **British Museum**. Thanks to decades of work by the Museum's Masson Project, led by Dr Elizabeth Errington, they have now been fully catalogued, and can be inspected in the Museum's Study Rooms, as well as through its online collection database: https://www.britishmuseum.org/collection.

The **British Library** holds most of Masson's surviving papers. That the collection is as extensive as it is, given how frequently Masson lost everything he possessed, is somewhat miraculous. There are sketches and journals, notes of joyful discovery and letters full of baffled anger. 'I am conscious there is much, indeed the greater portion,' wrote Masson of his own papers, 'intelligible to no one but myself.'* The Library has made an heroic attempt to bring order to the chaos, but volumes still jump from one year to another, and one place to another, seemingly at will. The majority of the Library's holdings are catalogued under MSS Eur. A.31, B.98–101, C.90, D.441–2, E.161–70 and F.61–5, and can be consulted through a splendidly idiosyncratic finding aid, the *Catalogue of European MSS*, volume II, available in the Library's Asian and African Studies Reading Room. The Library also holds extensive records from the East India Company: specific references are given throughout the text, but the Bengal Secret Consultations series, a compendium of the East India Company's more dubious deeds, is particularly valuable.

* National Archives (UK), FO 705/32, Masson to Pottinger, 18 October 1838.

The **National Archives of India** in New Delhi and the **Punjab Archives** in Lahore have important pieces of the puzzle in their collections, particularly in relation to the East India Company's invasion of Afghanistan. Masson's correspondence with Henry Pottinger is split between the British Library and the **National Archives, London**, where it is held with the Foreign Office papers under FO 705/32. The literary remains of Josiah Harlan – as full of tricks as the man himself – are held by the wonderful **Chester County Historical Society** in West Chester, Pennsylvania. The journal of Alexander Burnes is in the collections of **Worcester College, Oxford**. Masson's lowest moments can be traced in the Henry Rawlinson Papers at the **Royal Geographical Society**. The John Murray Archive in the **National Library of Scotland** holds the story of his misadventures in the world of publishing.

Bibliography

Al-Nadim, Ibn, trans. B. Dodge, *The Fihrist of al-Nadim: a tenth-century survey of Muslim culture*, Columbia University Press, New York, 1970

Alram, M., and D. E. Klimburg-Salter, *Coins, Art and Chronology: Essays on the pre-Islamic History of the Indo-Iranian Borderlands*, Österreichische Akademie der Wissenschaften, Vienna, 1999

Anon., *A Brief Memoir of an Officer of the Bengal Artillery*, L. B. Seely, London, 1834

Anon., *Accounts and Papers of the House of Commons, Session, 5 February–27 August 1839*, House of Commons, London, 1839

Anon., *Afghanistan: Ancient Land with Modern Ways*, Ministry of Planning of the Royal Government of Afghanistan, Kabul, 1961

Anon., *Alphabetical catalogue of the contents of the pre-mutiny records of the commissioner in Sind*, Commissioner's Printing Press, Karachi, 1857

Anon., *Correspondence Relating to Persia and Affghanistan*, J. Harrison, London, 1839

Anon., *Parliamentary Papers, Session 2, 31 May–13 August 1859*, House of Commons, London, 1859

Anon., *Return to an order of the Honourable the House of Commons, dated 24 June 1839: Accounts of all monies supplied from the revenues of India*, London, 1839

Anon., *The Bengal and Agra Annual Guide and Gazetteer for 1841*, William Rushton and Co., Calcutta, 1841

Anon., *The Law Relating to India and the East India Company*, W. H. Allen, London, 1842

Anon., *The Policy of the Government of British India, as exhibited in Official Documents*, W. H. Allen, London, 1839

Ata-Malik Juvaini, Alā' al-Dīn ʿAṭā Malik, trans. J. A. Boyle, *Genghis Khan: The History of the World Conqueror* [*Tarīkh-i Jahān-gushā*], Manchester University Press, Manchester, 1997

Atkinson, James, *Sketches in Afghaunistan*, H. Graves, London, 1842
—, *Character and Costume of Affghanistan*, H. Graves, London, 1843

Babur, Zahiruddin Muhammad, trans. Wheeler M. Thackston, *Baburnama*, Folio Society, London, 2013

Badian, E., *Alexandre le Grand, image et réalité*, Fondation Hardt, Geneva, 1976

Ball, Warwick, and Jean-Claude Gardin, *Archaeological Gazetteer of Afghanistan*, Recherche sur les civilisations, Paris, 1982

Barr, William, *Journal of a March from Delhi to Peshâwur: And from Thence to Câbul, with the Mission of Lieut.-Colonel Sir C.M. Wade*, J. Madden, London, 1844

Birdwood, G. C. M., *The Industrial Arts of India*, Chapman and Hall, London, 1880

Blakiston, John, *Twelve Years' Military Adventure in Three Quarters of the Globe*, Henry Colburn, London, 1829

Bloss, C. A., *Ancient History, illustrated by colored maps, and a chronological chart, for the use of families and schools*, Clark and Maynard, New York, 1869

Bopearachchi, O., *Monnaies gréco-bactriennes et indo-grecques*, Bibliothèque nationale, Paris, 1991

Buist, George, *Outline of the operations of the British troops in Scinde and Afghanistan*, Times Office, Bombay, 1843

Burford, Robert, *Description of a view of the city of Cabul, the capital of Affghanistan, with the surrounding country, now exhibiting at the Panorama, Leicester Square*, G. Nichols, London, 1842

Burgon, John William, *Petra, a Poem: To which a Few Short Poems are Now Added*, F. Macpherson, Oxford, 1846

Burnes, Alexander, *Travels Into Bokhara: Being the Account of a Journey from India to Cabool, Tartary, and Persia*, John Murray, London, 1834
—, *Cabool: A Personal Narrative of a Journey To, and Residence in that City, in the Years 1836, 7, and 8*, John Murray, London, 1843

Burnes, James, *Notes on his name and family*, printed for private circulation, Edinburgh, 1851

Byron, Lord, *The Works of Lord Byron: Including the Suppressed Poems*, A. & W. Galignani, Paris, 1828

Clarke, Edward Daniel, *The Tomb of Alexander, a Dissertation on the Sarcophagus brought from Alexandria, and now in the British Museum*, Cambridge University Press, Cambridge, 1805

Cohen, Getzel M., *The Hellenistic Settlements in the East from Armenia and Mesopotamia to Bactria and India*, University of California Press, Berkeley, CA, 2013

Cotton, Julian James, *General Avitabile*, Edinburgh Press, Calcutta, 1906

Creevey, William, ed. Sir Herbert Maxwell, *The Creevey Papers: A selection from the correspondence and diaries of the late Thomas Creevey, M.P.*, John Murray, London, 1903

Creighton, J. N., *Narrative of the Siege and Capture of Bhurtpore*, Parbury, Allen and Co., London, 1830

Crowe, Thomas Rain, *Drunk on the Wine of the Beloved: 100 Poems of Hafiz*, Shambhala, London, 2001

Dalrymple, William, *Return of a King: The Battle for Afghanistan*, Bloomsbury, London, 2013

—, *The Anarchy: The Relentless Rise of the East India Company*, Bloomsbury, London, 2019

Eden, Emily, *Up the Country*, Richard Bentley, London, 1867

Edwardes, Herbert Benjamin, *Life of Sir Henry Lawrence*, Smith, Elder, London, 1872

Egan, Pierce, *Life in London: Or, The Day and Night Scenes of Jerry Hawthorne, Esq., and His Elegant Friend Corinthian Tom*, Sherwood, Neely, and Jones, London, 1822

Elliot, Henry Miers, *The History of India, as Told by Its Own Historians*, Trübner and Co., London, 1871

Elphinstone, Mountstuart, *An Account of the Kingdom of Caubul, and Its Dependencies in Persia, Tartary, and India: Comprising a View of the Afghaun Nation, and a History of the Dooraunee Monarchy*, Longman, Hurst, Rees, Orme, and Brown, London, 1815

Errington, Elizabeth, *Charles Masson and the Buddhist sites of Afghanistan: explorations, excavations, collections 1832–1835*, British Museum Press, London, 2017

—, *The Charles Masson Archive: British Library, British Museum and Other Documents Relating to the 1832–1838 Masson Collection from Afghanistan*, British Museum Press, London, 2017

—, Vesta Sarkhosh Curtis and Joe Cribb, *From Persepolis to the Punjab: Exploring ancient Iran, Afghanistan and Pakistan*, British Museum Press, London, 2017

Eyre, Vincent, *Military Operations at Cabul, which Ended in the Retreat and Destruction of the British Army, January 1842*, John Murray, London, 1843

Forrest, George, ed., *Selections from the travels and journals preserved in the Bombay secretariat*, Government Central Press, Bombay, 1906

Fraser, P. M., *Cities of Alexander the Great*, Clarendon Press, Oxford, 1996

Gere, Cathy, *Knossos and the Prophets of Modernism*, University of Chicago Press, Chicago, 2010

Grey, C., and H. L. O. Garrett, *European Adventurers of Northern India, 1785 to 1849*, Languages Department, Patiala, 1970

Grote, George, *History of Greece*, John Murray, London, 1856

Hackin, J., and J. Carl, *Nouvelles recherches archéologiques à Bâmiyân: Mémoires de la Délégation Archéologique Française en Afghanistan*, G. Van Oest, Paris, 1933

Haghe, Louis, and Charles Haghe, after James Atkinson, *Sketches in Afghanistan*, Henry Graves, London, 1842

Harlan, Josiah, *Central Asia: Personal Narrative of General Josiah Harlan, 1823–1841*, Luzac and Co., London, 1939

—, *A memoir of India and Avghanistaun, with observations on the present exciting and critical state and future prospects of those countries*, J. Dobson, Philadelphia, 1842

Hiebert, Fredrik, and Pierre Cambon, *Afghanistan: Crossroads of the Ancient World*, British Museum Press, London, 2011

Higuchi, Takayasu, バーミヤーン: 京都大学中央アジア学術調査報告: アフガニスタンにおける仏教石窟寺院の美術考古学的調査 1970-1978 年 / 樋口隆康編 [*Bāmiyān: Kyōto daigaku chūō ajia gakujutsu chōsa hōkoku: Afuganisutan niokeru bukkyō sekkutsu jīn no bijutsu kōkogakuteki chōsa 1970 1978nen*], Dōhōsha Shuppan, Kyōto, 1983–1984

Honigberger, Johann Martin, *Thirty Five Years in the East: Adventures, Discoveries, Experiments, and Historical Sketches, Relating to the Punjab and Cashmere*, H. Ballière, London, 1852

Hultzsch, E., *Inscriptions of Asoka*, Clarendon Press for the Government of India, Oxford, 1925

Ibn Jubayr, Muḥammad ibn Aḥmad, trans. J. C. Broadhurst, *The Travels of Ibn Jubayr*, Jonathan Cape, London, 1952

Jacquemont, Victor, *Letters from India: Describing a Journey in the British Dominions of India, Tibet, Lahore, and Cashmere*, Edward Churton, London, 1834

Kaye, John, *Lives of Indian Officers: Illustrative of the history of the civil and military service of India*, A. Strahan, London, 1867

—, *History of the War in Afghanistan*, W. R. Allen, London, 1874

Kennedy, Richard Hartley, *Narrative of the campaign of the Indus, in Sind and Kaubool in 1838-9*, Richard Bentley, London, 1840

Kipling, Rudyard, *Under the Deodars*, Doubleday, Garden City, NY, 1914

Lal, Mohan, *Life of the Amir Dost Mohammed Khan of Kabul: With His Political Proceedings Towards the English, Russian, and Persian Governments, Including the Victory and Disasters of the British Army in Afghanistan*, Longman, London, 1846

—, *Travels in the Panjab, Afghanistan, Turkistan, to Balk, Bokhara, and Herat*, W. H. Allen, London, 1846

Landa, Gertrude (pseud. Aunt Naomi), *Jewish Fairy Tales and Legends*, Shapiro, Valentine and Company, London, 1900

Longworth Dames, M., *Popular Poetry of the Baloches*, Royal Asiatic Society, London, 1907

Macintyre, Ben, *Josiah the Great: The True Story of the Man Who Would Be King*, HarperCollins, London, 2004

MacKinnon, Daniel Henry, *Military Service and Adventures in the Far East*, Charles Oliver, London, 1847

Masson, Charles, *Narrative of Various Journeys in Balochistan, Afghanistan and the Panjab Including a Residence in Those Countries from 1826 to 1838*, Richard Bentley, London, 1842

—, *Narrative of a Journey to Kalât, Including an Insurrection at that Place in 1840: And a Memoir on Eastern Balochistan*, Richard Bentley, London, 1843

Mavor, William Fordyce, *Universal History, Ancient and Modern: From the Earliest Records of Time, to the General Peace of 1801*, Collins and Sons, Philadelphia, 1803

Mazari, Gholam Mahomed Khan, ed. T. L. J. Mayer, *Baloch Classics*, CMS Mission Press, Sikandra, Agra, 1906

Mitchell, Robert, *Plans, and views in perspective, with descriptions of buildings erected in England and Scotland*, Wilson and Co., London, 1801

Mitchiner, M., *Indo-Greek and Indo-Scythian Coins*, Hawkins, London, 1975–6

Mitford, William, *The History of Greece*, Cadell and Davies, London, 1818

Modi, Jivanji Jamshedji, *Oriental Conference Papers*, The Fort Printing Press, Bombay, 1932

Morgan, Llewelyn, *The Buddhas of Bamiyan*, Harvard University Press, Cambridge, MA, 2012

Morris, Henry, *The Governors-General of India*, Christian Literature Society for India, London, 1896

Murray, Craig, *Sikunder Burnes: Master of the Great Game*, Birlinn, Edinburgh, 2016

Noelle-Karimi, Christine, *The Interaction Between State and Tribe in Nineteenth-century Afghanistan*, University of California, Berkeley, CA, 1995

Norris, J. A., *The First Afghan War*, Cambridge University Press, Cambridge, 1967

Nott, William, *Memoirs and correspondence of Major-General Sir William Nott*, Hurst and Blackett, London, 1854

Oleksijczuk, Denise Blake, *The First Panoramas: Visions of British Imperialism*, University of Minnesota Press, Minneapolis, 2011

Osborne, William, *The court and camp of Runjeet Singh*, Henry Colburn, London, 1840

Parkes, Fanny, *Wanderings of a Pilgrim in Search of the Picturesque*, Manchester University Press, Manchester, 2001

Rattray, James, *The costumes of the various tribes, portraits of ladies of rank, celebrated princes and chiefs, views of the principal fortresses and cities, and interior of the cities and temples of Afghaunistaun*, Hering & Remington, London, 1848

Riddick, John F., *The History of British India*, Praeger, Westport, CT, 2006

Schmitz, Barbara, *Islamic manuscripts in the New York Public Library*, Oxford University Press, New York and Oxford, 1992

Shah, Idries, *The Pleasantries of the Incredible Mulla Nasrudin*, Octagon Press, London, 1983

Smith, Paul, *The Divan of Hafiz*, New Humanity Books, Melbourne, 1986

Stoneman, Richard, *The Greek Alexander Romance*, Penguin Books, London, 1991

—, *Alexander the Great: A Life in Legend*, Yale University Press, New Haven, CT, 2010

Suri, Lal Sohan Lal, *Umdat-ut-tawarikh*, S. Chand, Delhi, 1961

Thirlwall, Connop, *History of Greece*, Longman, London, 1840

Thomas, E., ed., *Essays on Indian Antiquities, Historic, Numismatic, and Palaeographic, of the late James Prinsep, F.R.S., Secretary to the Asiatic Society of Bengal*, Hertford, London, 1858

Thornberry, Walter, *Old and New London: The City Ancient And Modern*, Cassell, London, 1887

Traill, David, *Schliemann of Troy: Treasure and Deceit*, John Murray, London, 1995

Van Leeuwen, Richard, *The Thousand and One Nights: Space, Travel and Transformation*, Routledge, New York, 2007

Vasunia, Phiroze, *The Classics and Colonial India*, Oxford University Press, Oxford, 2013

Vigne, Godfrey, *A personal narrative of a visit to Ghuzni, Kabul and Afghanistan, and of a residence at the court of Dost Mohamed*, George Routledge, London, 1843

Von Schonberg, Erich, *Travels In India And Kashmir*, Hurst and Blackett, London, 1853

Walpole, Horace, ed. W. S. Lewis, *The Yale Edition of Horace Walpole's Correspondence*, Yale University Press, New Haven, CT, 1937–83

Waugh, Evelyn, *Labels*, Duckworth, London, 1974

Wheeler, Sir Robert Eric Mortimer, *Flames over Persepolis: Turning point in History*, Weidenfeld & Nicolson, London, 1968

Whitmarsh, Tim, and Stuart Thomson, *The Romance Between Greece and the East*, Cambridge University Press, Cambridge, 2013

Whitteridge, G., *Charles Masson of Afghanistan: Explorer, Archaeologist, Numismatist and Intelligence Agent*, Aris and Philips, Warminster, 1986

Widorn, V., U. Franke and P. Latschenberger, eds, *Contextualizing Material Culture in South and Central Asia in Pre-Modern Times*, Brepolis, Turnhout, 2016

Williams, John, *The Life and Actions of Alexander the Great*, J. & J. Harper, New York, 1830

Wilson, Horace Hayman, *Ariana Antiqua: A descriptive account of the antiquities and coins of Afghanistan*, Published Under the Authority of the Honourable The Court of Directors of The East India Company, London, 1841

Wolff, Joseph, *Travels and adventures of the Rev. Joseph Wolff*, Saunders, Otley and Company, London, 1861

Wordsworth, William, *The Poetical Works of William Wordsworth*, Edward Moxon, London, 1869

Xuanzang, trans. Samuel Beal, *Si-Yu-Ki: Buddhist Records of the Western World: Translated from the Chinese of Hiuen Tsiang*, Kegan, Paul, Trench and Company, London, 1884

Yapp, M. E., *Strategies of British India: Britain, Iran and Afghanistan 1798–1850*, Clarendon Press, Oxford, 1980

Picture Credits

SECTION 2

Acknowledgements

Stories leave marks. In my case, this story left me with: a lingering bruise to the head (a sleeper-train bunk, India); a stubborn orange stain (a motel dinner, Pennsylvania); a head-to-toe coating of Victorian dust (an archive, New Delhi); a missing tooth (an ill-advised evening, Egypt); a patchwork of profound debts, stretching across the world, to the people who have made this book possible.

Masson's story has been kept safe for almost two centuries thanks to librarians, curators and archivists on three continents. I am particularly grateful to everyone at the National Archives of India, the British Library, the Bodleian Library, the Chester County Historical Society and the British Museum, for guiding me through the twists and turns of the sources with infinite patience, and for helping me to sort the unreliable narrators from the very unreliable narrators.

At Bloomsbury, Michael Fishwick has, quite simply, been the editor of every author's dreams. Sarah Ruddick has generously guided the production of this book, and Richard Collins has copy-edited it with great kindness and insight. Hetty Touquet and Hannah Paget, who oversaw the marketing and publicity, have been amazing advocates for Masson's story.

At Peters, Fraser and Dunlop, Tessa David, Tim Binding, Caroline Michel and Laurie Robertson have guided this project with infinite generosity and wisdom. Thank you for encouraging me to follow this unlikely obsession for so many years, and for helping me to find my voice in ways which I never thought possible.

Jacqueline Smith and Robyn Reed at the BBC, along with everyone involved in the AHRC/BBC New Generation Thinkers scheme, encouraged me to turn Masson's story into a book, and to believe it might find an audience – and for that I am most grateful.

In Delhi, William Dalrymple and the late Bruce Wannell were kindness itself: scholars who carried, somehow, a little of a lost golden age with them, wherever they went – and whose hospitality still leaves me humbled.

My colleagues, past and present, in the Department of Classics and Ancient History at Durham have been wonderfully forgiving of my obsessions. Thank you, especially, to Barbara Graziosi for first taking a chance on my work, and to Kathryn Stevens for reminding me that, even in dark times, the stars are still there.

Over the course of ten years with Charles Masson, friends and family have been supportive beyond words. To my parents, Mary and Daniel: thank you for everything. To Meg Price, and to everyone who has listened to this story too many times: thank you for seeing the good things in it, especially when I could not. To Sophia: you know the rest. And to Yepoka Yeebo, who has seen this through with me, thank you above all. You never let me forget that, sometimes, our most impractical dreams are the finest ones of all.

And because stories often take a turn just before the end: thank you to Professor Sean Whittaker and his incredible team at Guy's Hospital, for being literal lifesavers when I was diagnosed with cancer in the middle of writing this book. These words have made it into the world because of you.

Index

A Note on the Author

Edmund Richardson is Associate Professor of Classics at Durham University. Before coming to Durham, he studied for his Ph.D. in Classics at Cambridge, then crossed the Atlantic for a postdoctoral fellowship at Princeton. In 2016, he was named one of the BBC/ AHRC New Generation Thinkers.

Richardson is fascinated by characters on the edge of most histories. He tells tales that seem a little too strange to be true. But in their truth, they change the way you see the world.

A Note on the Type

The text of this book is set in Adobe Garamond. It is one of several versions of Garamond based on the designs of Claude Garamond. It is thought that Garamond based his font on Bembo, cut in 1495 by Francesco Griffo in collaboration with the Italian printer Aldus Manutius. Garamond types were first used in books printed in Paris around 1532. Many of the present-day versions of this type are based on the *Typi Academiae* of Jean Jannon cut in Sedan in 1615.

Claude Garamond was born in Paris in 1480. He learned how to cut type from his father and by the age of fifteen he was able to fashion steel punches the size of a pica with great precision. At the age of sixty he was commissioned by King Francis I to design a Greek alphabet, and for this he was given the honourable title of royal type founder. He died in 1561.